WORLD CHRONOLOGY
OF
MUSIC HISTORY

Lira di Apollo

World Chronology
of
Music History

VOLUME IV

NAME INDEX
(Volumes I-III)

Compiled and Edited by
Paul E. Eisler

Foreword by Fritz Kramer

1976 OCEANA PUBLICATIONS, INC./Dobbs Ferry, New York

Library of Congress Cataloging in Publication Data (revised):

Eisler, Paul E.   1919-
   World chronology of music history.

   CONTENTS: v. 1. 30,000 B.C.-1594 A.D. v. 2. 1594-
1684. v. 3. 1685-1735 [etc.]
   1. Music—Chronology.   I. Title
ML161.E4   780'.9   72-4354
ISBN 0-379-16080-3 (series)
      0-379-16084-6 (v. 4)

Manufactured in the United States of America

To my beloved wife, Edith
and
to my earlier chronology
Judith
Paul III
Karen
and
Peter
with deepest affection

Foreword

The average music student, leaving school to enter life and embark on a career of his own, supposedly has a solid foundation of knowledge of the history of Eastern and Western music, both ancient and modern, and of the various musical styles and the ways to perform them. There is little doubt, however, that the sheer quantity of the material absorbed during the years of study is so overwhelming that for the young practicing musician it will take years for him to achieve true order and logic in his vision of historic perspective. There are also many professional musicians who pick up at random whatever they know about the different periods and styles of music, and the state of even their accumulated knowledge is deplorable.

The *World Chronology of Music History* is a concise survey of the art of music, especially its forms, its styles, the development of different theories, the ups and downs of music throughout the centuries and, of course, individual composers. Included, of necessity, are important highlights of what happened in other arts, what locations acquired transitory importance at any given time, and which crowned heads, emperors and kings and princes, and which theoreticians made their names known as relevant to music.

The importance of this particular *Chronology* lies in its comprehensiveness. Not only does it list the aforementioned items; it also gives literally thousands of examples of performances, premieres and — last but not least — performers. It is a gigantic undertaking. When it is complete, roughly 32,000 years of human evolution and culture will have been covered, starting with the Paleolithic Age and ending with electronic music.

Upon completion of the entire set (anticipated extent: 8-10 volumes) there will, of necessity, be added a separate index volume containing an alphabetical listing of the persons, works and events dicussed in the *Chronology*.

The use of the book ought to be described. If a reader wants information about a specific time period, he will find this time period covered in chronological sequence. Should a reader wish to obtain information about a personage whom he cannot locate as to the exact time in which he lived, he may find his name listed in the Index, together with the pertinent page in the volume. The first volume, covering the ages up to the latter part of the 16th Century, will, for instance, have more to say about the Renaissance period than, let's say, about the 9th Century, the century whose only towering personage was Charlemagne, the initiator of certain chant codifications and founder of the first music schools to teach strictly Western music.

From about the middle of the 16th Century on, the material is so abundant as to require a year-by-year coverage. Let us, for example, take the year 1590. What knowledge opens up on the first Madrigal opera, on Mr. Byrd, on the "Liber Secundum Sacrarum Cantionum," on the Council of Brunswick, the popularity of lute music, the painter Zuccari, *young* Monteverdi's doings, and the violin makers in Brescia! And after having read up on the multiple facts of the year 1590, we may proceed to pages and pages of happenings in 1591, and so on. In quoting examples, the standard practice has been followed of referring to major collections of published music.

Reading about music or listening to lectures about music without listening to the music itself is definitely a profitless undertaking. It is the music itself that matters above anything else. Our author, therefore, has taken special pains to emphasize the importance of certain works by various composers which are not to be overlooked. Parallel with the emphasis on masterworks run entries of the pertinent periods in general, such as Classical Antiquity, the Middle Ages (including the Gothic centuries), the Renaissance (as far as Vol. I covers) composers up to the heavenly heights of Byrd, Orlando di Lasso, Palestrina and Victoria.

Now, *to understand music it is also necessary to have some knowledge of the forces which have conditioned the various epochs during their growth.* Music can be grasped in its very depth only if coordinated with the sum total of the art of its time of origin, with literature, painting, sculpture and architecture. The *Chronology* offers assistance even above and beyond these features by also keeping close watch over the war-and-peace-makers of different time periods, their most cunning counsellors, their most eminent philosophers.

Fritz Kramer

Introduction

The preparation of this index of names for the first three volumes of the *World Chronology of Music History* has offered severe problems, several of which were unexpected. Needless to say, the Bach family presented difficulties requiring long and detailed research that hopefully will save considerable time for the users of this chronology. The problems stemmed essentially from the fact that the same names kept reappearing in succeeding generations. This would not have been difficult had it not been that frequently cousins with exactly the same names were composing in the same styles and for the same performing mediums. Some of the major sources have sadly failed to indicate clearly which Johann Christoph Bach or which Johann Christian Bach was responsible for a given work. In this index every effort has been made to clarify this by giving the generation and parenthood of those members of the family where a question might arise. Subsequent indices will be handled in the same manner.

Cross-referencing has been done where it seemed the least bit necessary and the main entry in each case has been placed under the heading most likely to be sought by the user. Thus the famed *castrati* Carlo Broschi carries a line "(see Farinelli)," the name under which this artist sang and was known to the public in his time. In the case of nobility or rulers the principal entry appears under the highest rank attained. Thus George, Elector of Hanover, carries the line "(see George I, King of England)." In some cases entries have been made under titles such as "London, Bishop of." On the surface this would appear extraneous, but in the opinion of the author the entry in the chronology was of sufficient importance to justify this usage, even though the man's name was unattainable. Needless to say there are but few index references of this nature.

An occasional entry has been made in which a page number is followed by a question mark in the following manner, "76(?)" to indicate that the reference is not positively concerned with the person listed. There are at most twenty such entries in the index.

In the matter of spelling arbitrary decisions have been made, and the most common usage has been selected, with alternate spellings cross-indexed. Names with patronymic prefixes have been entered under the family name, except in certain cases where the name is frequently spelled as one word. Here they have been cross-referenced as in La Lande which often appears as Lalande.

By and large procedures have been used that follow those in respected musical sources; the few exceptions are carefully covered with the expected cross-indexing.

NAME INDEX

A

ADLUNG, JACOB III-121,176,350,
    395
ADMON, PCW III-122
ADOLFATI, ANDREZ III-250,482
ADOLPH, of Burgandy I-277
ADREINI, ISABELLA I-502
ADRIAN I, POPE I-41,45
ADRIAN II, POPE I-50
ADRIAN III, POPE I-51
ADRIAN IV, POPE I-78
ADRIAN V, POPE I-99 *See illustration on p. 19*
ADRIAN VI, POPE I-271,272
ADRIANO, MESSER I-301
ADRIANSEN, EMANUEL (Hadrianus)
    I-476; II-58
ADRICHEM, FLORIS VAN I-442
ADRIO II-216
ADSON, JOHN II-91,136,202,224,
    264,268,292
AELRED, ABBOT, of Rievaulx (St.
    Aelred) I-74,79; II-45,403
AEMINGUS, SIEGFRIED COESUS VON
    III-240
AERTSENS, HENDRICK II-42,258
AERTSSENS (see Aertsens)
AESCHYLUS I-10,13
AETHELWOLD, ST. I-58
AFFILARD, MICHEL L' II-54,479,
    516; III-60,100,111,120,129,
    134,225,306
AFRANIO I-243
AGAPITUS I, POPE I-35
AGAPITUS II, POPE I-56
AGATEA, MARIO II-42; III-35
AGATHO, POPE I-41,42
AGAZZARI, AGOSTINO I-450; II-
    10,78,79,100,102,103,106,113,
    120,156,251,285,292
AGAZZI, GAETANO III-135
AGIAS I-16
AGINCOURT, FRANÇOIS D' II-523;
    III-273,276
AGINCOURT, PERRIN D' I-95
AGNELLI, CORENZO II-284

AGNELLI, SCIPIONE II-177

AGNES, ST. I-166

AGNES, MARIA GAETANO III-315

AGNESI, MARIA TERESA III-325,
    362

AGOSTINO, LUDOVICO (Reverendo
    Monsignore) I-296,410,426,
    465,470,471,509

AGOSTINI, PAOLO I-528; II-188,
    194,215,220,226,233,237,238,
    243,246,247

AGOSTINI, PIETRO SIMONE II-316,
    336,425,482,490; III-52

AGRELL, JOHAN JOACHIM III-165,
    354

AGRICOLA, ALEXANDER I-178,211,
    215,239,241,244,248,265,289,
    291,329

AGRICOLA, BENEDETTA EMILIA III-
    344

AGRICOLA, GEORG LUDWIG II-305,
    427,461

AGRICOLA, JOHANN (see Agricola,
    Paul)

AGRICOLA, JOHANN FRIEDRICH III-
    323

AGRICOLA, MARTIN I-196,213,215,
    275,279,284,287,305,307,318,
    320,368,369

AGRICOLA, PAUL (Johann) I-424;
    II-42,68,69,73,97,324,481;
    III-241

AGRICOLA, WOLFGAND CHRISTOPH
    II-42,281,321,337,341

AGUILERA, SEBASTIAN DE HEREDIA
    I-420

AGUILERA, SEBASTIAN DE HEREDIA
    I-514; II-42,79,182,389

AGUTTER, R. III-244

AHLE, JOHANN GEORG II-331,339;
    III-206,213

AHLE, JOHANN RODOLPH II-223,304,
    310,317,324,331,352,356,360,
    366,383,443,464

AICH, GOTTFRIED II-42,393
AICHINGER, GREGOR I-396,511; II-
    28,81,105,109,241
AIGNAN, ST. I-77
AILLY, PIERRE D' I-129
AINSWORTH, HENRY I-425; II-120,
    143,146,197,208
AJAX I-10,23
A'KEMPIX (see Kempis, A')
AKEROYDE, SAMUEL II-42; III-6,
    10,21,22,25,30,68,70,78,82,
    103,129
ALA, GIOVANNI BATTISTA I-344;
    II-142,175,182,226,265,268
ALAIN, JEAN I-128
ALAMANIA, ALEXANDER DE I-180,
    182,185,212
ALAMANIA, PIETRO (Da Vienna) I-
    181
ALARIC I-30
ALBAN (see Albani)
ALBAN, ST. I-74,97
ALBANESE, EGIDE JOSEPH IGNACE
    ANTOINE III-440
ALBANI, JOHANN MICHAEL II-467;
    III-424
ALBANI, MATHIAS II-200; III-133,
    257
ALBANO, MARCELLO II-169
ALBANO, ROSOLINA III-47,205
ALBERGATI, COUNT PIRRO CAPACELLI
    II-391,505,573; III-6,16,17,
    22,33,41,50,57,59,61,86,106,
    113,122,124,125,127,129,170,
    176,202,259,260,279,288,306,
    321,339,421,458,485
ALBERICI, GIACOMO II-93,125
ALBERT, ARCHDUKE, of the Nether-
    lands II-28,38,93,97,143,148,
    206
ALBERT V., DUKE of Bavaria I-
    283,362,363,368,370,402,405,
    434,453
ALBERT, DUKE of Brandenburg I-313

ALBERT III, DUKE of Brandenburg
    I-157
ALBERT, PRINCE of Prussia (Duke)
    I-235,272
ALBERT, HEINRICH II-85,86,232,
    235,257,284,287,310,319,339,
    340,352,361,364
ALBERTI, DOMENICO III-241
ALBERTI, GIUSEPPE MATTEO III-4,
    273,337
ALBERTI, INNOCENZIO DI II-35
ALBERTI, LEONE BATTISTA I-140,
    170,161,175,180,182
ALBERTI, PIETRO III-110,129,155
ALBICASTRO, ENRICO III-11,129,
    161
ALBINI, CHRISTOPHERI II-92
ALBINI, FILIPPO II-193,201,214,
    217,232
ALBINI, MATHIAS (see Albani)
ALBINONI, TOMMASO II-39,432,450,
    459; III-84,88,155,159,168,170,
    216,220,227,243,255,258,277,
    286,345,364
ALBINUS, JOHANN GEORG II-218,480
ALBIOSO, MARIO II-498; III-13
ALBRECHT, CARDINAL I-265,318
ALBRECHT V, DUKE of Bavaria I-
    393
ALBRECHT, DUKE of Prussia I-281
ALBRECHT, DUKE of Saxony I-159
ALBRECHT, JOHANN LORENZ III-450
ALBRECHT, JOHANN MATTHÄUS III-
    165,363,405
ALBRICI, BARTOLOMMEO II-42,392,
    400,483
ALBRICI, VINCENZO II-257,332,
    388,400,432,483,497,503; III-
    101
ALCANI II-363
ALCATIUS, LEO I-420
ALCOCK, JOHN I III-284
ALCUIN I-44,47
ALDEGATI, DOMENICO II-279

ALDEGREVER, H. I-306
ALDFORD, RECTOR OF II-271
ALDHELM, BISHOP I-40,41,42,43
ALDOBRANDINI, CARDINAL CINZIO
    I-455,519
ALDOBRANDINI, CARDINAL PIETRO
    I-522,530,535
ALDRED (Viol maker) I-231
ALDRICH, HENRY II-320,388,407,
    422,496; III-38,43,68,128,175,
    241
ALDROVANDINI, GIUSEPPE (Antonio
    Vincenzo) II-402,405; III-
    92,103,106,107,121,125,155,
    168,170,175,180,184,195,208,
    212,243,321
ALECTORIUS (see Hähnel, Johann)
ALEMAN, CARDINAL LOUIS I-150
ALEMANNO, HENRICO SAGITARIO II-
    139
ALEMBERT, JEAN LE ROND D' III-
    308
ALEOTTI, DETTO D'ARGENTA, GIOVANNI
    BATTISTA II-21,181,278
ALEOTTI, RAFFAELA II-284
ALESSANDRI, GIULIO D' II-42; III-
    15,48,106
ALESSANDRO, CATERINA II-35,121
ALESANDRO D'ESTE, CARDINAL (see
    Este)
ALESSANDRO, GENNARO D' III-304
ALESSANDRO, ROMANO I-348,379
ALEXANDER (Singer) I-181
ALEXANDER THE GREAT I-16,17,19;
    II-404
ALEXANDER I, POPE I-22
ALEXANDER II, POPE I-67
ALEXANDER IV, POPE I-78,96,100
ALEXANDER VI, POPE (Borgia) I-
    204
ALEXANDER VII, POPE II-358
ALEXANDER VIII, POPE III-37,43
ALEXIS I, CZAR II-250,316
AL FARABI see Farabi, Al

ALLISON, ROBERT II-124,125

ALMEIDA, FERNANDO DE II-185,285,
    374; III-135,349,389,470,489

ALMEYDA, CARLOS FRANCISCO DE
    III-135

ALOISI, GIOVANNI BATTISTA II-42,
    246

ALOVISIO (see Aloisi)

ALOVISIUS (see Aloisi)

ALOYSIUS (see Aloisi)

ALOYSON, M. ANGLUS (see Allison,
    Richard)

ALPHONSO VI, KING of Portugal
    II-510

AL-RAHMAN (see Jalíl)

ALRASHID, CALIPH HAROUN I-47

AL-SHIRWÁNÍ, II-231

ALSISE, GIACOMO II-1

ALSLOOT, DENIS VAN II-169

ALSTEDT (Alstedius), JOHANN HEIN-
    RICH II-127,136,149,284,397

ALTAEMPS, family I-223

ALTDORFER, ALBRECHT I-190,242,
    284,286,294,306

ALTENBURG, JOHANN CASPAR II-292;
    III-28

ALTENBURG, JOHANN ERNEST III-
    475

ALTENBURG, MICHAEL I-474; II-
    68,193,194,198,292

ALTNIKOL, JOHANN CHRISTOPH III-
    318,323

ALTOVITI, ANTONIO I-270,411,431

ALTOVITI, BINDO I-256,411

ALUREDUS I-98

ALVARADO, DIEGO DE II-306

ALXINGER, JOHANN BAPTIST III-
    135

ALYPIOS I-29

AMADE, LADISLAV VON III-180

AMADEI, FILIPPO (Pippo) II-517;
    III-251,318,326,335,339,354

AMADEI, MICHELE ANGELO II-35,161

AMEDO I-201

AMMANATI (Architict) I-254,416,
    527
AMMERBACH, ELIAS NIKOLAUS I-289,
    426,428,470,471; II-14
AMMON, BLASIUS II-69
AMNER, JOHN II-126,148,162,163,
    293,297
AMNER,RALPH II-87,120,213,395,
    414
AMODEI, CATALDO II-500; III-6,
    10,99
AMON, BLASIUS I-385
AMON RA (see RA, Amon)
AMOREVOLI, ANGELO III-294
AMOROSIUS, SIMON II-35,87
AMSFORTIUS, FRANCISCUS MARCELLUS
    I-373
AMYOT, JOSEPH (see Amiot)
ANA, FRANCESCO D' I-199,239,244
ANACLETUS, POPE I-21
ANASTASIUS I, POPE I-31,33
ANASTASIUS II, POPE I-33
ANASTASIUS III, POPE I-54
ANASTASIUS, IV, POPE I-78
ANBERT, (Mrs.) III-317
ANCHIETA, JUAN DE I-164,176,198,
    204,265,273
ANCHYTAS, of Tarentum I-14
ANCINA, PADRE GIOVENALE (Giovanni)
    I-479; II-28,30,33,74,85,434
ANDERSON, ANTHONY I-516
ANDILLY, ARNAULD D' II-335-1-9
ANDREAS, CARDINAL, of Austria
    II-12
ANDREINI, ISABELLA II-91,177
ANDREW OF CRETE, ST. I-40
ANDRIEV, J.F. D'(see Dandriev,J.F.)
ANERIO, FELICE I-383,399,416,
    438,442,448,455,480,481,503,
    504,532,533; II-45,57,63,75,
    79,81,99,100,103,106,110,112,
    113,119,120,121,125,126,134,
    136,137,148,149,153,155,156,
    169,175,188,191,194,202,233

17

ANERIO, GIOVANNI FRANCESCO   II-
    251
ANET, JEAN-BAPTISTE   II-343,386;
    III-64,162,240,373,376,390,
    418
ANFOSSI, PASQUALE   III-135,392,
    423
ANGELICO, FRA (Giovanni di Fie-
    sole)   I-127,151,152,156,157,
    158,171
ANGELO, ABBOT (St. Maria de Re-
    valdis)   I-129
ANGELO, (Signov)   II-392
ANGIERS   I-195
ANGIOLINI, GASPARO   III-353
ANGLEBERT (father)   II-450
ANGLEBERT, JEAN HENRI D'   II-53,
    246,271,382,383,397,450; III-
    16,40,42,56,150,162,305
ANGLES, HIGINI   I-84
ANGLES, NIGINION   III-203
ANGLICUS, AMERUS   I-98
ANGLICUS, BARTHOLOMAEUS   I-93
ANICETUS, ST.   I-23
ANIMUCCIA, GIOVANNI   I-211,213,
    363,376,385,393,404,410,414,
    421,422,425,451,456,497,501;
    III-467
ANIMUCCIA, PAOLO   I-344,392
ANJOS, DINIZ DOS   II-360; III-
    231
ANJOU, DUC D'   II-346
ANNA (Biblical)   I-110
ANNA, of Styria   II-139
ANNA (Anne) EMPRESS, of Russia
    III-77,435,486
ANNA, PRINCESS   I-58
ANNA AMALIA, PRINCESS of Prussia
    III-353
ANNE OF CLEVES   I-310,314
ANNE, PRINCESS of Wales   III-293
ANNE, QUEEN of Austria   II-309,
    408,501
ANNE, QUEEN of Bretagne   I-257

ANNE, QUEEN of Denmark II-124,
    150
ANNE, QUEEN of England (Boleyn)
    I-258,391
ANNE, QUEEN of England (Stuart)
    II-405,509,514; III-60,69,119,
    124,170,176,177,179,196,205,
    208,209,212,239,249,257,261,
    272,274,279,281
ANNE, ST. I-147,245,246
ANNIBALI, DOMENICO III-203,373,
    396,416
ANNO I-51
ANNUNCIACÃO, GABRIEL DA II-496;
    III-207
ANSAULT, MARIE ANNE III-39
ANSBACH, MARGRAVE OF II-405,446,
    447,457,476,483
ANSELMI, CAVALIERE II-220
ANTAEUS I-10,186
ANTEGNATI, family I-168,220
ANTEGNATI, COSTANZO I-370; II-
    113,119
ANTEGNATI, GIOVANNI BATTISTA
    I-328
ANTENOR I-8
ANTERUS, POPE I-26
ANTHEMIUS, of Tralles I-35
ANTHENODOROS, of Rhodes I-20
ANTHING, JULIANE FRIEDRIKE CHAR-
    LOTTE III-353
ANTHONY, ST. I-270
ANTICO, ANDREA I-228,250,251,
    255,263,264,267,269,271,297,
    299,301,303
ANTIER, MARIE III-396,397
ANTINORI, LUIGI III-109,372,373,
    383,385,451
ANTIOCHUS IV, of Syria I-19
ANTIOPE I-280
ANTIQUIS,GIOVANNI D' I-348,436,476
ANTOINE, "GRAND BATARD", of Bur-
    gundy (Son of Philip the Good)
    I-152,172

ANTONELLI   II-117,161,320

ANTONII, PIETRO DEGLI   II-323,462,
   465,483·   III-183,325

ANTONIO, DON   III-458

ANTONIO, FRATE   (see Cesti, Marcantonio)

ANTONIOTTO, GIORGIO   III-69

ANTONITES   I-255

ANZALONE, ANTONIA (Scarlatti)
   II-472,485

APHAIA   I-11

APHRODITE   I-12,17,19

APOLLINARE, ST.   I-35,36

APOLLO   I-8,9,10,11,16,18,19,27   *See frontispiece*

APOLLONI, APOLLONIO   II-418

APPENZELLER, BENEDICTUS   I-300,
   320,337

APRILE, GIUSEPPE   III-452

APULEIUS   I-400

AQUASPARTA, DUCHESS OF   I-508

AQUIAR, ALEXANDRE DE   II-92

AQUILA, MARCO, D'   I-301

AQUILA, SERAFINO DALL'   I-205,
   212

AQUIN, D'   (see Daquin)

AQUINAS, ST. THOMAS   I-92,97,98

ARAGON, YOLANDE D'   I-94,145

ARAIA, family   III-135

ARAIA, FRANCESCO   III-161,421,
   422,481,484,486

ARANDA, LUIS DE   II-375

ARANIES, JUAN   II-218,220

ARBEAU, THOINOT (Tabourot, Jehan)
   I-265,287,329,436,497,504,514;
   II-2

ARBUTHROT, J.   III-324,325,468

ARCADELT, JACQUES   I-225,241,
   295,303,304,305,306,307,308,
   310,312,318,319,320,322,326,
   329,356,358,363,371,372,377,
   412,429,492; II-114,226,238,
   240,352

ARCADIUS   I-24

"ARCANGELO DAL VIOLINO"   (see
   Stradivarius, Antonius)

22

ARCHILOCHOS I-7,8
ARCHINTO, COUNT III-103
ARCHYTAS I-15
"ARCIMELO" III-205
ARCOLEO III-13
"ARCOMELO" III-205
ARDANAZ, PEDRO II-453; III-206
ARDASHIR I-25
ARDEMANIO, GIULIO CESARE II-169,
    182,243,331
ARELLANO, ALONZO RAMIREZ DE
    (see Ramirea)
ARENA, ANTONIO DE I-303
ARESTI (see Arresti)
ARETINI I-196
ARETINUS, GUIDO I-61,63
AREZZO, GUIDO D' I-58,59,61,62,
    63,64,65,72,74,196,346
ARGENTA, D' (see Aleotti)
ARGENTINO, OTTOMARO LUSCINIO
    I-301
ARGENTIS, O.T. DE II-32,34
ARGENTORATI (see Argentino)
ARGYLL III-2
ARIETTO, family II-44
ARIETTO, FRANCESCO II-44
ARIETTO, SIMONE II-44,251
ARIETTO, SIMONE II II-44
ARIGONI, CARDINAL II-156
ARION, of Methymna I-8,9
ARIOSTI, ATTILIO II-380,407,
    418; III-16,46,74,77,84,94,
    102,106,110,113,115,151,155,
    166,167,170,176,178,181,183,
    189,193,195,202,210,212,213,
    216,222,232,251,278,294,295,
    302,322,326,337,345,351,358,
    359,361,362,363,371,392,393,
    405,407
ARIOSTO I-261,264,296,356,386,
    395,441,522
ARISI I-93
ARISTIDES II-344
ARISTION I-10

BISHOP AMBROSE AND EMPEROR THEODOSIUS *25*

ARTEAGA II-37
ARTEMIS I-16
ARTHUR, KING I-36; II-468,516
ARTORIUS I-27
ARTUSI, GIOVANNI MARIA I-315,
    348,489· II-30,58,60,79,81,
    88,106,114,147
ARUNDELL, LORD III-1
ARUNDELL, (Lady) Elizabeth I-
    223
ARUNDELL, SIR JOHN I-223
ASCANIO, JUSQUIN D' (see Pres,
    Josquin De)
ASCENSIUS, JODACUS BADIUS I-247
ASCHAM, ROGER I-259,331,415,423
ASCHENBRENNER, CHRISTIAN HEIN-
    RICH II-351,445,471,516;
    III-46,98,272,452
ASHBURY JOHN III-162
ASHMOLE II-383
ASHTON I-291
ASHURBANIPAL I-8
ASHWELL, THOMAS I-222,290,346
ASOLA, GIOVANNI MATTEO I-348,
    383,402,423,440,450,462,476,
    487,490,523,524; II-24,106,
    119
ASPLMAYR, FRANZ III-139,337,404
ASPROYS, J. I-128
ASSISSI, FRA PIERAZZO D' I-118
ASSOUCY, CHARLES D' II-92,326,
    331,332,334,335,348,437,466,
    469
ASTON, HUGH I-190,272
ASTORGA, EMANUELE D' II-486;
    III-120,220,231,232,258,259,
    277,286,290,297,304,316,337,
    342,352,389,442
ASTORGA, JEAN OLIVER OF III-
    135
ASURNASIRPAL III,. KING I-6
ATLANTE I-199
ATANAGI, DIONIGI I-403
ATFIELD, JOHN III-135,493

ATHALARIC   I-33
ATHANASIOS, ST.   I-26
ATHELSTAN, KING   I-52,55
ATHENA   I-13,15,19
ATHENAIOS   I-24
ATKINS, THOMAS   III-332
ATTAIGNANT, PIERRE   I-216,283,
    284,285,286,287,288,291,292,
    293,295,296,297,298,304,306,
    308,309,311,312,318,320,323,
    368,372,380,416,436
ATTEY, JOHN   II-209,296
AUBERT, ISABELLA   III-293
AUBERT, JACQUES   II-474; III-
    37,319,379,396,405,423,493
AUBERT, LOUIS   III-324,448
AUDINOT, NICHOLAS-MÉDARD   III-
    427
AUDLEY, (Lady) KATHERINE   II-389
AUFSCHNAITER   III-94,184,191,320,
    418
AUGUST, DUKE of Braunschweig   II-
    301
AUGUST, MORITZ   III-319
AUGUSTIN, LIEBER   II-481
AUGUSTINE, ST.   I-29,30,32,37,177,
    189,376
AUGUSTUS, EMPEROR of Rome   I-20
AUGUSTUS II, KING of Poland   III-
    114,248,313,374,392,452,468
AUGUSTUS III, KING of Poland   III-
    115,272,295,317,463,465,468,
    471,474,475,476,483
AULEN, JOHANNES   I-178,241
AULETTA, PIETRO   III-116,147,314,
    379,387,407,409,418
AULNOY, MME. D'   II-481; III-434
AURELI, AURELIO   II-518; III-4,
    63,71,394
AURELIUS, MARCUS   I-23,24,299
AURISICCHIO, ANTONIO   III-246,481
AUSTEN   I-222
AUTORI   I-410
AUTREAU, JACQUES   II-365; III-315

AUXCOUSTEAUX, ARTUS   I-514; II-153,237,257,264,267,280,288, 306,339,360,361,367

AUXERROIS, ST. GERMAINE L'   I-146

AUALOS, DONNA MARIA D'   I-486

AVENANT, CHARLES D'   (see Davenant, C.)

AVENARIUS, (Dr.) JOSEPH   II-9

AVERARA, D'   III-114

AVILA, GIACOMO   II-153

AVILEZ, MANUEL LEITÃO DE   (see Leitao)

AVISON, CHARLES   II-55; III-140, 233

AVOGIO   III-135

AVOSSA, GIUSEPPE   III-295

AYLWARD, THEODORE   III-427

AYRER, JAKOB   I-229; II-182,194

AYRTON, EDMOND   III-477

AYRTON, WILLIAM   III-385

AZZAIVOLO, FILIPPO (Azzaivolo)   I-372,373

AZZAIVOLO   (see Azzaivolo)

B

BABÁN, GRACIÁN   II-42,366

BABB, SAMUEL   III-135

BABELL, WILLIAM   III-52,139,352

BABST, VAL   I-329

BACCUSI, IPPOLITO   I-216,342,345, 510; II-10,119,175

BACH, ABRAHAM   II-313

BACH, AMBROSIUS   II-432

BACH, ANNA ELISABETH   III-36

BACH, ANNA MAGDALENA   III-153, 167,328,336,347,353,359,371, 373,374,376,377,394,403,415, 452,462,464

BACH, ANNA SCHMIED (wife of Jo-
hannes son of Veit) II-271
BACH, BARBARA KATHARINA II-486
BACH, C.P.E. (see Bach, K.P.E.)
BACH, CASPAR (Shepherd) II-322,
359
BACH, CASPAR, I (2nd generation)
II-64,74,186,193,260,264,267,
271,280,305
BACH, CHRISTIAN GOTTLIEB III-
371,403
BACH, CHRISTIANE BENEDICTA III-
415,424
BACH, CHRISTIANE DOROTHEA III-
438,452
BACH, CHRISTIANE SOPHIE HENRI-
ETTE III-353,384
BACH, CHRISTINE DOROTHEA II-
472
BACH, CHRISTOPH (3rd generation)
II-147,155,296,301,302,313,
339,347,352,355,382,383,421,
431,432,480,503,509; III-1,
88,108,324,335,344
BACH, DOROTHEA II-472
BACH, DOROTHEA MARIA (4th gen-
eration) II-347,480
BACH, ELISABETH III-79
BACH, ELISABETH JULIANE FRIDER-
ICA (6th generation) III-383
BACH, ELISABETH LÄMMERHIRT III-
82
BACH, ERNESTUS ANDREAS (6th gen-
eration) III-394
BACH, EVA HOFFMAN II-168
BACH, GEORG CHRISTOPH (4th gen-
eration) II-301,418,421,479,
510; III-29,40,90,108,197,
213,266,324
BACH, GEORG MICHAEL (5th gener-
ation) III-167,182
BACH, GOTTFRIED (5th generation)
III-44,56
BACH, GOTTLIEB FRIEDRICH (6th
generation) III-276,353,494

LES CLAVECINISTES

● CHARLES PHILIPPE EMMANUEL BACH ●
Né à Weimar en 1714 — Mort à Hambourg en 1788

BACH, JOHANN CASPAR II-472

BACH, JOHANN CHRISTIAN (4th gen-
    eration) II-292,401,402,418,
    432,435,443,479,503; III-64,
    101,182,395

BACH, JOHANN CHRISTIAN (son of
    George Christoph, 5th gener-
    ation) III-213

BACH, JOHANN CHRISTIAN (son of
    Johann Christian, 5th gener-
    ation) III-117

BACH, JOHANN CHRISTIAN (grand-
    son of Lips Bach, 5th gener-
    ation) II-479

BACH, JOHANN CHRISTIAN (son of
    Johann Christian, 6th gener-
    ation) III-101

BACH, JOHANN CHRISTIAN (son of
    Johann Nikolaus, 6th genera-
    tion) III-304

BACH, JOHANN CHRISTIAN (son of *See illustration on p. 37*
    Johann Sebastian, 6th gener-
    ation) III-485

BACH, JOHANN CHRISTOPH (son of
    Christoph, 4th generation)
    II-313,431,433,481,486,497,
    509; III-1,4,13,45,56,71,82

BACH, JOHANN CHRISTOPH (son of
    Heinrich, 4th generation)
    II-302,317,402,413,422,426,
    449,462,463,472,481,490,503;
    III-4,14,36,46,60,83,153,162,
    175,180,183,270,427

BACH, JOHANN CHRISTOPH (son of
    Johann Aegidius, 5th genera-
    tion) II-454; III-2,486

BACH, JOHANN CHRISTOPH (son of
    Johann Ambrosius, 5th gener-
    ation) II-432,474; III-46,
    82,91,92,93,152,335

BACH, JOHANN CHRISTOPH (son of
    Johann Christian, 5th gener-
    ation) II-443; III-73,182,
    326,395

BACH, JOHANN CHRISTOPH (son of
Johann Christoph, 5th generation) II-449,462; III-36,
46,435

BACH, JOHANN CHRISTOPH (son of
Johann Christoph II, 6th generation) II-516; III-174

BACH, JOHANN CHRISTOPH (son of
Johann Nicolaus, also known
as Johann Christian, 6th generation) III-304

BACH, JOHANN CHRISTOPH FRIEDRICH
III-452,453,456

BACH, JOHANN ELIAS (6th generation) III-197

BACH, JOHANN ERNST (5th generation II-509; III-213,215,
220,373

BACH, JOHANN ERNST (6th generation) III-344,351

BACH, JOHANN FRIEDRICH (5th generation) II-459,503; III-
225,427

BACH, JOHANN FRIEDRICH (6th generation) III-188,207

BACH, JOHANN GEORG (son of Georg
Christoph) II-510; III-266

BACH, JOHANN GEORG (son of Aeg-
idius) II-485

BACH, JOHANN GOTTFRIED BERNHARD
III-284,427,486

BACH, JOHANN GÜNTHER (son of
Heinrich, 4th generation)
II-347,501,503,504,509;III-81

BACH, JOHANN GÜNTHER (6th generation) III-182,487

BACH, JOHANN HEINRICH (5th generation) III-13

BACH, JOHANN HEINRICH (son of
Johann Christoph, 6th generation) III-214

BACH, JOHANN HEINRICH (son of
Johann Valentin, 6th generation) III-249

*See illustrations on pp. 51,
60-61, 165*

32,48,151,212,270,273,312,313,
326,328,375,441,442,453,459,
460,482,500,511,518; III-1,2,
24,29,30,55,73,77,82,83,88,
91,93,96,102,107,134,138,141,
148,149,150,152,159,160,162,
164,165,167,174,175,177,179,
180,181,183,187,191,193,195,
196,197,199,204,206,207,208,
213,214,215,216,220,221,222,
224,225,227,229,230,235; III-
240,246,247,249,252,258,261,
263,264,266,267,268,273,274,
276,277,279,282,284,285,286,
288,289,292,293,295,296,297,
298,303,305,306,307,309,310,
311,312,313,314,316,317,319,
322,323,324,325,326,327,328,
330,332,333,334,335,336,337,
343,344,345,346,347,350,351,
352,353,354,356,357,359,360,
361,362,363,365,367,371,372,
373,374,376,379,380,381,382,
383,384,385,386,387,390,391,
392,393,394,398,399,401,402,
403,405,407,409,411,412,413,
415,416,417,418,421,423,425,
426,427,428,429,430,432,436,
437,438,439,440,441,442,443,
445,446,448,449,451,452,454,
456,458,461,462,463,464,465,
466,467,468,470,472,473,474,
475,476,477,478,479,483,485,
489,493,494

BACH, JOHANN STEPHAN III-43
BACH, JOHANN VALENTIN (5th gen-
    eration) II-421; III-80,90,
    197,249,324
BACH, JOHANN WILHELM (7th gener-
    ation) III-453
BACH, JOHANNA JUDITHA II-485;
    III-13,215
BACH, JOHANNES (son of Caspar,
    2nd generation) II-74,86,147,

BAILLE, ALEXANDER   III-135,490
BAILLE, (Lady) GRIZEL   II-405
BAILLOT   III-256
BAINI, GIUSEPPE   I-216,363
BAKER (spinet-maker)   II-460
BAKER, THOMAS   III-169,184,227
BAKFARK, VALENTIN   I-245,272,281,
    312,336,338,354,356,400,402,
    409,425,444; II-452
BALA, FRIAR   I-23
BALASSI, VALENTIN   I-352,429,532
BALBASTRE, CLAUDE   III-395,415
BALBI, ALVISE   II-274
BALBI, LODOVICO (Luigi)   I-225,
    331,447,484,485; II-86,93,100,
    112,121
BALBULUS, NOKTER   I-50,51,54
BALDI   III-135,374,380,385,396,
    405
BALDINI   I-471
BALDOVINETTI, ALESSO   I-149,157,
    165,210
BALDUNG (Grien), HANS   I-194,249,
    262,264,286,331
BALDWIN, JOHN   I-443,516,517,518,
    519,521; II-99,101,162
BALE   I-342
BALELLI   III-135
BALL (Miss)   III-424
BALL, ELIZABETH   II-502
BALLABENE, GREGORIO   III-135,326
BALLARD, family   III-162,299,314,
    346,366,419
BALLARD (see also Leroy and Bal-
    lard)
BALLARD, JEAN-BAPTISTE CHRISTOPHE
    II-521; III-84,93,94,126,184,
    187,196,209,217,218,224,253,
    285
BALLARD, PIERRE   II-128,280
BALLARD, ROBERT   I-283,346,350,
    410,427; II-35,46,49,83,99,
    114,128,129,137,154,176,180,
    206,208,235,296,424,434,463;
    III-138,285

BALLESTRA, RAIMUNDO II-126
BALLETTI, MANON III-326
BALLETTI, MARGHERITA III-255
BALLI, DOMENICO (Belli?) II-186
BALSAMINO, SIMONE I-534
BALSART, T. (see Baltzar, T.)
BALTAGERINI (see Baltazarini)
BALTAZARINI I-448,461,469
BALTZAR, THOMAS (Balsart) II-44,255,356,359,360,366,371,
    383,385,391,392
BANASTRE, GILBERT I-188,196,200
BANBURY, EARL OF III-4
BANCHI, GIULIO CESARE II-196
BANCHIERO, ADRIANO I-239,409,
    494,519; II-3,22,23,30,57,58,
    63,66,67,69,73,81,84,93,94,
    96,105,106,113,120,121,127,
    135,137,140,144,149,152,155,
    157,162,164,169,189,193,194,
    195,197,209,215,226,229,233,
    243,267
BANCO, MASO DI I-117
BANCO, NANNI DI I-124
BANCROFT, JOHN III-49,59,62
BANDINI, OTTAVIO I-468
BANNISTER, JEFFERY II-465
BANISTER, JOHN I, II-251,360,386,
    389,392,393,395,402,406,408,
    411,412,413,419,423,434,437,
    439,441,444,445,447,463,465,
    467,473,475,479,482; III-186
BANISTER, JOHN II II-498; III-
    6,57,94,97,151,486
BANKS, BENJAMIN III-395
BANNIUS, JOANNES ALBERTUS II-
    14,310
BAPTIST, SIGNOR JO. (see Draghi)
BARAHONA, JUAN DE ESQUIVEL II-
    35,112,144
BARBANDT, CARL III-135
BARBAPICCOLA, NICOLA III-121,124
BARBARELLI, GIORGIO (see Gior-
    gione)

BARBARIN, MANFRED I-373
BARBARINO, BARTOLOMEO ("detto
  el Pesarino") II-35,127,137,
  144,155,157,169,174,176
BARBARINO, FLORIDE DE WILVESTRIS
  A (see Silvestris)
BARBARO II-40
BARBÉ, ANTOINE II-30,275
BARBELLA, EMANUELE III-309,381
BARBELLA, FRANCESCO III-296,401
BARBARELLI, GIORGIO (see Gior-
  gione)
BARBERIIS I-338
BARBERINI, family II-312
BARBERINI, (Cardinal) ANTONIO
  II-354
BARBERINI, (Cardinal) FRANCESCO
  II-208,276,287,300
BARBERINI, MATTEO II-348
BARBET, ANSELME II-74
BARBETTA(?) I-418
BARBETTA, GIULIO CESARE I-417,
  467,515; II-79,81
BARBIREAU, JACQUES I-135,161,
  166,167,199,202,256
BARBIAN, GUGLIELMO III-54
BARBONI II-182
BARCROFTE, GEORGE I-293,453;
  II-35,126
BARCROFTE, THOMAS I-293,300
BARDELLA, ANTONIO NALDI I-516
BARDI, GIOVANNI I-296,486,488,
  524; II-6,7,12,14,58,65,142
BARDZIŃSKI, ALANUS III-129,217
BAR'-EBHRAJA (see Hebraeus, Bar)
BARGAGLI, GIROLOMO I-429,502
BARGAGLI, SCIPIONE I-314,348,
  492; II-42,146
BARGES, ANTONIO I-343
BARLEY, WILLIAM II-10,22,30,31,
  32,35,59,88,91,114,120,121,
  155
BARNABAS, ST. I-195
BARNABEI, G.E. II-413

BARTLETT, JOHN (see Bartlet)
BARTOLDO, SPERINDIO I-291
BARTOLI, COSIMO I-410
BARTOLINI, VINCENZIO III-135
BARTOLUCCI, FRA RUFFINO I-251
BARTON, DR. III-281
BARTON, WILLIAM III-428
BARYPHONUS, HEINRICH II-121,
    164,195,235,355
BASCHENIS, EVARISTO II-179,471
BASEDOW, JOHANN BERNHARD III-
    359
BASEVI (see Cervetto)
BASIL IV, CZAR (see Shuiski)
BASIL, ST. I-28
BASILE, ADRIANA (Baroni) II-
    131,215
BASILI, ANDREA III-188,416
BASILY, ANDREA (see Basili)
BASIRON I-247,248
BASSANDINE, THOMAS II-3
BASSANO (Basson, de Basson),
    family II-35,298
BASSANO, GIOVANNI I-480,481,518;
    II-2,23,27,75,105,162
BASSANO, JACOPO I-251,385,395,
    524
BASSÉ, ADAM DE LA I-100
BASSELIN, OLIVIER I-139
BASSANI, GIOVANNI BATTISTA II-
    193,363,364,467,469,474,477,
    478,507,519; III-29,86,128,
    184,258,294
BASSETT, (Sir) RICHARD II-497
BASSEVI (see Cervetto)
BASSINI, GIAMBATTISTA II-427
BASSIRON, PHILIPPE I-133
BASSO, I-311
BASSUS, JUNIUS I-29
BASTA, GENERAL II-72
BASTON, JOHN III-135,437
BASTON, JOSQUIN I-235,406
BATAILLE, GABRIEL II-57,114,117,
    118,174,250

BATCHELAR, DANIELL (see Batch-
    eler)
BATCHELER, DANIELL (Batchelar)
    I-514; II-127
BATES, WILLIAM III-135,448
BATESON, JANE II-92
BATESON, JOHN II-142
BATESON, SARAH II-105
BATESON, THOMAS I-443: II-29,34,
    69,74,79,81,88,92,105,112,118,
    140,142,144,162,182,207,250,
    257,258
BATESON, THOMAS II II-79
BATESON, MRS. THOMAS II-250
BATESTON (see Bateson)
BATHE, JOHN I-396
BATHE, WILLIAM I-353,396,476;
    II-2,58,87,99,137,142,154
BÁTHORI, (Prince) SIGLSMUND I-
    428,502; II-148
BATHORI, KING STEPHAN I-447; II-
    82
BATHORY, (Cardinal-Prince) AN-
    DREA (Bathori) I-470,477;
    II-29
BATI, LUCA I-504,533,537; II-
    6,23,56,66,112
BÂTON (father) III-301
BÂTON, CHARLES III-301,468
BÂTON, HENRI III-246,301
BATTEN, ADRIAN II-155,219,272,
    279,281,283
BATTEN, EDWARD II-279
BATTEN, JOHN II-279
BATTEN, WILLIAM II-279
BATTI, PIETRO IACOMO II-434
BATTISTA, ST. GIOVANNI I-451;
    III-279
BATTISTINI, GIACOMO III-95,97
BAUCHIER, JOSIAS II-501
BAUGIN II-256
BAULDEWEYN, NOEL (Baulduin) I-
    249,255,256,262,266,285
BAULDUIN, NOEL (see Bauldeweyn)

BAULLONGE, VALENTIN DE II-198

BAUMANN (publisher) I-493; II-202

BAUMGARTEN, GOTTLIEB ALEXANDER III-276

BAURATH, ANNA AMALIA III-110, 266

BAVARIA, ELECTRESS OF III-63, 70,77

BAVIERA (nephew) III-338

BAVIERA, VIOLANTE BEATRICE DI III-338

BAYLE (?) I-353

BAYLE, PIERRE II-322; III-98, 114

BAYLEY,ANN III-19,20

BAYLEY, WILLIAM III-20

BAYLY, ANSELM III-318

BAYNARD, JOHN III-70

BAYNE, ALEXANDER III-306

BAYNES, (Sir) THOMAS II-375

BAZZANI, FRANCESCO MARIA II-42, 447,484,491; III-74

BAZZINI, FRANCESCO II-56,275, 375

BÉ, GUILLAUME LE I-312,315,328

BEACON, THOMAS I-356

BEAN, APHRA III-106

BEARD, JOHN III-246,487

BEATRICE, QUEEN of Hungary I-134,186,192,197,198,278

BEATRICE, VIOLANTE (see Baviera, de)

BEATRIX, of Burgundy I-78

BEAUCHAMP, CHARLES LOUIS II-275, 426; III-199,378

BEAULIEU I-461

BEAUMARCHAIS, PIERRE AUGUSTIN III-450

BEAUMAVIELLE II-427; III-28

BEAUMONT, FRANCIS I-478; II-26, 127,173; III-23,44,51

BEAUNE, CLAUDE DE I-395

BEAUNEVEU, ANDRÉ I-126

BEAUVARLET (see Charpeutier, Jean Jacques)
BECCARI, AGOSTINO I-360
BECCAU, JOACHIM III-320
BECH, FRANZ (see Beck)
BECK, FRANZ (François) III-351, 427
BECKER (?) I-211
BECKER, DIEDRICH II-42,310,418, 419
BECKET, THOMAS À I-78,79
BEDE, VENERABLE I-38,39,41,44
BEDFORD, (Rev.) ARTHUR III-252
BEDOS, DOM I-197
BEECKE, IGNAZ VON III-464
BEETHOVEN, family III-138
BEETHOVEN, CORNELIUS VAN II-519; III-2,183,295
BEETHOVEN (Mrs.) CORNELIUS VAN III-183
BEETHOVEN, CORNELIUS VAN (II) III-224,441,474
BEETHOVEN, JOHANN VAN III-167
BEETHOVEN, LUDWIG VAN III-258, 259,313,374,440,454,462,463, 465,466,474,476,485
BEETHOVEN, LUDWIG, VAN (II) I-226; III-2,128,258,259,277, 382,465,466
BEETHOVEN, MARIA BERNARDINA LUD-OVICA VAN III-476
BEETHOVEN, MARIE LOUISE VAN III-224,259
BEETHOVEN, MICHAEL VAN II-518, 519; III-2,215,224,259
BÈGUE, NICOLAS ANTOINE LE II-251,414,469; III-26,70,74,174
BEHAIM, MICHAEL I-137,145,183
BEHN, APHRA II-428,463,465,475, 490,505,506; III-15,89
BEISSEL, CONRAD JOHANN III-46, 326,333,435,446
BEL, FIRMIN LE I-307,310,311, 385

BEL, JACQUES (Jacotin) LE I-294,
   312,317
BEL, PHILIPPE LE I-100
BÉLA, KING of Hungary I-81
BELARDINO (Pierluigi) I-359,360
BELATIUS, FRANCESCO (see Bella-
   zzi)
BEL'AVER VINCENZO I-454,485
BELDEMANDIS PRODUSCIMUS DE I-
   107,142,148,207
BELED, SHEIKH EL I-2
BELEM, ANTONIO DE II-193,413;
   III-153
BELGIOIOSO, BALDASSARE DA I-
   359
BEL'HAUER, VINCENZO (see Bel'-
   aver)
BELISONIUS, PAUL I-435
BELLA, DOMENICO DELLA III-129,
   193
BELLANDA, LODOVICO II-35,75,88,
   106,127,137,149
BELLANTE, DIONISIO II-35,248,
   307
BELLASIO I-451
BELLAZZI (Belatius) FRANCESCO
   II-35,185
BELLAY, JOACHIM DU I-272,339,
   340,381
BELLECHOSE, HENRI I-145
BELLENGUES, RICHARD DE I-144
BELLÈRE I-422,471,472,482,512,
   521,526,529,535
BELLERMANN (Director) I-232
BELLERMANN, CONSTANTIN III-101
BELLERMANN, HEINRICH I-232
BELLET, HUGH I-431
BELLI, DOMENICO (Balli?) II-35,
   110,130,170,172,180,186
BELLI, GIROLAMO I-383,470,474;
   II-104,176
BELLI, GIULIO I-391; II-58,73,88,
   94,105,106,114,135,148,153,202,
   282

BELLI, P.G. II-274

BELLINI, GIOVANI I-152,175,176,
    180,185,195,196,198,201,208,
    242,252,256,261,373

BELLINZANI III-305,306,314,328,
    345,387,396,426,432,468,477,
    493

BELLONI, GIOSEFFO II-35,81,88,
    94,100,137

BELLOTTO, BERNARDO (see Canal-
    etto, G.A.)

BELLSTEDT, JOHN GOTTFRIED II-490

BEMBO, family I-480

BEMBO, (Cardinal) PIETRO I-180,
    241,255,296,310,335,458

BENCI, ANTONIO (see Pollaiuolo)

BENCI, GINEVRA I-188

BENCOVITCH, FEDERICO II-471

BENDA, FRANZ (František) III-
    232,313,466

BENDA, GEORG III-337

BENDA, J. ANTONÍN III-344,403,
    487

BENDA, JAN JIŘÍ III-4,285

BENDA, JOSEF III-363

BENDELER, JOHANN PHILIPP II-380;
    III-15,30,53,115,208,225

BENDELER, SALOMON II-571; III-
    259,363

BENDIDIO, LUCREZIA I-334,385,
    389,421

BENDLER, S. (see Bendeler, Sol-
    omon)

BENEDETTI, (Singer) III-135,323,
    332,338,345,372

BENEDETTI, PIETRO II-35,44,135,
    137,139,150,176,250,327

BENEDETTI, ROCCO I-437

BENEDETTO, STEFANO II-436

BENEDICT I, POPE I-36

BENEDICT II, POPE I-42

BENEDICT III, POPE I-50

BENEDICT IV, POPE I-52

BENEDICT V, POPE I-57

BENEDICT VI, POPE   I-57
BENEDICT VII, POPE   I-57
BENEDICT VIII, POPE   I-63
BENEDICT IX, POPE   I-64,65
BENEDICT XI, POPE   I-109
BENEDICT XII, POPE   I-116; III-
    386
BENEDICT, XIII, POPE   III-379,
    386,446
BENEDICT, ST.   I-35,209
BENEDICTIS, JACOB DE   I-81,101
BENELLI, ALEMANNO (see Bottri-
    gari)
BENEVOLI, ORAZIO   II-91,92,244,
    296,309,316,317,436,437,499
BENINI   III-135
BENNET, JOHN   I-424; II-30,34,35,
    69,88,162,202
BENSER, J.D.   III-135
BENSERADE, ISAAC DE   II-142,337,
    352,362,414
BENSON, JOHN   II-343
BENTE, MATTEO   II-66
BENTIVOGLIO, GINEVRA   I-190; II-
    217
BENTLEY (?)   I-473
BENTLEY, RICHARD   II-390
BENTZON, NIELS VIGGO   III-263,
    264
BEOWULF   I-35,43,61
BERARDI, ANGELO   II-42,418,455,
    497; III-22,26,38,48,73
BERCHEM, JACQUES (Jachet van)
    I-242,300,310,321,332,333,364,
    385,386,396; II-56
BEREGANI   II-516; III-255,368
BERENGER, RAYMOND   I-95
BERNSTADT, GAETANO   II-36; III-
    302,305,350,363
BERENT, SZYMON   II-285,327,328
BERG, ADAM   I-315,419,432,434,
    436,440,445,468,504,520,534;
    II-23,67,126
BERG, GEORGE (Georg)   III-135

BERG, JOHANN I-345,370

BERGHE, JÉRÔME VAN DEN (see
   Jérôme)

BERGONZI, CARLO II-517; III-302

BERGONZI, MICHEL ANGELO III-344

BERHARD II-343

BERKELEY, DR. III-364

BERKOSKE, LAURENS III-460,469

BERMUDO, JUAN I-251,339,341,364

BERN, (Mr.) III-194

BERNABEI, ERCOLE II-199,390,417,
   423,441,450,453,467,478,490;
   III-15,19,20

BERNABEI, GIUSEPPE ANTONIO II-
   327,437,467,475,478,482,490;
   III-56,243,451

BERNABEI, VINCENZO II-519; III-
   48,57

BERNACCHI, ANTONIO I-225; III-
   2,167,238,245,293,302,309,
   319,332,345,415,416,417,424,
   442,448

BERNARD "THE GERMAN" I-166

BERNARD, JOHN I-161

BERNARD, ST. I-62,189,202

BERNARD, ST. (composer and writer) I-69,76,78

BERNARD, SAMUEL III-467

BERNARDI, BARTOLOMEO II-282,
   380; III-39,69,175,181,183,
   246,453

BERNARDI, FRANCESCO (see "senesino")

BERNARDI, STEFFANO II-131,135,
   164,208,268,271

BERNARDINO, GIOVANNI I-345,363,
   383; II-9

BERNARDINO, ST. I-160,182

BERNARDONI, PIETRO ANTONIO III-
   174,181,212,222

BERNASCONI, ANDREA III-207

BERNERS, LORD I-279

BERNHARD (organist) I-180

BERNHARD, CHRISTOPH II-237,328,

356,381,397,400,403,424,472;
III-26,62

BERNHARD I, PRINCE III-206

BERNIER, NICOLAS II-396; III-
83,117,188,196,476

BERNINI, GIANLORENZO II-27,262,
366,369,395,416,492

BERNO I-62

BERNRODER, HERM. I-406

BERRY, (Duke) JEAN DE I-143,
145

BERSELLI, MATTEO III-129,325,
338

BERSHEH, EL I-4

BERTALI, ANTONIO II-92,259,324,
328,334,345,350,371,377,382,
384,393,396,403,409,411,422,
425

BERTAND I-493

BERTATI, GIOVANNI III-492

BERTEZEN, SALVATORE III-136

BERTHAUME III-136

BERTI, GIOVANNI PIETRO II-218,
220,222,226,269,280,284,285,
365

BERTIE, PEREGRINE III-1,4

BERTIN DE LA DOUÉ II-493; III-
201,209,243,283,298,315,320

BERTINI, SALVATORE III-337

BERTOLLI, FRANCESCA III-129,416,
422,424,438,454,466,487

BERTOLOTTI II-186

BERTON III-136

BERTONI, FERNANDO GIUSEPPE III-
371,409,434,472

BERTRAM (Master) I-119,125

BERTRAND, ANTHOINE DE I-332,451,
491

BERTANDUS(?) (see also Vaqueras)
I-193

BERWALD, JOHANN FRIEDRICH III-
250

BERWILLIBALD, GIORGIO GIACOMO
III-294

BESARD, JEAN BAPTISTE I-412;
   II-75,81,82,88,107,176,178
BESARDUS(?) I-247; II-81,176
BESLER, SAMUEL I-435; II-75,
   131,144,202,223
BESLER, SIMON II-263
BESOZZI, family (Bezozzi) III-
   135
BESOZZI, ALESSANDRO III-95,97,
   103,173,182,483,487,491
BESOZZI, ANTONIO III-277,393,
   491
BESOZZI, CHRISTOFORO III-167,
   175,372,383
BESOZZI, GAETANO III-395
BESOZZI, GIUSEPPE III-14,249,
   402,462
BESOZZI, PAOLO GIROLAMO III-189,
   303,487,491
BESSON III-416
BÉTHUNE II-493
BÉTHUNE, CANON DE I-77,89,91
BETSON, RICHARD II-140
BETTERTON, THOMAS III-51,89,125
BETTINO II-307
BEVERINGEN, ANDRIES (see Pev-.
   ernage, A)
BEVERNAGE, ANDRIES (see Pev-
   ernage, A)
BEUILAEQUA I-393
BEVILACQUA, COUNT MARIO I-458,
   468,482,486,490,525
BEVIN, EDWARD II-53,66; III-134,
   162,256
BEVIN, ELWAY I-502,503; II-36,
   91,99,135,193,280,292
BEYS, CHARLES DE II-354
BEZE (Beza) THÉODORE DE I-265,
   350,351,352,353,355,359,394,
   398,402,403; II-96
BEZOZZI, family (see Besozzi)
BEZZI, GIROLAMO III-293,317
BIANCHETTI, LODOVICO I-474
BIANCHI,GIOVANNI BATTISTA III-136

BIANCHI (Bianco, Blanchis), PI-
ETRO ANTONIO II-36
BIANCHI, VINCENZO II-290,300
BIANCHINI I-332
BIANCIARDI, FRANCESCO II-104,
105,111
BIANCO, NANNI DI I-142,146
BIAT, MONCO II-117
BIAT, PAOLO II-115,117
BIBBIENA (architect) III-222
BIBBIENA, CARDINAL I-255
BIBER, HEINRICH IGNAZ FRANZ VON
(see also Birben) II-310,
405,456,463,497,498,523;
III-22,25,40,75,116,189,238
BIBIENA, GALLI (brothers) III-
110
BICCI, ANTONIO I-533; II-12,20
BICCHI (Bichi), CARDINAL II-318,
433
BICHI, CARDINAL (see Bicchi)
BICKNOR, ALEXANDER DE I-113,252
BIEGER, (father) I-453
BIEGER, EUPHROYSYNE I-453
BIEST, "MERTEN" VAN DER I-374
BIFFI, A. III-465
BIFFI, GIOVANNI II-10,23
BIGGS, EDWARD II-268
BIGONGIARI, MARCO II-167,275,
307,348,352,354,364; III-11
BIGONZI III-368
BIHZAD I-170,198
BILAL iKN-RIYAH I-40
BILHON, JEAN DE I-298
BILLAINE, P. II-222
BINCHOIS, GILLES I-130,148,149,
152,153,173,174
BINDER, CHRISTLIEB SIGMUND III-3
352
BINI(?) III-154
BINI, PASQUALE III-294
BIONDI, G.B. II-109,180
BIONI, ANTONIO III-116,341,349,
363,379,428,447,456

JOHANN SEBASTIAN BACH AND HIS FAMILY *61*

BIRBEN, CARLO HENRICO DI III-
    238
BIRCHENSHA (Birkenshaw), JOHN
    II-42,298,301,397,398,406,411,
    430,433,435,439; III-70
BIRCKNER, JOHANN II-239
BIRDE, JULIANA (see Byrd)
BIRKENSHAW (see Birchensha)
BIRKENSTOCK, JOHANN ADAM III-
    18,233,238,345,374,428,462
BIRLEY, JULIANNA (see Byrd)
BIRNIE, WILLIAM II-187
BISAGNO II-361
BISCHOFF, JAN II-260,307,367,
    426
BISHOP, JOHN II-402; III-21,29,
    93,416
BISSARI III-336
BISSE, (Dr.) THOMAS III-363
BITON I-9
BIZCARGUI, GONZALO MARTINEZ DE
    I-252
BLACKHALL (Blakhall, Blakehall)
    ANDREW I II-118,237
BLACKHALL, ANDREW II II-237
BLACKWELL, ISAAC II-42,456
BLAGRAVE, THOMAS II-360
BLAHOSLAV, (Bishop) JAN I-386
BLAIKIE II-516
BLAINVILLE(?) III-213
BLAINVILLE, CHARLES HENRI DE
    III-255
BLAISE, ST. I-47,149
BLAMONT, FRANÇOIS COLIN DE
    III-45,215,319,352,359,376,
    383,418,430,443,456,481

BLANC, DIDIER LE I-454,467
BLANCHARD, ESPRIT JOSEPH AN-
    TOINE III-100,305,345,428,
    480

BLANCKS, EDWARD I-524; II-24
    36,202
BLAND, HUMPHREY III-399

BLANKENBURG, QUIRINS GERBRANDT
    II-351,469,521; III-225,418,
    460,468
BLAS DE CASTRO, JUAN (see Cas-
    tro)
BLAVET (Blauet), MICHEL III-151,
    354,407,443
BLIND RORY (see Roderick)
BLITHEMAN, WILLIAM I-397,517,
    518
BLONDEL (architect) II-179,441;
    III-17
BLONDEL DES NESLES (see Nesles)
BLOUNT II-361
BLOW, ELIZABETH III-318
BLOW, HENRY (father of John)
    II-317,320,340,355
BLOW, HENRY II (son of Henry)
    II-320
BLOW, HENRY (son of John) II-
    462
BLOW, JOHN II-317,323,327,336,
    355,381,393,397,400,401,411,
    419,422,449,450,462,467,474,
    479,482,488,492,498,503,504,
    505,508,511,513,519,520,521,
    523; III-1,3,6,11,15,18,38,
    40,42,55,66,72,73,91,94,103,
    108,109,111,118,124,125,126,
    132,153,155,156,157,165,180,
    193,223,226,256,318,427
BLOW, JOHN JR. (son of John)
    III-73
BLOW, KATHERINE (mother of John)
    II-317,320,340
BLOW, KATHERINE (sister of John)
    II-340
BLOW, KATHERINE (daughter of
    John) III-427
BLUME I-228
BLUNDEVILLE, JOHN II-401
BOCCACCIO I-119,120,165,242,
    332
BOCCAPADULE, ANTONIO I-437

BOCCARDI, MICHELE A.   III-439
BOCKSHORN, SAMUEL (Friedrich)
    II-242,328,356,359,364,368,
    372,373,377,389,401,423,430;
    III-227
BODDECKER, PHILIPP JAKOB   II-340;
    III-11,129,168
BODE, JOHANN JOACHIM CHRISTOPH
    III-424
BODENSCHATZ, ERHARD   I-223,424;
    II-30,57,79,82,94,100,107,
    112,114,137,164,182,202,204,
    239,265,275,284
BODINUS, SEBASTIAN   III-136,164
BODMER, JOHANN JACOB   III-121
BOEMUS, JOHANN   I-212,259
BOESSET, ANTOINE   I-484; II-162,
    176,180,193,202,206,213,239,
    248,265,306,352,373,409,414,
    424,434
BOESSET, CLAUDE JEAN BAPTISTE
    II-396; III-102
BOESSET, JEAN BAPTISTE (de De-
    hault)   II-154,309,323,332,
    366,521; III-4,102
BOEST, GASPARD   II-407
BOETHIUS   I-7,33,34,35,71
BOËTHUS   I-18
BOETIUS, AUGUST   II-521
BOFFRAND   II-416; III-98
BOGURODZICA   I-70
BÖHM, GEORG   II-382,455,474,519;
    III-73,117,462
BOILEAU, NICOLAS   II-278; III-34
BOISMORTIER, JOSEPH BODIN DE
    III-56,363,435,480
BOISSARD, JEHAN (see Verdelet)
BOIVIN, (Mme.)   III-465
BOLECHOWSKI, JÓZEF   III-136
BOLEYN, (Sir) WILLIAM   I-258
BOLLES (viol maker)   I-231
BOLLOHOWSKI, JÓZEF (see BOLECH-
    OWSKI)
BOLOGNA, ANTONIO DA   I-323

BOLOGNA, GERONINO DI I-271
BOLOGNA, GIOVANNI DA (Boulogne)
    I-286,411,455; II-117,286
BOLOGNA, JACOPO DA I-104,107,
    119,120
BOLSENA, ANDREA ADAMI DI II-392;
    III-251,252,254
BOLT, JOHN I-533; II-96,117,135,
    292
BONA, of Savoy I-186,191
BONA, VALERIO II-9,68,135,155,
    187
BONACOSSI, F. II-300
BONAGIONTA, GIULIO I-409,410,
    416,507
BONANNI, F. III-339
BONAVENTURA, ST. (composer) I-
    91,95,98; III-399
BONCOMPAGNI, GIACOMO I-441,457,
    464
BONCOMPAGNI, PRINCE II-302
BONDONE, GIOTTO DI (see Giotto)
BONENIENSIS, JOANNIS GUIDETTI
    I-467
BONFADINO II-204
BONHOMME, PIERRE II-174
BONHOUR, MARGUERITE II-8
BONI II-220
BONIFACE (English missionary)
    I-41
BONIFACE I, POPE I-32
BONIFACE II, POPE I-35
BONIFACE III, POPE I-39
BONIFACE IV, POPE I-39
BONIFACE V, POPE I-39
BONIFACE VI, POPE I-52
BONIFACE VIII, POPE I-102
BONIFACE IX, POPE I-127
BONIFACE, ST. I-41,45
BONINI (?) II-105,107,111,112,
    114,121,148,150,164,229
BONINI, SEVERO II-299,303,391
BONIS III-79
BONIVENTI, GIUSEPPE II-430; III-
    50,57,179,263,316,320

BONLINI II-283; III-430

BONNER, BISHOP I-332

BONNET-BOURDELOT (see also Bourdelot)

BONNET-BOURDELOT, JAQUES III-
201,288,363,376,387

BONNET-BOURDELOT, PIERRE II-284;
III-201,224

BONNEVIL, ÉTIENNE DE I-100

BONNEVIN, GIOVANNI I-235

BONNO, GIUSEPPE III-239

BONO, PIETRO I-134

BONOMETTI, GIOVANNI BATTISTA
II-36,135,163,164,165,187

BONOMINI II-262

BONONCINI, brothers III-251

BONONCINI, ANTONIO MARIA (Marc'
Antonio) II-454; III-101,
103,106,113,167,175,190,196,
205,206,209,210,213,217,219,
223,235,240,251,253,285,293,
294,296,302,312,324,331,336,
338,384,410,423

BONONCINI, GIOVANNI MARIA II-
301,409,410,414,419,424,433,
434,439,440,445,451,456,459,
467,468,469,471,473,475

BONONCINI, GIOVANNI II-426; III-
11,20,21,22,30,33,48,50,56,
60,68,69,77,79,81,86,88,94,
97,106,110,116,121,122,127,
151,158,161,166,167,171,172,
175,176,178,179,180,184,189,
190,195,198,202,205,212,213,
214,221,222,228,231,239,240,
241,243,245,251,255,266,268,
278,319,321,325,326,327,331,
335,336,337,338,339,341,343,
344,345,347,351,353,363,367,
380,382,392,396,398,400,406,
443,448,449,452,456,458,483,
487

BONONCINI, MARC' ANTONIO (see
Antonio Maria)

BONPORTI, FRANCESCO ANTONIO II-436; III-54,92,103,110,118, 176,184,201,209,217,261,286, 287,296,305,329,335,396

BONTEMPI, GIOVANNI ANDREA (Angelini) II-218,309,320,332, 334,377,389,390,407,423,433, 435,439,445,488; III-48,94, 198

BORA, CATHERINE VON I-278

BORASSA, LUIS I-130

BORBONI, NICOLO II-36,273,287

BORCH, TER II-179,339,500

BORCHGREVINCK, MELCHOIR II-9, 29,30,57,94,100,107,181,185, 214,260

BORDENAVE, JEAN DE II-307

BORDONE, PARIS I-213,427

BORDINI, FAUSTINA III-73,153, 296,319,345,353,363,383,405, 417,428,442,448

BORETTI, GIOVANNI ANDREA III-69, 387,409,414,419,428,434,439, 445,459,482

BORGHESE, ANTONIO (Borghesi) III-136

BORGHESE, CARDINAL II-197

BORGHI, GIOVANNI BATTISTA III-273

BORGHI, LUIGI III-136

BORGHINI, VINCENZO I-456

BORGIA, LUCREZIA I-236,241

BORGO II-76

BORIS, ST. I-101

BORJON (?) II-437,439

BORJON, CHARLES EMMANUEL (de Scelleny) II-264; III-54

BORLASCA, BERNADINO II-36,121, 126,137,142,174,206,219

BORN, BERTRAN DE I-72

BORNEIL, GUIRANT DE (Bornelh) I-72,91

BOROSINI, ANTONIO II-380,480; III-14,64,211,250,251

GRAVEVR, le papier de ce liure,
Où BACON a peint son scauoir,
Aura sur le temps ce pouuoir,
Quil durera plus que ton cuiure.

Crisp van Paß. Iun. Fecit.

BOROSINI, ELEONORA   III-282,305,
    360
BOROSINI, FRANCESCO   III-52,78,
    225,263,325,354,362,363,371,
    373
BOROSINI, ROSA (d'Ambreville)
    III-78,268,291,319,342,354
BORREN, DEN   II-226
BORRI, GIOVANNI BATTISTA   II-
    42; III-22,30
BORROMEO, (Cardinal) CARLO   I-
    395,416,437,467,497
BORROMEO, ST. CHARLES (? Card-
    inal)   I-111
BORROMINI, FRANCESCO   II-34,287,
    305,346,416
BORRONO   I-332
BORROWDELL, GILES   II-509
BOS, (Abbé) JEAN-BAPTISTE DU
    III-322
BOSCH, HIERONYMUS   I-164,198,213,
    215,244,252,261
BOSCHERVILLE, ST. GEORGE DE   I-60
BOSCHETTI, GIOVANNI BOSCHETTO
    II-150,170,182,187,193,207
BOSCHI, GIUSEPPE   III-136,233,
    242,243,249,252,327,336,338,
    351,363,405
BOSCHOP (Boskop), CORNELIUS   I-
    414,415,432
BOSSE, ADAM LE   I-85
BOSSINENSIS, FRANCISCUS   I-249
BOSSUET (Bishop) JACQUES-BÉNIGNE,
    II-237
BOSTEL, LUCAS VON   II-330; III-
    301
BOSWELL   III-44
BOTEAUVILLE, MICHEL DE   I-208
BOTELER, (Sir) WILLIAM   II-362
BOTELLI   III-302
BOTTEGARI, COSIMO   I-440,441
BOTTICELLI, SANDRO   I-159,185,
    186,187,188,189,191,194,195,
    196,197,198,206,251

BOTTRIGARI, COSIMO (see Botte-
    gari, Cosimo)
BOTTRIGARI, ERCOLE (Benelli)
    I-291,350,534; II-30,33,76,
    141
BOUCHARDON, CLAUDE DE I-438
BOUCHER, FRANÇOIS III-186
BOUCON, ANNE-JEANNE III-225,
    454
BOUFLEURS III-90
BOULOGNE, JEAN DE (see Bologna,
    G.)
BOULLOGNE, VALENTIN DE I-522;
    II-198,270
BOURBON, DUKE OF III-319,337
BOURBON, LOUIS DE, PRINCE of
    Conde (Coysevox) III-34
BOURDALOVE, LOUIS II-262
BOURDELOT, PIERRE (Uncle of Pi-
    erre Bonnet) II-126; III-1,
    201
BOURET III-372,376
BOURGEOIS, LOUIS I-242,317,319,
    320,322,329,334,335,339,342,
    350,351,353,355,371,383,385,
    386,397
BOURGEOIS, LOUIS-THOMAS II-461;
    III-183,207,251,267,276,284,
    296,313,336,337,374,419,428,
    486,494
BOURGES, CLEMENTINE DE I-216,
    379,385
BOURNONVILLE, JACQUES DE II-
    466; III-253
BOURNONVILLE, JEAN-VALENTIN DE
    II-154,163,181,193,296
BOUTMY, family III-136
BOUTMY, GUILLAUME III-352
BOUTMY, JACQUES ADRIEN II-508;
    III-248,277,317
BOUTMY, JEAN BAPTISTE JOSEPH
    III-373
BOUTMY, JOSSE III-108,338,
    416

BOUTS, DIERIC I-144,165,176,178,
    181,184
BOUVARD, FRANCOIS II-430; III-
    178,201,209,354,411,421,460
BOUYS, A. III-192
BOUZIGNAE III-139
BOVICELLI, GIOVANNI BATTISTA
    I-534; II-36
BOVIER, BERNARD LE, DE FONTEN-
    ELLE (see Fontanelle)
BOWER, RICHARD I-392
BOWLE, RAPHE I-374
BOWMAN, HENRY II-469,475,483,
    513; III-129
BOWMAN, JOHN II-340; III-73,84
BOWWENS, ELIZABETH II-23
BOXBERG, CHRISTIAN LUDWIG II-
    426; III-64,111,115,118,155,
    168,175,177,193,416
BOXE, WILLIAM I-333
BOXE, (the younger) I-503
BOYCE, JOHN I II-299; III-102,
    136,138,139
BOYCE, JOHN II III-251,284,350,
    478,493
BOYCE, WILLIAM II-160,239
BOYER, ABBÉ II-334; III-66,96
BOYES, THOMAS II-36,79
BOYLE, ELIZABETH I-536
BOYVIN III-288
BRACACCIO, GIULIO CESARE (see
    Brancaccio)
BRACCINO DA TODI, ANTONIO II-
    114
BRACCIOLI, GRAZIO III-281,400,
    461
BRACEGIRDLE, MRS. III-62
BRACK, JORG I-261
BRADDOCK, EDWARD II-450; III-
    29
BRADDOCK, ELIZABETH II-450
BRADE, CHARLES II-232
BRADE, CHRISTIAN II-237
BRADE, HIERONYMUS II-148

BRADE, STEPHEN II-252
BRADE, WILLIAM I-379; II-9,29,
    103,107,112,121,130,132,148,
    155,157,176,177,181,189,193,
    202,208,224,232,237,251,252
BRADSTREET, JOHN I-517
BRADWELL, JOSEPH II-271
BRADY, NICHOLAS III-105,157,159,
    469
BRAHMS, JOHANNES I-226; II-277
BRAITTENSTEIN, JOHANN I-402
BRAMANTE, DONATO I-159,196,204,
    215,237,245,258
BRAMBILLA, PADRE III-105
BRANCACCIO (Bracaccio), GIULIO
    CESARE I-359,462,470
BRANCHI, SILVESTRO II-165
BRANDENBURG, ELECTOR OF II-238,
    408
BRANDOLINI, AURELIO I-202
BRANDT, ANNA MARGARETHA III-80
BRANDT, ISABELLA II-124,255
BRANDT, JAN II-68
BRANDT, JOBST VON I-262,420
BRANDT, PER III-268,405
BRANT (see Brandt)
BRASART (see Brassart)
BRASSART, JEAN I-130,153,159,
    179
BRASSART, OLLIVIER I-398
BRASSEUR II-281
BRASSICANUS (Brassianus), JOHAN-
    NES II-36,164,167,269,332,
    372
BRASSÓ I-243
BRATTLE, THOMAS III-35,251,268
BRAVO, JUAN I-368,386
BREBOS, JAN II-119
BRECOURT, G. MARCOUREAU DE (see
    Marcoureau de Brecourt, G.)
BREDEMERS, (Bredeniers) HENRY
    I-182,268,269,288
BREDENIERS, HENRI (see Bredem-
    ers)

74

BRÉHY, HERCULE II-443; III-215
BREITENGRASER, WILHELM I-298
BREITINGER, JOHANN JACOB III-171
BREITKOPF AND HARTEL III-130
BREITKOPF, BERNHARDT CHRISTOPH
    III-89
BREITKOPF, JOHANN GOTTLOB IMMAN-
    UEL III-318,322
BREMBANA DEL VAL, ZAMBO I-432
BREMNER, ROBERT III-273,332,405
BRENDTNER, JOSEPH III-257
BREQUIN, COPIN DU I-118
BRESCIA, BONAVENTURA DA I-212,
    282,283
BRESSAND, FRIEDRICH CHRISTIAN
    II-431; III-45,85,128
BRETON, PIERRE MONTAN III-392
BRETONNE, ANTOINE III-480
BRETT, R. III-64
BREUNICH III-332,398,491
BREVAL, JOHN DURANT III-462,466
BREVI, GIOVANNI BATTISTA II-42,
    444; III-59,78,125
BREWER, THOMAS II-134,161
BREWSTER, WILLIAM II-306
BRIAD III-215
BRIAN, A. (see Bryne, A.)
BRIARD, ÉTIENNE I-210,287,290,
    293
BRICE, GERMAIN III-272
BRICEÑOS (see Brizeño)
BRIDGE, RICHARD III-422
BRIEGEL, WOLFGANG (Karl) II-230,
    308,344,375,427,469,483; III-
    22,235,258
BRIERE, DE LA III-171
BRIGNOLI, GIACOMO I-345
BRIND, RICHARD III-242,312
BRINI(?) III-268
BRISEUX (architect) II-492; III-
    411
BRISSAE, MARSHAL DE I-359,448
BRITO, ESTEVÃO DE II-42
BRITTON(?) III-428

BRITTON, THOMAS II-309,474; III-
    80,275,276
BRIVIO, BERTONI III-391,422,434,
    472
BRIVIO, GIUSEPPE FERDINANDO III-
    161
BRIXI, FRANTISEK XAVER III-449
BRIXI, SIMON III-72,350,396,485
BRIXI, VIKTORIN IGNAC III-294
BRIZEÑO, LUIS DE II-42,209,233,
    235
BROADWAY, RICHARD III-136
BROADWOOD, JOHN III-359,453
BROCKES, BERTHOLD HEINRICH II-
    487; III-261,289,296,302,376
BROCKWELL, HENRY II-494
BRODERIP, JOHN III-318
BRODERIP, WILLIAM II-511; III-
    165,268,270,383
BROJIN DE SCELLERY, CHARLES EM-
    MANUEL (see Scellery, Charles
    Emmanuel Brojin de)
BROLO, BARTOLOMEO I-153
BROME, RICHARD III-443
BROMPTON I-70
BRÖNNEMULLER, ELIAS III-129,
    235,243
BRONNER, GEORG II-407; III-75,
    84,124,177,178,288,363
BRONZINO, ANGELO I-239
BROOME, JOSIAS II-242
BROSCHI, CARLO (see Farinelli)
BROSCHI, RICCARDO III-161,351,
    374,407,409,426,428,430,443,
    469,490
BROSCHI, SALVATORE III-211
BROSCIUS, JAN II-343
BROSSARD, SEBASTIEN DE II-354,
    355,431,439,474,516; III-21,
    36,59,94,95,97,98,116,118,
    184,185,187,247,374,419,425
BROSSE, DE (architect) I-367;
    II-167,235
BROSSES, CHARLES DE III-237

BROUN, JOHN   I-183

BROUNKER, LORD WILLIAM   II-349

"BROUNO"   I-392

BROUWER, ADRIAEN   II-48,96,98,
    236,246,259,262,287; III-34

BROWN, JOHN   III-285

BROWN, ROBERT   I-467,503,509,
    517

BROWN, TOM   III-176

BROWN, THOMAS(?)   III-76

BROWNE, BENEDICT   II-80

BROWNE, RICHARD   II-9,161,390,
    397

BROWNE, (Sir) THOMAS   II-96,240,
    270,283,300,319,369,507

BROWNE, WILLIAM   II-153,160,173,
    308

BROZEK, JAN   (see Broscius, Jan)

BROZINO, ANGELO   I-430

BRUCK, ARNOLD DE (Von)   I-189,
    213,287,296,319,359

BRUDIEU, JOAN   I-304,323,444,450,
    481,517

BRUEGEL, PIETER (the elder)   I-
    279,344,352,362,367,375,395,
    400,404,405,408,411,416,417,
    419

BRUÈRE, LE CLERC DE LA   III-308

BRUHIER   I-330

BRUHNS, NIKOLAUS   II-402; III-
    110

BRUHNS, PETER   II-297; III-116

BRULÉ, GACE   I-91

BRUMEL, ANTOINE   I-189,192,208,
    210,238,242,246,248,278,323

BRUMEL, JACHET   I-323

BRUNETTI, ANTONIO I   III-136,317

BRUN, CHARLES LE   II-191,212,304,
    379,477; III-51

BRUNELLESCHI, FILIPPO   I-125,139,
    146,147,149,152,160

BRUNELLI, ANTONIO   II-36,99,100,
    126,127,150,155,157,170,176,
    189,233,239

BRUNETTI, ANTONIO II III-333
BRUNETTI, DOMENICO II-36,100,
    120,121,193,202,264
BRUNETTI, GIOVANNI II-36,229
BRUNETTI, GIOVANNI GUALBERTO
    III-292,368,469,470,490
BRUNETTI, GIUSEPPE III-136
BRUNNE, ROBERT DE I-110
BRUNO, COUNT of Egisheim (see
    Leo IX, Pope)
BRUNO, GIOVANNI BATTISTA I-358,
    361,372
BRUNSWICK, DUKE OF II-456,482
BRUSA, GIOVANNI FRANCESCO III-
    161,384
BRUYÈRE, JEAN DE LA II-315,419;
    III-30
BRUYNINX (Dutch Ambassador) III-
    258
BRYAN, MR.(?) II-465
BRYAN, A. (see Bryne, A.)
BRYDGES, JAMES (see Chandos,
    Duke of)
BRYNE, ALBERTUS II-287,383,408,
    418,419,435,465
BRYNE, ALEXANDER III-411
BRYSON, JAMES II-293
BUCCHIANTI, C.P. II-239
BUCHAN (Bughan), JOHN II-36,112
BYCHAW(?) I-415
BUCHNER, HANS I-192,199,239,256,
    304,307,332,351; II-228
BUCHNER, PHILIPP FRIEDRICH II-
    155,305,421
BUDDAH I-28,31,41,42,87,96
BUFFARDIN, PIERRE GABRIEL III-
    46,269,285,323
BUINI, GIUSEPPE MARIA III-99,
    309,328,338,434
BUISSON, ROBERT DU II-35
BULIFON, ANTONIO III-173
BULKLEY, STEPHEN II-389
BULL, DR. JOHN I-391,453,466, *See illustration on p. 77*
    479,480,485,518,523,524; II-

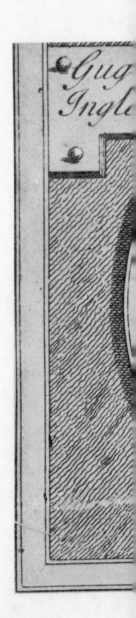

9,13,14,44,68,98,99,104,105
130,132,135,139,141,147,148,
154,174,192,193,200,213,241,
244,248,318,341,356

BULL, WILLIAM II-42,408,468,471,
488; III-11,99,126,153

BULLEYN, WILLIAM I-398

BULLOCK III-299

BULTINCK, MARIE CLÉMENCE III-
222

BÜNAW (Bünau) RUDOLPH COUNT VON
II-225,264

BUNS, BENEDICTUS (a Sancto Josepho) II-410,462,467,469,
471,475,513; III-75,99

BUNYAN, JOHN II-245,378,410,
477,492,507; III-34

BUONAMENTE, GIOVANNI BATTISTA
II-233,235,275,276,281,282,
306

BUONARROTI (see Michelangelo)

BUONAVITA, ANTONIO I-493

BUONINSEGNA, DUCCIO DI I-96,
100,101,113

BUONTALENTI I-509

BURCHARD, ULRICH I-264

BURCHIELLA (see Molino, Antonio)

BURETTE, BERNARD III-347,357,
387

BURETTE, CLAUDE III-99,161

BURETTE, PIERRE JEAN II-401;
III-99

BURGHLEY, LORD I-453,466

BURGK, JOACHIM À I-332,414; II-
10,125,129,138,145,168

BURGKMAIR I-295

BURGOLT, SABINA KATHARINA II-
496

BURGOS I-91

BURGUNDY, DUKE OF III-83

BURKE, EDMUND III-421

BURMEISTER II-33

BURNABY III-186

BURNET, WILLIAM   III-396
BURNEY, CHARLES   I-67,94,234,288,
    491; II-285,290; III-22,62,
    132,138,191,225,235,333,337,
    342,348,383,429
BURT, WILLIAM   II-91
BURTIUS   I-196
BURTON, ANNE   II-479
BURTON, JOHN   III-427
BURTON, ROBERT   I-449; II-205,
    295,304
BURY, BERNARD DE   III-324
BURZIO, NICOLO   I-163,264
BUS, GERVAIS DE   I-111
BUSBY, DR. RICHAD   II-242(?);
    III-89,204
BUSHY, DR. RICHARD (Busby ?)   II-
    242(?)
BUSNOIS, ANTOINE (Antonius)   I-
    85,124,157,177,178,185,191,
    203,234
BUSSANI, GIACOMO FRANCESCO   II-
    458; III-35,359
BUSTI   (see Busto)
BUSTO, PIETRO   II-14
BUTERNE, JEAN   II-331; III-74
BUTI (librettist)   II-320,386
BUTLER, CHARLES   II-121,189,264,
    269,276,320
BUTLER, THOMAS   I-428
BUTLER, (Sir) WILLIAM   (see Bot-
    eler)
BUTTSTADT, J.H.   (see Buttstett,
    J.H.)
BUTTSTETT, FRANZ VOLLRATH   III-
    484
BUTTSTETT (Buttstädt), JOHANN
    HEINRICH   II-406,519; III-21,
    270,328
BUTTSTETT, H.M.   III-56
BUTZBACH, JAKOB   I-192
BUUS, JACQUES (Bohusius, Von
    Paus)   I-317,319,335,339,342,
    350,352,400

BUXTEHUDE, DIETRICH I-214; II-
    155,402,418,447,477; III-103,
    110,179,184,199,206,213
BUXTEHUDE, HANS JENSEN II-74,
    448
BUYSERO, DIRK II-476,490
BUYTEN, MARTIN VAN I-485,488
BYFIELD, JOHN III-136,386,417
BYNG, ADMIRAL III-312
BYNG, (Sir) GEORGE III-321
BYRD, CHRISTOPHER I-417; II-
    1,28,162,268
BYRD, ELIZABETH I-425; II-1
BYRD, ELLEN I-486
BYRD(E), HENRY I-254
BYRD, JUCIANA I-412,448,461,
    486
BYRD, RACHEL II-1,268
BYRD, THOMAS I-447; II-68,268
BYRD, WILLIAM I-216,227,260, *See illustration on pp. 82-83*
    269,275,290,323,345,358,359,
    362,378,388,389,392,396,412,
    417,425,428,429,434,438,439,
    440,441,443,444,447,448,450,
    453,455,461,462,463,465,466,
    469,471,472,473,474,476,478,
    479,481,485,486,490,493,496,
    497,498,499,500,501,502,504,
    505,507,509,510,511,514,515,
    516,517,519,520,523,524,528,
    532,533,534; II-1,2,7,15,19,
    21,22,23,68,82,94,105,107,
    111,112,126,132,137,139,146,
    154,157,162,200,207,212,218,
    255,268,299,318,339,340,341,
    344,356,368,423,434

C

CABALLONE, MICHELE III-64,296,
    395

CABANILLAS, JOSE II-427; III-373

CABANILLES, JUAN II-310,417, 459; III-257

CABARTE II-182

CABEZÓN, ANTONIO DE I-250,289, 359,405,451

CABEZÓN, HERNANDO DE I-451; II-74

CACCINI, FRANCESCA (La Cecchina) II-87,140,142,202,222,226, 231

CACCINI, GIULIO (Giulio Romano) I-376,450,537; II-7,12,15,44, 56,57,58,62,66,68,69,72,73, 74,75,76,77,84,87,91,123,125, 126,127,150,157,161,170,180, 181,182,185,186,189,191,206, 220,292

CADÉAC, PIERRE I-304,323,345, 360,368

CADWALADR, KING I-38

CAESAR (see Smegergill, William)

CAESAR, JULIUS I-20

CAFARO, PASQUALE III-292,487

CAFFARELLI, FRANCESCO (see Maiorano, F.)

CAFFARELLI (Gaetano Maierano) III-182,240,385,405,428,477, 478

CAFFIAUX, PHILIPPE, JOSEPH III-450

CAIGNET, DENIS II-16,107,219, 220,223

CAIMO, GIOSEPPE I-395,397,398, 406,456,458,467,474,475,496

CAIN I-360; II-334

CAIUS, POPE I-26

CAIX D'HERVELOIS, LOUIS DE II-426; III-377

CALANSON, GUIRAUT DE I-89

CALCAGNINI, MARIO II-262

CALDARA, ANTONIO II-426; III-138,139,235,244,258,293,301,

367,400,434,446,447,459,471,
472,482,492

CALDERÓN II-49,67,249,353,389,
490,499

CALEGARI, FRANCESCO ANTONIO III-
129,175,180,188

CALEGARI, MARIA CATERINA II-
310,372,381,397

CALESTANI, VINCENZIO II-36,170,
176

CALETTI-BRUNI, PIER FRANCESCO
(see Cavalli, P.F.)

CALÌ II-94

CALIARI, PAOLO (see Veronese)

CALICCHIO, CAMILLA II-466

CALIGINOSO II-64,332

CALIGULA I-486,504

CALISTA, LELIO II-42,511;III-85

CALIXTUS III, POPE (see Callistus)

CALLICRATES I-13

CALLIÈRES, FRANÇOIS DE III-40

CALLISTUS I, POPE I-25

CALLISTUS II, POPE I-74

CALLISTUS III, POPE I-172

CALLOT, JACQUES I-527; II-270

CALMO, ANDREA I-250,330,337,
410,425

CALORI, ANGIOLA III-453

CALVI, DONATO (Calvis) II-221,
397

CALVIN, JOHN I-249,265,303,306,
310,317,318,320,321,335,350,
355,399

CALVISIUS, SETH I-367,456,467,
512,533,534,537; II-3,10,16,
30,58,76,82,135,137,144,162,
163,164,170,176,252

CALVO, D. LAURO II-196

CALZABIGI, RANIERO SIMONE DE
III-276

CAMARGO, JEAN-BAPTISTE CUPIS
DE (see Cupis, (de Camargo),
J.B.)

CAMARGO, MARIA ANNA CUPPI III-241

CAMARGO, MIGUEL GOMEZ I-345

CAMBEFORT, JEAN DE II-92,349,352,383

CAMBERT, ROBERT II-246,335,359,365,370,371,384,389,403,408,422,426,432,435,436,430,440,443,449,450,451,452,467,470

CAMBRENSIS, GIRALDUS (Gerald de Barri) I-70,76,80,82,90

CAMDEN, WILLIAM I-88,352; II-207,217

CAMERLOHER, PLACIDUS VON III-395

CAMETTI II-455

CAMIDGE, JOHN III-486

CAMILLA, of Aragon I-184

CAMILLO I-420

CAMPANILE, OTTAVIO III-159

CAMPANUS, JOHANNES II-68,88,182,201,207

CAMPBELL, WILLIAM III-136

CAMPEGGI, COUNT RUDOLFO II-96,115,116,130,151,177,178

CAMPIAN, THOMAS I-409,528; II-3,10,69,70,76,78,97,107,110,128,144,150,151,152,153,154,160,180,183,189,191,192,356,357,398; III-139

CAMPIN, ROBERT (Master of Flemalle) I-124,142,147,159

CAMPIOLI (Gualandi, Antonio) III-129,225,327,385,439,441,450

CAMPION, EDMUND I-463

CAMPION, FRANÇOIS III-269

CAMPION, THOMAS (see Campian, Thomas)

CAMPIONI, CARLO ANTONIO III-326

CAMPISTRON II-448; III-19,73

CAMPO, DON DIEGO DE II-1

CAMPRA (?) II-191 (?)

CAMPRA, ANDRE II-374,375,469,
    481,497,511; III-80,83,99,
    109,111,113,115,116,118,121,
    127,152,153,155,158,166,174,
    177,179,181,186,188,189,190,
    193,195,197,198,209,221,222,
    227,239,240,244,246,253,257,
    258,262,267,279,303,311,328,
    335,344,345,349,362,371,400,
    402,407,414,438,443,455,458,
    480,484
CAMPRA, JOSEPH II-387; III-124,
    396
CAMUS, SEBASTIEN LE II-131
CANALETTO, GIOVANNI ANTONIO
    (Bellotto, Bernardo) III-
    114
CANALI (Canale), Floriano (de
    Brescia) II-36,58,70,76,82,
    141
CANCINEO, MICHEL ANGELO II-36,
    114
CANGE, CHARLES DU II-126,475;
    III-28
CANIS, CORNELIUS I-316,319,337
CANNABICH, M.F. III-454
CANNICIARI, POMPEO II-426; III-
    233
CANNONS, EDGWARE III-327
CANO, ALONSO II-73,416
CANOBI, C. III-68
CANOVA DA MILANO, FRANCESCO
    (see Milano)
CANTONE, GEROLAMO II-475
CANUTE, KING I-59,63
CANUTI III-366
CAPACELLI (Count) PIRRO (see
    Capecelli)
CAPECE, ALESSANDRO ("Romano")
    II-36,153,155,179
CAPACELLI, (Count) PIRRO (see
    Albergati)
CAPECI, CARLO SIGISMONDO III-
    222,223,224,235,237,239,249,

CARCE III-126

CARDANO, GIROLAMO I-234,393,
444

CARDONNE, PHILIBERT III-440

CARDOSO, MANUEL I-417,496; II-
150,176,226,276,320,324,331

CARÊMPRENANT I-354

CARESANA, CRISTOFORO II-296,
367,413,498; III-34,124,199,
232

CAREST, JOSSE I-265,274,371

CARESTINI, GIOVANNI III-203,
310,338,355,364,374,385,405,
428,442,464,472,487

CAREU III-352

CAREW, THOMAS II-27,264,267,270
291,429

CAREY (see "Randall, John")

CAREY, HENRY (Savile) II-472;
III-20,147,222,246,272,290,
328,349,350,353,355,366,388,
407,408,414,419,432,452,456,
457,459,464,480,486

CARISSIMI, GIACOMO II-45,48,91,
92,167,222,236,245,252,267,
321,328,338,381,448; III-77,
184,189

CARLETON, (Sir) DUDLEY II-180,
223

CARLIER, CLAUDE II-125

CARLO, GERONIMO I-289,362

CARLOMAN I-51

CARLOS II, KING III-152,157

CARLTON, (Rev.) RICHARD I-448;
II-70,73,141,287

CARO, ANNIBALE I-407

CAROLAN III-343,382,465

CAROLAN, MARY (see Maguire,
Mary)

CAROLAN, TURLOUGH II-427; III- *See illustration on p. 93*
139

CAROLI, ANGELO ANTONIO III-166,
403,454

CARON, ANTOINE I-425,437,460;
II-7

See illustrations on pp. 105, 115

CASTILLEJA, PEDRO FERNANDEZ DE
I-257,325
CASTILLO, BERNARDO CLAVIJO DEL
II-87,231
CASTILLO, DIEGO DEL II-64
CASTRO, JUAN BLAS DE I-335,383,
420,421,445,456,537; II-3,
10,31,88,92,121,201,202,208,
257,280; III-478
CASTROVILLARI, DANIELE II-379
CASTRUCCI, PIETRO II-480; III-
284,286,293,300,302,315,327,
368
CASULANA, MADDALENA I-415,419
CASONE, GIROLAMO I-482,512
CATHERINE, of Alexandria I-111,
185
CATHERINE, of Braganza, QUEEN
of England II-256,386,407,
468,496,518; III-61,65
CATHERINE, of St. Susanna (sis-
ter II-390
CATHERINE I, EMPRESS of Russia
II-523
CATO, DIOMEDES II-82
CATONE, SERAFINO I-520
CATTANEO, CLAUDIA (see Monte-
verdi, Claudia)
CAUMEZ, JEAN I-127
CAURROY, FRANÇOIS EUSTACHE DU
I-338,417,420,447,470; II-
16,29,119,121,128; III-147
CAUS, SOLOMON DE II-97,143,163,
164,166
CAUSSIN, ERNOUL I-285
CAUSTUN, THOMAS I-353,393,417
CAVACCIO, GIOVANNI I-368,370,
463,466,524; II-16,137,231
CAVALIERI, EMILIO DE' I-341,
473,481,496,503,510,512; II-
4,57,58,62,74
CAVALLI (Pietro), FRANCESCO I-
339; II-73,174,180,199,213,
283,285,288,289,290,293,295,

299,300,301,303,304,306,307,
308,309,312,313,315,317,319,
326,329,330,335,339,340,342,
343,344,345,347,350,352,353,
354,355,356,359,361,366,370,
374,375,376,377,378,385,386,
388,389,395,401,402,406,409,
419,425,434,438,456,461,475,
477,480; III-88

CAVALLINI, PIETRO I-95

CAVAZZONI, GIROLAMO I-269,331

CAVAZZONI, MARCO ANTONIO I-200,
   254,255,262,268,272,273,274,
   285,302,312,319,320,322,323,
   400,417,424; II-94

CAVENDISH, family II-44

CAVENDISH, MICHAEL I-524; II-
   23,24,31,33,241

CAVERON, ROBERT I-117

CAXTON, WILLIAM I-185,186,187,
   192,193,194,202

CAZZATI, MAURIZIO II-52,199,
   299,301,320,332,345,348,362,
   364,366,369,371,393,399,404,
   409,415,420,424,425,428,433,
   444,467

CABALLOS, FRANCISCO I-300

CABALLOS, RODRIGO I-368,385

CECCHI, GIOVANMARIA I-503

CECCHINI, TOMASO II-42,80,132,
   144,153,155,170,176,244,310

CECI, (Canon) ATTILIO I-420

CECIL, JOHN III-75

CECIL, (Sir) ROBERT II-2

CECILIA, ST. I-24,25,48,166,
   193,206,237,260,534; II-33

CELANO, THOMAS OF (see Thomas
   of Celano)

CELESTINE I, POPE I-32

CELESTINE II, POPE I-76

CELESTINE III, POPE I-81

CELESTINE IV, POPE I-94

CELESTINE V, POPE I-102

CELIANO, LIVIO I-493; II-6

CELLARIUS, JOHANNES II-2,187

CELLES, FRANÇOIS BÉDOS DE III-231,385

CELLINI, BENVENUTO I-213,255,325,427

CELTIS, CONRAD I-137,173,206,211,248,288

CENAMI, GIOVANNA I-154

CENCI II-320

CENCORIAUS I-25

CENE, MICHEL CHARLES LE III-296,373

CENTLIVRE, MRS. III-185,201

CENTONELLI, A. II-203

CERCEAU, DU III-359

CEREROLS, JUAN II-181,462

CERESANA II-503

CERESINI, GIOVANNI II-36,105,107,176,182,215,237,239,285

CERF, JEAN-LAURENT LE II-450; III-148,191,192,194,201,202,203,208,209,338,385

ČERNOHORSKÝ, BOHUSLAR MATĚJ II-517; III-183,487

CERONE, DOMENICO PIETRO I-406,422,524,528; II-22,80,112,118,119,121,126,148,150,181,223

CERQUETTA, MADDALENA II-393

CERRE II-114

CERRETO, SCIPIONE I-342,348; II-68,70,114,202,233,257,258

CERSNE, EBERHARD I-141

CERTON, PIERRE I-133,285,289,293,296,312,322,326,332,354,360,374,376,429

CERVANTES I-334; II-49,173

CERVETTO (the elder) II-503; III-405

CESANA, (Count) BARTOLOMEO II-36,150

CESARINI (?) III-202

CESARINI, GIULIANO I-480

CÉSARIS I-145

CESTI, MARCANTONIO (Pietro Antonio) II-44,181,213,280,
296,315,317,327,331,332,337,
340,341,342,344,349,351,352,
353,355,357,367,370,373,383,
385,387,392,401,404,406,408,
409,410,411,413,414,416,417,
418,421,422,430,439,440,452,
490; III-77

CESTI, REMIGIO (Regio?) II-42,
387,393,404,439(?)

CHABANCEAU (see Barre)

CHABANEAU DE LA BARRE, PIERRE
(see Barre)

CHABANON, MICHEL PAUL GUIDE
III-427

CHABRA, CHARLES (Chiabrano, Carlo) III-360

CHALCIS I-7

CHAMBERLAIN, JOHN II-223

CHAMBERLAIN, LORD II-385,411,
442,478,510; III-4,19,38,54

CHAMBERS, WILLIAM I-528

CHAMBERS, WILLIAM (architect)
III-390

CHAMBONNIÈRES, CHAMPION DE, family II-36

CHAMBONNIÈRES, JACQUES CHAMPION
DE I-295; II-53,67,74,259,
297,316,335,337,338,397,427,
428,429,437

CHAMBONNIÈRES, NICOLAS CHAMPION
DE I-295

CHAMBONNIÈRES, THOMAS CHAMPION
DE II-67

CHAMBRE, ANNE DE II-45

CHAMPAGNE, THIBAUT DE I-72

CHAMPAIGNE (Champagne), PHILIPPE
DE II-64,77,335,390,453

CHAMPION (see Chambonnières)

CHAMPION, JACQUES DE LIEGE I-
255,265

CHAMPMESLÉ, MARIE DESMARES II-
312

CHANDOS, DUKE OF (James Brydges)
   III-260,316,327,329
CHANNAY, JOHANNES I-293
CHAO-NÜ, KING I-90
CHAPATY, ANNE II-192
CHAPERON, FRANÇOIS III-115
CHAPMAN, GEORGE II-27,34,149
CHAPMAN, JOHN II-270
CHAPMAN, LWEWELL II-345
CHAPOTON II-295,326
CHAPPELL, MR. I-398
CHAPPINGTON, JOHN II-15,98
CHARANTON, ENGUERRAND I-143,
   161,171,175
CHARDE, JOHN I-264
CHARDAVOINE, JEAN I-441,445
CHARDIN II-40,405
CHARDIN, JEAN-BAPTISTE SIMEÓN
   III-127,412,472
CHARES, of Branchidae I-8
CHARKE, RICHARD III-136,419,430
CHARLEMAGNE I-44,45,46,47,48,
   74,175
CHARLES ("Mr. Charles") III-136
CHARLES, ARCHDUKE of Austria
   I-529; II-229
CHARLES, ARCHDUKE of Graz I-417
CHARLES, CARDINAL of Lorraine
   (see Charles, Duke of Guise)
CHARLES (the Bold) DUKE of Bour-
   bon and Burgundy I-161,177,
   178,179,187,289
CHARLES, DUKE of Guise (Cardinal
   of Lorraine) I-363
CHARLES, DUKE of Orleans I-144
CHARLES VI, EMPEROR of Austria
   (see Charles III, King of
   Spain)
CHARLES IV, EMPEROR of Luxembourg
   I-111,116,118
CHARLES II, HOLY ROMAN EMPEROR
   (see Charles I, King of France)
CHARLES III, HOLY ROMAN EMPEROR
   (see Charles II, King of France)

Der unter den Namen Space Camino
scherzhaft berüchtigte Spieler.

Ih verspiel meine chriftliche Chevallü
all mein Münzerei.

CHARTERIS, HENRY   II-4

CHARTON, QUARTON   (see Charanton, Enguerrand)

CHARTRIOT, ANNE   II-67

CHARTRIOT ROBERT   II-67

CHAUCER, GEOFFREY   I-54,108,117, 120,121,123,125,126,127,130, 148,158,187

CHAUMONT, LAMBERT   III-95

CHECHA   III-121

CHÉDEVILLE   III-82

CHELEBÍ, EVLÉYÁ   II-44,49

CHELL, WILLIAM   I-275,361

CHELLERI, FORTUNATO   III-45,220, 286,339,341,344,345,362,374, 383,385,438,447,458

CHEMIN, NICOLAS DU   I-252,315,339, 342,344,351,368,407,444

CH'EN JUNG   (see Jung)

CHÊNG, CH'IAO   (see Ch'iao)

CHERUBINI, MARIA LUIGI   III-368, 422,434,447,459,472

CHESNAYE, NICOLE DE LA   I-187, 200,245

CHETWOOD, (Brother) RUGUS WIL-LIAM   III-345,430,444

CHEVALIER(?)   I-494; II-36,97

CHEVALIER, ESTIENNE   I-166

CHEYNEY, LADY   II-159

CH'I, MU   I-87

CHIABRANO, CARLO   (see Chabra, Charles)

CHIABRERA   II-114

CH'IAO, CHENG   I-73,78

CHIARAMONTI, NIOBID   I-15

CHIARINI, PIETRO   III-292,483

CHIEPPO, ANNIBALE   II-112

CHILCOT   III-466

CHILE, WILLIAM   II-99,257,260 261,272,288,289,306,337,344, 361,375,377,381,391,392,414, 439; III-91,110

CHILDE   I-130

CHILESOTTI   II-184

CHILMEAD, EDWARD   II-323

CHILSTON I-107

CHIN, TAI I-152

CHINDASVINTHUS, KING I-40

CH'ING DYNASTY II-312

CHINZER, GIOVANNI III-99,448,
    487

CHNEMHOTEP I-3

CHOJNACKI, LUKASZ II-501

CHOPIN, FREDERICK I-220

CHOU I-6

CHRISMANN, FRANZ XAVER III-373

CHRIST, JESUS I-24,29,34,35,
    49,52,60,62,70,71,75,76,77,
    81,91,98,99,110,112,117,125,
    147.150.154.156,159,177,186,
    214,240,244,271,308,318,322;
    II-456

CHRISTIAN, DUKE of Saxe-Weiss-
    enfels III-295,298

CHRISTIAN IV, KING of Denmark
    II-12,22,27,29,34,57,72,111,
    117,185,265

CHRISTIAN, IREEN II-358

CHRISTIAN ALBERT, DUKE of Sles-
    vig-HOLSTEIN II-445,447,
    489; III-39

CHRISTIAN ERNST, MARGRAVE of
    Kulmbach and Bayreuth II-84

CHRISTIAN LUDWIG, MARGRAVE of
    Brandenburg III-335,477

CHRISTIAN WILHELM, MARGRAVE of
    Brandenburg II-199,287

CHRISTIANE, ELECTRESS of Saxony,
    QUEEN of Poland-Saxony (see
    Eberhardine)

CHRISTIANI (violinist) III-344

CHRISTINA, of Lorraine I-502,
    503,504,508

CHRISTINA, QUEEN of Sweden I-
    116; II-332,353,359,370,490,
    498,504; III-21,38,39,123

CHRISTO, ESTAEVÃO DE II-4,154

CHRISTO, LUIZ DE II-224; III-
    71

CHRISTOFFEL, HANS JACOB (see
    Grimmelshausen)
CHRISTOFORI, BARTOLOMEO DI FRAN-
    CESCO II-127,355,411; III-
    46,74,234,251,252,296,321,
    327,350,377,385,386,429,438,
    441,458
CHRISTOFORO I-325,409,450
CHRISTOPHER, ST. I-148
CHRISTUS, PETRUS I-159,161,162
    165,182
CHROSTKOWSKI, ALBERT, JR. II-
    236,427
CHRYSANDER I-234,235; II-492;
    III-337,419
CHRYSOSTOM, ST. I-27
CHRYSOSTUM, ST. JOHN I-29
CHU CH'UAN I-161
CHU, TSAI-YJJ II-134
CHUEH I-5
CHUNG I-8
CHURCH, JOHN II-459; III-191,
    357
CHURCH, RICHARD III-123
CHURCHILL, JOHN III-180
CHYLIŃSKI, ANDREZEJ II-64,255
CIAIA, AZZOLINO BERNARDINO DELLA
    II-432; III-152,170,177,398
CIAMPI, FRANCESCO III-99,308,
    376,386,389,416,419,481,491,
    494
CIAMPI, VINCENZO LEGRENZIO III-
    323
CIBBER, COLLEY III-74,104,156,
    177,178,217,289,299,412,416,
    419
CIBBER, SUSANNA MARIA (Arne)
    III-276,451,466,478
CIBBER, THEOPHILUS III-101,466,
    478
CICOGNINI, G.A. II-352,360
CICOGNINI, JACOPO II-180,206,
    212

CICONIA, JOHANNES I-177,123,143
CIECO, BENEDETTO CLARIO I-298
CIFRA, ANTONIO I-443; II-6,8,
    97,117,119,141,157,189,197,
    203,207,229,230,246,285; III-
    132
CIMA, GIOVANNI PAOLO I-424; II-
    27,36,100,120
CIMA, TULLIO II-21,142,224,323,
    371
CIMABUE, GIOVANNI I-94,95,98,
    109
CIMAROSA, DOMENICO III-422,434
CIMELLO, TOMASO I-331
CINI, GIOVANNI BATTISTA I-400,
    417; II-113
CINZIO I-318
CIONE, ANDREA DI (see Verrocch-
    io)
CIPRIANI, LORENZO III-136
CIRILLO, FRANCESCO II-212,274,
    350,351,353,357,360,388,420
CIRULLO, GIOVANNI ANTONIO II-
    36,111,170
CISNEROS, (Cardinal) FRANCISCO
    XIMENEZ DE I-201,212
CLAES (Clos), MARIE MADELEINE
    III-207,415
CLAESZ, PIETER II-330,385
CLAESZ, WILLIAM I-536; II-493
CLAGGET, CHARLES III-144
CLAIR, LE (see Lecclair)
CLARA EUGENIA, INFANTA I-528
CLARESCHAW, MARTIN I-199
CLARI, GIOVANNI II-466; III-
    95,139,264,288,327,329,377
CLARK, FRANCIS III-23,25
CLARKE, family (Windsor) III-
    129
CLARKE (Clark) JEREMIAH II-
    370,443,511; III-5,54,68,93,
    95,106,108,111,113,118,123,
    125,126,127,151,155,156,162,
    164,168,170,180,184,189,193,

CLEMENT IV, POPE   I-97
CLEMENT V, POPE   I-110
CLEMENT VI, POPE   I-117
CLEMENT VII, POPE   I-274,292
CLEMENT VIII, POPE   I-519,524,
    525,527,533; II-93
CLEMENT IX, POPE   II-288,417
CLEMENT X, POPE   II-430,465
CLEMENT XI, POPE   III-160,208,
    296,342
CLEMENT XII, POPE   III-435,446
CLÉRAMBAULT, CÉSAR FRANÇOIS NI-
    COLAS   III-161,414,444
CLÉRAMBAULT, LOUIS NICOLAS   II-
    347,461; III-242,245,336,463
CLÉREAU   I-335
CLERIA, MADONNA   I-427
CLETUS, POPE   (see Anacletus)
CLÈVE, JOHANNES DE   I-285,358,
    376,420,466
CLEVE, JOOS VAN (the elder)   I-
    194,314
CLIQUOT, family   III-136
CLICQUOT, JEAN BAPTISTE   III-273,
    282
CLICQUOT, L.A.   III-404,478
CLICQUOT, ROBERT   III-17,171,191,
    251,273
CLIFFORD, (Rev.) JAMES   II-37,
    208,261,263,382,389,392,393,
    395,397,398,455,504; III-84,
    116
CLIFFORD, LORD   II-183
CLIFFORD, THOMAS   II-263,302,314
CLINIO, TEODORO   II-4,78
CLIVE, CATHERINE   III-250,404,
    412,416,441,476
CLIVE, GEORGE   III-476
CLIVE, ROBERT   III-379
CLODIUS, CHRISTIAN   II-320
CLOS   (see Claes)
CLOTHIER, DEVEREUX   II-390
CLOTHIER, JOHN   III-123,317
CLOUET, school   I-395

CLOUET, FRANÇOIS I-270,391,427,
    430
CLOUET, JEAN I-195,285,315,316
CLUER, ELIZABETH III-359
CLUER, JOHN III-264,286,329,
    359,404,435
CLYNN I-88
COATTINO (Coattinus, Coattinum)
    I-507,508,512,526,535,536
COB(B), JAMES II-375,483; III-
    109
COBB, JOHN II-42,285,324
COBB, THOMAS III-359,360,428,
    483
COBBOLD, WILLIAM I-379,516; II-
    34,70,112,288
COBHAM, HENRY I-456
COCCHI, CLAUDIO II-36,232,233,
    237,239,261
COCCHI, GIOACCHINO III-292,422,
    447,487
COCHLAEUS, JOHANNES I-188,261,
    353
COCK, HIERONYMUS I-344,402
COCK, SYMON I-314
COCKAIN, (Sir) ASTON II-367
COCLICUS, (Coclico) ADRIEN PETIT
    I-213,329,332,334,353,354,370,
    392
COCQ, JEHAN LE I-316
COCQ, MADELEINE LE III-330
COCX, JAN II-255,288,407,428,
    431,445,468,473
CODDE, ANNA I-286
COELHO, MANNEL RODRIGUES I-470;
    II-80,176,195,217,264
COELLO, ALONSO SANCHEZ I-292,
    455,501
COFFEY, CHARLES III-409,410,
    419,430,441,444,446,469,490,
    491
COGGLESHALL II-323
COINCI, GAUTIER (DE) I-74,94
COLANDER, HEINRICH I-456; II-15

COLASSE, PASCAL II-326,327,455,
    468,511; III-5,19,21,25,27,
    35,39,40,42,44,55,62,66,90,
    95,100,102,107,152,193,206,
    228,232

COLBERT, JEAN BAPTISTE II-191,
    423,516
COLBRON, JAMES II-6
COLE, B.(?) III-136
COLE, BENJAMIN III-136
COLEBY, THEODORE II-450
COLEMAN, CHARLES II-275,339,
    346,360,368,396; III-88,108
COLEMAN, EDWARD II-12,57,349,
    360,361,386,389,422,439; III-
    425
COLEMAN, MRS. II-401
COLERUS II-94
COLET, JOHN I-265
COLFS, ANTOINE III-305,374
COLIGNANI, FRANCESCO III-317
COLIGNY, ADMIRAL I-428
COLISTA (see Calista, Lelio)
COLLA, GIUSEPPE III-439
COLLÉ III-471
COLLEGE, STEPHEN II-495
COLLEONI, BARTOLOMMEO I-197
COLLINS, WILLIAM III-342
COLMAN (see Coleman)
COLOGNE, ELECTOR OF II-239
COLOMBANI, ORAZIO I-216,447,
    524
COLOMBE, JEAN I-176
COLOMBI, GIUSEPPE II-271
COLOMBE, ST. I-460
COLOMBI, (Colombo) VINCENZO I-
    338,388
COLOMBINI, FRANCESCO II-217
COLONNA, FABIO II-182,331
COLONNA, FABRIZIO, (Duke of Tag-
    liacozzo) I-337
COLONNA, G. A. II-195
COLONNA, GIOVANNI PAOLO I-225;
    II-279,371,436,439,441,449,

CASANOVA LIVED TO A GREAT AGE.
IN THE END HE BECAME A LIBRARIAN
AND SMALL BOYS HURLED ROCKS AT HIM
BECAUSE HE LOOKED SO ODD.

COOKE, JOHN II-214,224
COOKE, THOMAS III-409
COOPER, JOHN (see Coperario)
COOPER, RICHARD III-380,382,
    408,428,480
COOPER, ROBERT I-236; II-16
COPE, (Sir) ANTHONY II-356
COPERARIO, (Cooper) GIOVANNI
    I-421; II-44,87,100,132,147,
    148,157,170,231,232,237,238,
    324
COPPETTA, FRANCESCO I-442
COPPINI, A. II-109
COPPOLA, GIALOMO I-303
CORADINI, FRANCISCO III-441,
    448
CORAILL, MLLE. III-315
CORBET, MRS. III-266
CORBETT, (Corbetta) FRANCISQUE
    II-199,360,423,450,496
CORBETT, W. III-95,125,159,186,
    200,203,204,251,266,269,274,
    301,423
CORBETTA, FRANCESCO (see Cor-
    bett)
CORDANS, BARTOLOMEO III-161,
    400,411,420,424,433,481,485
CORDES, JEAN DE II-69
CORDIER, BAUDE I-130
CORDIER, JACQUES I-459; II-133,
    413
CORDIER, MADELAINE I-237
CORDOT, NATALIS II-55
CORDOUVAL, JEHAN DE I-155
CORDOVA, CONSALVO FERNANDES DI
    I-394
CORELLI, family II-42
CORELLI, ARCANGELO (I) II-346
CORELLI, ARCANGELO (II) II-44,
    45,337,346,364,375,399,408,
    410,423,427,433,436,438,455,
    456,462,467,471,474,478,480,
    484,488,489,492,497,498,500,
    502,504,505,506,507,512,519;

III-3,5,6,9,10,13,18,19,21,
24,38,39,40,41,43,45,46,54,
57,73,83,84,86,90,93,95,97,
103,115,123,132,138,150,151,
152,153,154,155,156,162,165,
167,169,172,173,175,178,184,
188,191,193,194,197,198,200,
201,202,205,208,211,215,221,
224,225,226,227,230,231,232,
234,237,242,244,250,251,259,
261,265,272,277,279,284,285,
286,287,291,292,294,301,313,
329,339,346,375,382,408,422,
438,456

CORELLI, GIACINTO   III-199,207
CORELLI, IPPOLITO   III-173,285
CORELLI, RUDOLFO   II-262
CORELLI, (Marchese) VITTORIO
   EMMANUELE   III-199
CORER (see also Correr)   II-399
CORI, ANGELO MARIA   III-354
CORIOLANUS   II-399
CORKINE, WILLIAM   II-36,128,144
CORNACCHIOLI, GIACINTO   II-249
CORNAGO, JOHANNES   I-134,171,
   178
CORNARO, FRANCESCO   I-262
CORNARO, GIORGIO   II-324
CORNARO (Bishop) MARCO (Padua)
   II-186
CORNEILLE, PIERRE   II-102,274,
   279,331,332,334,335,400,431,
   446,448,454,472,476,484,494,
   522; III-72
CORNEILLE, THOMAS   II-448
CORNELIA (see Calegari, M.C.)
CORNELIUS, POPE   I-26
CORNELYS, THERESA   III-182,354
CORNET, PIERRE   I-528; II-36,
   134,135,218,223,231,264
CORNET, SEVERIN   I-315,335,462,
   463,466,528
CORNISH, HENRY   II-488
CORNUEL, JEAN   I-210

CORNYSHE, ROBERT   I-177,273

CORNYSHE, WILLIAM   I-179,200,204,
    240,247,250,251,263

CORRADI, GIULIO CESARE   II-477,
    484

CORRADINI   III-161,347,367,377,
    403,436,437,440

CORREA DE ARAUXO, FRANCISCO
    II-22

CORREA, HENRIQUE CARLOS   II-487

CORREA, MANUEL   II-64,233,264,
    275,347

CORREGGIO (Antonio Allegri)
    I-198,205,266,280,282,290,
    298

CORREGGIO, NICCOLÒ DA   I-191

CORRER, COUNT   I-202

CORRETTE, MICHEL   III-136,463,
    475

CORRI   III-422

CORSELLI, FRANCESCO   III-436,
    492

CORSI, JACOPO   I-533,534; II-7,
    12,15,20,62,65,86

CORT, BARTOLOMÉ DEL   II-224

CORTE, DELLA   III-130

CORTECCIA, FRANCESCO   I-251,269,
    291,307,308,309,310,320,328,
    335,400,422,425,427

CORTELLINI, CAMILLO   II-4,36,
    122,164,176,233

CORTONA   II-12,363,425

CORVINUS, J.M.   II-318

CORVINUS, (King) MATTHIAS   I-
    157,181,186,194

CORYATE   II-174

COSIMO I. DUKE   I-320,321,373

COSIMO II, GRAND DUKE   II-87,125

COSIMO III, GRAND DUKE of Tus-
    cany   II-422; III-21

COSIMO, PIERO DI   I-175,271

COSIN, BISHOP   II-239,274,383

COSSA, FRANCESCO DEL   I-156,179,
    187

COSSÉ, CHARLES DE   I-307

COSSONI, CARLO DONATO   II-381;
    III-39,150

COSTA, ALFONSO VAZ DA   II-34

COSTA, ANDRÉ DE   III-136,227,
    342

COSTA, ANTONIO DA   III-277

COSTA, FRANCESCO   II-233

COSTACUTI, MARCHESE   III-114

COSTANTINI, ALESSANDRO   II-306

COSTANTINI, FABIO   I-424; II-10,
    144,155,157,159,169,171,181,
    182,202,204,209

COSTANZI, GIOVANNI BATTISTA   III-
    189,377,419,421

COSTAZUTI, V.   II-289,299

COSTELEY, GUILLAUME   I-291,410,
    421,426,453; II-98

COSYN, BENJAMIN   I-481; II-36,
    67,98,200,212,230,232,306

COSYN, JOHN   I-481

COTGRAVE   II-135

COTTE, ROBERT DE   II-362; III-
    244

COTTE, ROGER   III-374

COTTERELL   III-13

COTTON, DR.   III-278

COTTON, JOHN   II-321,322

COTTON, JOHN (Joannes of Liége)
    I-69

COTTON, ROBERT BRUCE   I-427; II-
    259

COTUMACCI, DON CARLO   III-116,
    319

COUCHET, ABRAHAM   II-408

COUCHET, JAN   II-302,317,354,
    355,356

COUCHET, JOZEF   II-408

COUPER, JOHN   I-146,290

COUPER, WILLIAM   III-447

COUPERIN, family   II-335; III-
    135

COUPERIN, ARMAND-LOUIS   II-256;
    III-371

COUPERIN, CHARLES (I) II-66, 264

COUPERIN, CHARLES (II) II-264, 284,316,383,386,417,480

COUPERIN, DENIS II-66

COUPERIN, FRANCOIS (I) II-259; III-171

COUPERIN, FRANÇOIS (II, "Le Grand") I-350; II-66,417, 481,504; III-5,39,44,46,48, 53,65,66,69,74,78,83,94,98, 100,110,111,113,115,121,124, 138,149,150,160,162,164,167, 168,172,177,187,193,196,200, 201,209,215,242,247,248,253, 256,266,267,269,270,271,272, 273,279,281,283,286,288,298, 300,305,306,307,308,346,347, 350,355,357,364,366,372,376, 377,388,397,408,416,428,430, 463,465,473

COUPERIN, LOUIS II-224,256,316, 358,364,371,382,383

COUPERIN, MARGUERITE-ANTOINETTE III-198,200,428

COUPERIN, MARGUERITE-LOUISE II-465; III-160,404

COUPERIN, MARIE-MADELEINE III-44

COUPERIN, MATHURIN II-66

COUPERIN, NICOLAS II-487; III-355,466,473

COUPERIN, NICOLAS-LOUIS III-215

COUPERIN, PIERRE-LOUIS III-215

COURTEVILLE, RALPH III-53,56, 70,75,82,92,494

COURTEVILLE, RAPHAEL (I) II-375,455

COURTEVILLE, RAPHAEL (II) III-487

COURTOIS, JEAN I-235,294,297, 303,307,308,313,325,332

COURTRAI I-452

CREIGHTON, (Rev.) ROBERT (Bish-
op of Bath and Wells) II-
291,388,427,450; III-474
CREMA, GIOVANNI MARIA DA I-332
CREQUY, AMBASSADOR II-272
CRESACRE, ANNE I-284
CRESCIMBENI II-408
CRESPEL, GUILLAUME I-166,305
CRESPIN, JOHN I-369
CRESSET, J. III-122
CRÉTIN I-239,248
CRISPIAENEN I-208
CRISTOFORI, BARTOLOMMEO DI FRAN-
CESCO (see Christofori, Bar-
tolommeo)
CRIVELLATI, CESARE II-36,220
CRIVELLATI, DOMENICO II-36,244
CRIVELLI, ARCANGELO II-305
CRIVELLI, CARLO I-206
CROCE, GIOVANNI I-373,479,480,
502,512,513,524,528,533,534;
II-4,10,12,13,16,20,23,31,
70,80,82,84,88,94,96,105,107,
114,119,122,128,129,137,144,
149,150,182,253
CROES, HENRI DE III-198,355,
416
CROESUS, of Lydia I-10
CROFT, WILLIAM II-473; III-
122,151,154,156,159,168,177,
184,189,190,191,195,197,226,
227,249,259,261,267,279,286,
289,361,374,393,398
CROIX, PIERRE DE LA I-85,102
CROMBERGER I-264
CROMWELL, OLIVER II-33,312,
315,350,354,359,367,369,373,
374,376; III-114
CROMWELL, RICHARD II-235,262,
369
CROMWELL, THOMAS I-250,306; II-
124
CROSS, MB. LETITIA III-93
CROSS, NATHANIEL III-287

CROSS, THOMAS, I II-312,338
CROSS, THOMAS, II II-511,516,
    517; III-57,70,78,108,111,
    115,128,129,155,327,468
CROTTI, FRANCESCO II-114
CROUCH, JOHN III-49
CROUILLY, SIEUR DE (see Coup-
    erin, François)
CROWLEY, ROBERT I-339
CROWNE, JOHN II-434; III-10,61,
    64
CRÜGER, JOHANN II-22,45,208,209,
    220,226,233,253,269,293,311,
    321,325,329,332,341,377,386,
    409,419; III-48,96
CRUIRANO III-242
CRUSO, J. II-290
CRUZ, AGOSTINHO DA II-119,261,
    263; III-94
CUGAT, ST. I-230
CUISINIÉ III-227
CULLEN, JOHN III-136,180,210,
    215,217,218,248,271
CUMBERLAND, EARL OF II-183
CUMMINGS II-488
CUPEDA, DONATO III-173,189
CUPIS, CARDINAL DE I-299
CUPIS, FRANÇOIS III-318
CUPIS (de Camargo), JEAN-BAPTISTE
    III-249
CUPPI, MARIA-ANNA (see Camargo)
CURIONI, ROSA III-136
CUSANI, family III-310
CUSTOS II-313
CUTELL, RICHARD I-137
CUTTING, FRANCIS II-10,36,67
CUTTING, THOMAS II-10,36,105,
    111,117,134,142
CUYP, ALBERT II-198; III-59
CUYPERS, JOHANNES THEODOSIUS
    III-362
CUZZONI, FRANCESCA III-153,297,
    313,319,351,374,396,405,417,
    428,454,475,482,493

CYBEL   I-18
CYNAN, GRYFFUDD AB   I-59
CYNEWULF   I-44,45
CYPRIAN, ST.   I-107
CYRIL   I-46
CYRUS, of Persia   I-10
CYSIS, JEAN-BAPTISTE   III-414,
    417
CZERNOHORSKY, BOHUSLAU   III-454

D

DA BOLOGNA   (see Bologna)
DABORNE, ROBERT   II-124
DACHSTEIN, WOLFGANG   I-275
D'AGINCOURT   (see Agincourt, D')
DAHMEN, WILHELM   III-440
DAHURON   III-322
D'ALESSANDRI, GIULIO   (see Ales-
    sandri, d')
DAL GAUDIO   (see Gaudio, Dal)
DALHAM   (see Dallam)
DALL'ABACO   (see Abaco, Dall')
DALLA CASA, GIROLAMO   (see Casa,
    Girolamo dalla)
DALLAM, family   II-43
DALLAM, GEORGE   II-437; III-14
DALLAM, RALPH   II-437,443,444,
    445
DALLAM, ROBERT   II-74,222,268,
    271,272,302,401
DALLAM, THOMAS (I)   II-22,34,96,
    133,148,163,174,260,261,281,
    383
DALLAM, THOMAS (II)   II-383
DALLAM, TOUSSAINT   II-383
DALLANS   (see Dallam)
DALLERY, CHARLES   III-174
DALLERY, PIERRE   III-484
DALLUM   (see Dallam)
DALYELL, (Sir) J. GRAHAM   I-209

DANYEL, JOHN (see Daniel, John)

DANZI, INNOCENZ (Innocente)
   III-436

DAQUIN, LOUIS (Claude) III-79,
   207,396,397,454,490

DAQUIN, PIERRE-LOUIS (de Chat-
   eau-Lyon) III-331

DARDESPIN III-14

DARIUS, of Persia I-11,19,198

DA SALÒ (see Salo, Da)

DASER, LUDWIG I-371,389; II-
   176

DASHORST, ANTHONIS MOR VAN (see
   Moro, A.)

D'ASSOUCY (see Assoucy D')

D'ASTORGA (see Astorga, d')

DAUBE, JOHANN FREDERICK III-
   436

DAUN, COUNT III-213,224,266

DAUPHIN (France, 1679) II-481

DAUVERGNE, ANTOINE III-136,267

DAVANTE I-380

DAVENANT, CHARLES II-272,276,
   292,360,361,362,368,390,394,
   412,415,416,419,420,432,447,
   463,465,467; III-7,44,186

DAVENANT, (Sir) WILLIAM II-
   102,287,288,308,335,360,378,
   382,388

DAVID I-6,7,27,60,81,153; II-
   166,500

DAVID, GERARD I-165,193,208,
   209,237,239,249,250,260,274

DAVIDICI I-471

DAVIDSON, PATRICK II-279; III-
   111

DAVIDSON, THOMAS II-455

DAVIE II-439

DAVIES, HUGH II-217

DAVIS (violinist) II-360

DAVIS, E.G. III-368

DAVIS, THOMAS (composer) III-
   136

DAVY, RICHARD I-222,251,258,269

DAY, C.L.   II-343
DAY, (Daye) JOHN   I-341,356,380,
    381,382,386,391,393,394,395,
    411,427,453,467,474,481
DAY, THOMAS   II-265
DAYE, STEPHAN   II-295
DAZA, ESTEBAN   I-445
DE ABBATIS (Abbates)   (see Ab-
    batis)
DEAN, REVEREND   II-382
DEANE, THOMAS   II-43; III-184,
    234,439
DE ANTIQUIS, GIOVANNI   (see An-
    tiquis)
DE BACILLY   (see Bacilly)
DE BERTRAND, ANTHOINE   (see
    Bertrand)
DE BÈZE, THEODORE   (see Beze)
DEBOLECKI, WOJCIECH   II-170,
    182,313
DE BOUCHARDON, CLAUDE   (see
    Bouchardon)
DE BROSSARD   (see Brossard, De)
DE BURY, BERNARD   (see Bury)
DEBUSSY, CLAUDE   I-226
DE CABEZÓN, ANTONIO   (see Cab-
    ezon)
DE CAMARGO   (see Cupis)
DE CASTRO, JEAN   (see Castro)
DE'CAVALIERI, EMILIO   (see
    Cavalieri)
DE CHRISTO   (see Christo, De)
DE CLEVE, JOHANN   (see Cleve)
DECORUS, VOLUPIUS   (see Schon-
    sleder, Wolfgang)
DECROIS   III-338
DEDEKIND, CONSTANTIN CHRISTIAN
    II-241,352,357,364,368,389,
    392,393,395,398,400,403,404,
    409,410,414,428,430,439,446,
    453,463,497,498,513; III-285
DEDEKIND, HEINRICH (Enricus)
    II-187
DEDEKIND, HENNING   II-156,208,
    239,255,304,325

132

DEDEKIND, MUSOPHILUS (see Dede-
    kind, Henning)
DEDEKIND, STEPHAN II-278
DEERING, RICHARD (see Dering)
DE FALCO, MICHAEL (see Falco)
DE FESCH, WILLEM (see Fesch)
DEFOE, DANIEL II-378; III-114,
    171,179,196,322,332,349,368,
    390
DE'FRANCESI, SAN LUIGI (see Fran-
    cesi)
DE GATTI, TEOBALDO (see Gatti)
DE GÓIS, DAMAIÃO (see Góis)
DE GRANDIS (see Grandis, De)
DEGRINIS II-377
DEHAULT, SEIGNEUR DE (see Boes-
    set, Jean Baptiste)
DE HEREDIA (see Aguilera)
DEINIRA I-185
DEISS, MICHAEL I-398
DEITRICHSTEIN, CARDINAL II-232
DE JUDICE, CESARE (see Judice,
    Cesare de)
DEKKER, THOMAS II-262
DE KONING, DAVID (see Koning,
    David De)
DELAIR III-46
DE LANGA, FRANCISCO SOTO I (see
    Soto)
DELANGE, HOMAN-FRANÇOIS III-304
DE LAPORTE, JOSEPH (see Laporte)
DEL CORT, BARTOLOME (see Cort,
    Bartolome Del)
DELFT, J. VERMEER VAN (see Ver-
    meer van Delft, J.)
DELLA BELLA (see Bella)
DELLA CIAIA (see Ciaia)
DELLA CORTE (see Corte)
DELLA PORTA, FRANCESCO (see
    Porta)
DELLA ROVERO, GIULIO FELTRIO
    (see Rovero)
DELL'ARPA, GIAN LEONARDO (see
    Arpadell')

DELLA TAVOLA, ANTONIO (see Tavola, A. della)

DELLA VIOLA (see Viola, Della)

DELLER (Teller) JOHANN FLORIAN III-413

DELMOTTE I-420

DELONEY, THOMAS II-20

DELORME (architect) I-260,399, 423

DE LYON, CORNEILLE (see Lyon)

DEMACHI, GIUSEPPE III-136

DEMANTIUS, CHRISTOPH I-409,526; II-2,13,21,70,87,114,150,258, 305,306

DEMARTINECOURT, CLAUDINE II-252

DE MEDICI, DUKE FRANCESCO (see Medici)

DEMETER I-16

DEMETRIUS, of Phalerum I-17

DEMETRIUS I, CZAR OF RUSSIA II-96

DE MONTAIGNE, MICHEL (see Montaigne)

DE MONTANOS, FRANCISCO (see Montanos)

DE MORALES, LUIS (see Morales)

DEMOSTHENES I-17

DEN BORREN (see Borren, Den)

DENHAM, HENRY I-465

DENHAM, JOHN II-166

DENIS, CLAUDE II-493; III-430

DENIS, MICHAEL III-422

DENIS, ST. I-72,75,145

DENNER, JACOB III-428,486

DENNER, JOHANN CHRISTOPH II-355,392; III-53,163,213

DENNIS, JOHN III-91,194

DENSS, ADRIAN II-36

DENT, E.J. III-225

DENTICE, family II-36

DENTICE, LUIGI I-356

DENTICE, SCIPIONE II-271

DE RAICK, DIEUDONNÉ (see Raick)

DE RIBERA, JOSÉ (see Spagnoletto, Lo)

DERING (see also Harvey, Mary)

DERING (Dancing Master) III-
483

DERING, (Deering) RICHARD I-
424,444,451,452,462; II-16,
31,45,126,142,174,176,183,
189,193,195,208,224,235,250,
251,252,269,354,369,389

DERMODY, DONALD O' (see O'Dermody)

DERRICK II-43

DE SANCTA MARIA, TOMÁS (see Sancta Maria)

DESBROSSES II-470

DESCARTES, RENE II-1,183,277,
330,332,349,419

DESCOTEAUX II-313; III-404

DESMARETS (Desmaret), HENRI II-
390; III-71,86,97,108,118,154,
189,193,195,226,237,302,331,
346,372

DE SORESINA, MARGHERITA (see
Soresina)

DES PRÉS, JOSQUIN (see Pres, Josquin des)

DESPUIG, GUILLERMO (Guillermus
de Podio) I-206

DESQUESNES, JEAN II-36,82,252

D'ESTE (see Este, D')

DESTOUCHES, (Cardinal) ANDRE
II-387,437; III-69,109,111,
113,122,123,152,158,168,181,
188,196,258,262,269,276,289,
298,312,320,336,362,367,377,
383,405,411,452

DEUDON, JEANNE-FRANÇOIS III-61

DEUSDEDIT (Adeodatus I) POPE
(see Adeodatus)

DEUTSCH, NIKLAUS MANUEL I-193,
272,275,289

DE VARGAS, LUIS (see Vargas)

DE VEGA, LOPE (see Vega, Lope de)

DE VENTO, IVO (see Vento)
DEVIS, ARTHUR III-255
DE VISÉE, R. (see Visée, R. De)
DEYER, JAMES (see Dyer, James)
D'HERVELOIS, LOUIS DE CAIX (see Caix)
DIACONUS, PAULUS I-45
DIANA, the Huntress I-349
DIAZ, GABRIEL I-514; II-99,135, 169,201,219,257
DI BAGNO, MONSIGNOR (see Bagno)
DI CAPUA, RINALDO (see Capua)
DICKENS, CHARLES III-219
DIDEROT, DENIS III-138,267
DI DINO, FRANCISCO (see Dino)
DIDYMOS I-20
DIDYMUS I-21,22
DIETRICH, SIXTUS I-200,256,264, 279,312,318,330,336,345
DIETRICH, (Archbishop) WOLF II-146
DIEUPART III-162,188,200,221, 247,250,334,490
DI GHERARDI, PINELLU (see Gherardi)
DI LASSUS (see Lasso)
DILHERR II-330
DILICHIUS, PHILIPP II-213
DILKE III-111
D'INDIA, SIGISMONDO (see India, Sigismondo D')
DINELY, THOMAS II-498
DINO, FRANCISCO DI I-189
DINTEVILLE, JEAN DE I-296
DIOBONO, POMPEO I-359
DIOCLETIAN I-26
DIOCRÈS, RAYMOND II-319
DIODORUS I-29
DIOMEDES, CATO II-68,101,128, 144,162,164
DION I-120
DIONIGI, LUIGI II-43,325,414
DIONYSIOS, of Halikarnassos I-19
DIONYSIUS I-9,10,16

DIONYSIUS, POPE   I-26

DI PESARO, DOMENICO   (see Pesaro)

DIRUTA, AGOSTINA   II-36,175,176,
    183,198,209,253,255,258,265,
    317,321,420

DIRUTA, GIROLAMO   I-371,428,529;
    II-15,16,19,114,120,122,125,
    142,147,164,175,224,226,233

DI SALO, GASPAR   (see Salo)

DITFURTH, F.W.   I-233

DITTERSDORF   III-165

DIVITIS, ANTOINE (Antoine le
    Riche)   I-185,210,234,240,
    241,257,259,280,287,297,313,
    351

DIXON, CLEMENT   II-225,262

DIXON, JOHN   II-247,262

DLUGORAJ, ALBERT (Adalbert, Wo-
    jciech)   II-82,189

DODD, EDWARD   III-203

DOEBRICHT, JOHANNA ELIZABETH
    III-269

DOGNAZZI, FRANCESCO   II-36,107,
    115,156,157,186,192,306,307

DOISI DE VELASCO   II-64,294

DOLCE, LODOVICO   I-407

DOLES, JOHANN FRIEDRICH   III-
    284

DOLMETSCH, ARNOLD   II-130

DOMANOIR, GUILLAUME (I)   II-161

DOMBET, GUILLAUME   I-144,160

DOMENICHI, LODOVICO   I-333

DOMENICI, DOMENICO   II-156

DOMENICO OF PIACENZA   (see Pia-
    cenza, Domenico)

DONATELLO   I-127,145,151,153,154,
    159,160,171,178

DONATI (Donato), BALDASSARE   I-
    289,342,344,389,414,454,510,
    513,524,533; II-8,16,23,31,
    58,79,84,150,195,276

DONATI (Donato), IGNAZIO   II-80,
    101,122,142,144,150,169,170,
    183,187,189,203,209,210,212,

215,226,232,233,239,248,250,
253,259,265,269,276,299,314,
318,349

DONFRIED II-210,211,212,215,238,
239,244; III-458

DONI, ANTONFRANCESCO I-326; II-
6

DONI, GIOVANNI BATTISTA I-532;
II-208,272,273,274,293,297,
320,321

DONNE, JOHN I-433; II-12,56,205,
230,259

DONNINI III-319,320,355,454

DONTARINI II-40

DONUS, POPE I-41

DOPPELMAYR, J.G. III-428,429,
430,432

DORICI, brothers I-361,394,411,
419,422,430

DORICO, ALOYSIO I-292,361,365,
430

DORICO, VALERIO I-292,361,365

DORMULI, VIRGINIA I-461

DORNEL, LOUIS ANTOINE III-4,235,
242,253,444

DORNEVCEL III-348

DOROTHY, ST. I-139

DORYPHORUS I-13

DOSSI, DOSSO I-190,321

DOU, GERARD II-153,458

DOUÉ, BERTIN DE LA (see Bertin)

DOUEN I-308

DOUWES, K. III-125

DOVÉ, T. BERTIN DE LA (see Bertin)

DOW, DANIEL III-453

DOW, ROBERT I-462,466

DOWLAND, JOHN I-338,456,460,
465,469,475,496,524,533,536;
II-1,2,3,10,15,16,18,20,22,
23,24,27,29,31,57,59,63,68,
80,82,84,85,91,94,98,99,101,
107,114,123,127,128,129,130,
141,142,144,145,148,150,157,

435,441,453,457,458,477,483,
484,490,496,499,507,514,516;
III-2,4,6,9,10,13,21,22,23,
51,55,59,60,62,63,64,72,78,
81,87,92,97,104,159,316
DÜBEN, ANDREAS (the Elder) II-
2,161,201,223,224,293,387
DÜBEN, ANDREAS, (the younger)
II-443; III-171
DÜBEN, CARL GUSTAF III-153
DÜBEN, GUSTAF (the elder) II-44,
218,321,392; III-45
DÜBEN, GUSTAF (the younger) II-
370; III-47,117,259,313,370,
384
DÜBEN, JOACHIM II-462; III-427
DÜBEN, KARL VILHELM II-462; III-
361,427
DÜBEN, MICHAEL II-64
DUBOURG, MATTHEW III-138,182,
259,275,286,315,364,368,393,
404,412
DUBUISSON, PIERRE I-401
DU CANGE, CHARLES (see Cange)
DU CAURROY, FRANÇOIS (see Caur-
roy, François)
DUCCIO I-111,112
DUCHÉ III-157,171,177,209
DU CHEMIN, NICOLAS (see Chemin)
DUCIS, (Protestant Clergyman)
I-293
DUCIS, BENEDICTUS I-251,259,291,
293,301,305,308,310,313,325,
330
DUDDYNGTON, ANTHONY I-265
DUDLEY, ROBERT I-483
DUETO, ANTONIO I-475
DUFAY, GUILLAUME I-123,125,126,
130,136,144,146,147,148,150,
151,152,154,155,156,157,158,
160,161,164,170,171,173,176,
178,179,183,190,214,238,294,
324
DUFFETT II-447,465

DURANTE, FRANCESCO II-517

DURANTE, OTTAVIO II-114

DURANTE, SILVESTRO II-344,397,
    421

DURASTANTI, MARGHERITA III-10,
    234,259,291,318,323,324,332,
    335,342,344,351,364,464,474

DURAZZO, COUNT GIACOMO III-304,
    308

DURELLI, FERDIANO II-136

DÜRER, ALBRECHT I-181,204,209,
    210,213,237,240,245,246,248,
    258,260,265,266,268,271,279,
    282,284

DÜRER, HANS I-213

D'URFEY, THOMAS (see Urfey,
    Thomas D')

DURÓN, SEBASTIÁN II-490; III-
    56,109,122,129,175,250,286,
    295

DURVAL II-250

DUSART I-239

DUŠEK, FRANTIŠEK XAVER III-439

DUVAL, MLLE. III-88,136

DUVAL, FRANÇOIS II-448; III-
    193,196,209,220,314,329,402

DUVAL, MARC I-290,464

DYCK, ANTHONY VAN II-34,173,198,
    205,206,212,217,240,262,275,
    287,300

DYER, ANNE II-68,80

EYER, (Sir) EDWARD I-348; II-
    110

DYER, ELIZABETH II-68,80

DYER, JAMES II-56,68,74,80

DYGON, JOHN (clergyman) I-249,
    306,320

DYGON, JOHN (composer) I-209,
    254

DYGON, JOHN of Kent I-275

DYSON, ADAM I-278

E

EARL, THOMAS   II-98
EARLE, WALTER   II-187
EARSDEN, JOHN   II-36,183
EAST, LUCRETIA   II-257
EAST, MICHAEL   II-68,88,99,101,
    128,183,189,220,285,322,323
EAST (Este) THOMAS   I-383,444,
    480,491,499,500,501,502,505,
    507,509,510,523,524,525,526,
    530,535,537; II-11,16,17,18,
    19,20,23,24,25,26,57,58,59,
    61,71,81,82,83,88,90,94,107,
    110,114,118,119,120,128,137,
    204,222,257
EBELING, JOHANN GEORG   II-279,
    280,388,410,419,457,462
EBERHARDINE, ELECTRESS CHRISTI-
    ANE   III-393,398
EBERLIN, DANIEL   III-5
EBERLIN, JOHANN ERNST   III-173,
    380,396,417
EBERSDORFF, PETER VON   I-100
-EBHRAJA, BAR'   (see Hebraeus,
    Bar)
EBNER, WOLFGANG   II-131,268,279,
    325,392,401
EBREO, SALOMONE ROSSI   (see Ros-
    si)
EBSWORTH, J.W.   III-6
EDDARD, JOHANNES   I-273,295,358,
    426,436,450,451,455,456,470,
    484,503,506,507; II-10,15,16,
    17,23,29,30,31,59,87,112,114,
    122,128,134,138,234,269,303,
    305,307,311,316,319,343,349,
    393,394,459,513
ECCLES, HENRY   II-431,450,453;
    III-5,39,329,488
ECCLES, JOHN   II-418,506; III-
    48,52,57,66,75,78,82,83,84,

EDWARD II, KING of England, (Plantagnet) I-100,110

EDWARD III, KING of England, (plantagenet) I-112,115, 116,118,121,140

EDWARD IV, KING of England, (York) I-158,175,181,241

EDWARD V, KING of England, (York) I-179,193

EDWARD VI, KING of England, (Tudor) I-259,304,311,336,337, 338,340,354,355,356,456; II-96

EDWARDE, MARTYR II-36

EDWARDS, JONATHON III-435

EDWARDS, RICHARD I-273,311,334, 348,392,405,406,446

EDWARDS, TOM II-411

EDWIN, KING of Northumbria I-39

EDWY (The Fair), KING of England I-56

EEDEN, GILES VAN DEN III-405, 414

EEDEN, HEINRICH VAN DEN III-93, 100,346

EFFLER, JOHANN III-249,250

EFFREM, MUZIO (Mutio) II-36, 175,177,208,232,234

EGAS, ENRIQUE DE I-190,205,298

EGBERT, KING of England I-45, 47,49

EGENOLFF, CHRISTIAN I-297,299, 357

EHE, HANS LEONHARD III-117

EILMAR, GEORG CHRISTIAN III-285

EINESHAM I-93

EISENHUT, THOMAS II-43,450,451, 513; III-177

EISENTRAUT, MARTHA ELIZABETH II-481

EITNER I-227,235,287; III-59

EKKEHARD II, MARGRAVE I-96

EKKEHARD IV (Monk) I-58,66

ELEANOR (wife of Francis I) I-288

ELEANOR, of Aquitaine I-77

ELEONORA (wife of Hercules I) I-134

ELEONORA, EMPRESS II-396

ELEANORA (Leonora), of Toledo I-307,308,309,321

ELECTRA I-20

ELEONORA MADALENA THERESA, EMPRESS of Austria II-470

ELERT, PIOTR II-35,266,307,347

ELEUTHERIUS, POPE I-24

ELFORD, RICHARD III-172,173,275

EL GRECO (Theotokopoulos) I-319,478,489; II-6,28,91,117, 160; II-133

ELIGIUS, ST. I-162

ELIJAH (The Prophet) I-128

ELIOT, JOHN II-384

ELIZABETH, of Austria I-427

ELIZABETH, of Hungary (Saint) I-127

ELIZABETH, EMPRESS of Russia III-237

ELIZABETH, PRINCESS (daughter of James I) II-141,147,150, 152

ELIZABETH I, QUEEN (Tudor) I-106,253,259,295,311,355,361, 370,374,375,384,405,409,411, 417,426,433,437,438,450,452, 464,477,483,491,518,519,523, 526; II-8,38,68,71,73,78,81, 83,85,496,502

ELIZABETH, QUEEN (wife of Charles III) III-232

ELIZABETH, QUEEN (wife of Henry VII) I-204,236

ELISABETTA, QUEEN of Spain III-222

ELLERTON III-447

ELLIS, A.J. II-46,97

ELLIS, WILLIAM II-360; III-34

ELMENHORST, H.   III-73

ELPHEGE, BISHOP   I-56

ELSBETH, THOMAS   II-64,75,103,
    169,173

ELSTS, J. VAN DER   II-365

ELTON, RICHARD   II-335,372

ELVINUS   I-81

ELYOT, (Sir) THOMAS   I-292

ELYS, EDWARD   II-404

ELZEVIR   II-345

EMERIC, KING   I-85

EMMERAM, ST.   I-99,155

ENCINA, JUAN DEL   I-157,179,183,
    203,208,266,274,287

ENCLOS, SIEUR DE L'   II-251

ENDA, JOHANN VON   II-6

ENDEL, CHRISTOFFER   I-280

ENDEL, WILLIAM   I-397

ENDERLE, WILHELM GOTTFRIED   III-
    343

ENGEL, CARL   II-48

ENGELMANN, GEORG   II-13,173,257

ENRICHELLI   III-136

ENZIO, MARQUIS   II-237

EPHRAIM, ST. (hymn composer)
    I-30

ÉPIE, L'   III-215

EPINE, MARGHERITA DE L'   III-
    65,69,74,180,181,182,188,200,
    207,216,229,242,259,269,313

ERASMUS   I-184,236,263,274,289,
    301,313,435

ERASMUS, ST.   I-278

ERBA, DIONIGI   III-65,83,95,97,
    129

ERBACH, CHRISTIAN   I-383,431;
    II-59,66,75,88,101,109,153,
    224,228,242,271,272

ERCOLE I, DUKE of Ferrara   I-134,
    183,184,193,297,210,241,266

ERCOLE II, DUKE of Ferrara   I-
    284,297,336,346,370,372

ERDMANN, GEORG   III-152,426,428

ERECHTHEUM   I-14

EREDI, (Heredi) FRANCESCO II-
    36,59,214,215,247,248
EREMITA II-20
ERHARDI II-372
ERICH, DANIEL III-129,256
ERLEBACH, PHILIPP HEINRICH II-
    363; III-110,111,244,274,419
ERMANGARDE, of Narbonne I-80
ERNEST, ARCHDUKE of Bavaria I-
    395,492
ERNEST, DUKE (Governor of the
    Netherlands) II-252
ERNST, COUNT of Buckeburg II-
    130
ERNST AUGUSTUS, ELECTOR of Han-
    over (Duke of Braunschweig)
    II-493; III-2,120,216,296
ERNST, JOHANN III-101,285
ERNST LUDWIG, DUKE of Hesse-Darm-
    stadt and Meiningen III-242,
    260,366,368
ERNESTI, JOHANN AUGUST III-454,
    476,478
ERNESTI, JOHANN HEINRICH II-519;
    III-355,414,415
ERRICHELLI III-136
ERTHEL, SEBASTIAN II-43
ESCH, J. I-273
ESCHENBACH, WOLFRAM VON I-79,
    82,89,91
ESCOBAR, ANDRÉ I-342
ESCOBAR, PEDRO DE I-247
ESCOBEDO, BARTOLOMÉ I-251,301,
    317,359,392
ESCRIBANO, JUAN I-247,374
ESCUREL, JEHANNOT DE L' I-109
ESLAVA, MIGUEL HILARION I-234
ESPINOSA, ANTONIO DE I-376
ESPINOSA, JUAN DE I-257
ESQUIER, AUBREY veare I-434
ESQUIVEL, JUAN DE (see Barahona)
ESSENGA, SALVATORE I-386,407
ESSEX, EARL OF II-12
ESSEX, JOHN I-306

ESSEX, LADY II-151
ESTE (English publishers) (see East)
ESTE D', family I-219,263,272, 361,398,532; II-22,158,179
ESTE, (Cardinal) ALESANDRO D' II-1,58,74
ESTE, ALFONSO D' I-236,265,403, 454,461,486
ESTE, CESARE D' I-486,488
ESTE, (Cardinal) IPPOLITO D' I-280,310,384,387,396,404, 418,419,421,425,429,457,475, 532
ESTE, ELEONORA D' I-533
ESTE, ISABELLA D' I-199,210
ESTE, LEONORA D' I-418
ESTE, LIONELLO D' I-158
ESTE, LUCREZIA D' I-418
ESTE, (Cardinal) LUIGI D' I-453,455,485
ESTE, (Duke) RINALDO D' III-338
ESTÉBAN, FERNANDO I-142
ESTERHÁZY, PAUL III-241
ESTERHÁZY (Prince) PAUL ANTON III-65,241,253,268,271
ESTOCART, PASCHAL DE. L' I-315
ESTUICK, SAMPSON II-363,468, 489; III-65,101,111,167,259
ETHELBALD I-50
ETHELBERT (King of England) I-50
ETHELBERT (King of Jutish King-dom of Kent) I-37,38
ETHELRED I, KING of England I-50
ETHELRED II, (The Unready), KING of England I-57,63
ETHELWOLD, BISHOP of Winchester I-57
ETHELWULF I-49
ETHEREGE II-463
ETHERIA (Aquitanian pilgrim) I-30

FABER I-295,356
FABER, BENEDIKT II-78
FABER, J. III-487
FABER, J.A.J. III-332
FABER, NICHOLAS I-121
FABIAN, POPE I-26
FABIAN, R. III-490
FABRI, ANNIBALE PIO III-110,
    319,417,429,441
FABRI, GUILLAUME I-329
FABRI, NICCOLA I-176
FABRIANO, GENTILE DA I-121,142,
    148,149,150,151,153
FABRICIUS, JAN (see Fabrycy,
    Jan)
FABRICUIS, WERNER II-263,332,
    360,367,401,478
FABRITIUS, CAREL II-211,315,
    354
FABRIZIO, DON I-509
FABRYCY, JAN II-252
FACIEN, JEHAN (elder) I-438
FACIO, ANSELMO II-70
FAGO, LORENZO III-189,351,448
FAGO, NICOLA ("Il Tarantino")
    II-466; III-64,73,166,189,
    190,191,199,203,217,219,233,
    237,238,254,261,262,271,280,
    289,419
FAIDIT, GAUCELM I-79,80,89,90,
    93

FAIGNENT I-335
FAIGINENT, NOÉ II-6
FAIL, NÖEL DU I-483
FAIRFAX, (Sir) THOMAS II-312,
    315,362
FALCA, PIETRO (see Longhi)
FALCO, MICHELE DE III-52,237,
    257,261,308,357,367
FALCONE II-58

FARNESE, ANTONIO III-175
FARNESE, ELISABETTA (see Elisabetta, Queen of Spain)
FARNESE, (Cardinal) ODOARDO II-103
FARNESE, (Duke) OTTAVIO I-386
FARNESE, (Duke) RANUCCIO (of Parma) I-320; II-181,241,246, 271
FARONELL II-519,522
FARQUHAR III-169,174,177,212
FARRANT, DANIEL II-62,66,104
FARRANT, JOHN I-409,426; II-27,140,181
FARRANT, RICHARD I-225,279,296, 356,396,397,417,451,456; II-104
FARRENC, LOUISE I-220
FASCH, JOHANN FRIEDRICH III-26, 124,171,250,278,323,338,346
FASOLO, GIOVANNI BATTISTA II-239,244,314,371,372
FATTORINI, GABRIELE II-24,59,66, 70,76,88,114,164
FAUSTA I-294
FAUSTINI, G. II-416
FAVART, CHARLES SIMON III-240, 245,393,454,458,482

FAWKES, GUY III-55
FAYETTE, MARIE DE LA II-270; III-77
FAYRFAX, ROBERT I-169,177,200, 202,207,212,222,235,236,239, 251,253,267,268,270,287,288
FEBURE, JEAN LE II-12,63
FEDE, (Count) ANTONIO MARIA III-221,224
FEDELI, CARLO III-5
FEDELI, RUGGIERO II-358,444,468; III-5,25,51,187,200,374
FEDELI, VITO I-326
FEDERICO GENNARO ANTONIO III-459,463,486

FEI, MI   I-66,73
FEIND, BARTHOLD   II-477; III-201,227,342
FEILDING (Viceconte), BASILIO   II-283
FEINHOLD, THEODOR CHRISTLIEB   II-503
FEKE, ROBERT   III-204
FEKETE, ANDREW   I-384
FEL, ANTOINE   III-82
FEL, MARIE   III-267,466,476
FÉLIBIEN   III-211
FELICIANI   II-20
FELIS, STEFANO   I-436,520; II-78
FELIX I, POPE   I-26
FELIX III (II), POPE   I-33
FELIX IV (III), POPE   I-35
FELIX V, POPE   I-157
FELL, DR.   II-415,513
FELSTIN, SEBASTIAN DE   I-190, 245,267,298,312,325,326
FELTON, WILLIAM   III-285,488
FELTRE, CHRISTOFORO DA   I-148
FELTRIO, FEDERICO DELLA ROVERE (see Rovere)
FEN, MA   I-60
FENAROLI, FEDELE   III-424
FENELL, THOMAS   II-395,405,468; III-43,87,232
FÉNELON, ARCHBISHOP of Cambray   III-205,211,231
FENTON, LAVINIU   III-225,384, 386,402
FEO, FRANCESCO   III-56,190,239, 265,271,280,289,303,316,323, 353,355,358,360,367,389,408, 410,421,424,434,444,447,469, 477
FEODOR (see Theodore)
FERABOSCHI, FRANCESCA   II-413
FERABOSCO, DOMENICO MARIA   I-255,311,320,326,332,435
FERDINAND, of Austria   II-213, 347,348,392

FERDINAND, of Bavaria I-406
FERDINAND, ARCHDUKE of Graz II-
    91,156,163
FERDINAND, ARCHDUKE of Tyrol
    II-5
FERDINAND, GRAND-DUKE of Tuscany
    II-15,87
FERDINAND I, HOLY ROMAN EMPEROR
    I-287,325,362,369,398,470
FERDINAND II, HOLY ROMAN EMPER-
    OR I-450; II-4,42,78,126,188,
    191,192,222,262,275,283,340
FERDINAND III, HOLY ROMAN EMPER-
    OR II-42,192,270,275,279,
    280,283,284,325,329,332,363,
    402
FERDINAND V, KING of Spain I-
    157,164,183,184,190,198,201,
    204,209,261,273
FERDINAND, PRINCE of Florence
    (son of Grand Duke Cosmo III)
    III-21,46,74,234,271,296
FERDINAND KARL, ARCHDUKE of Aus-
    tria II-324,371
FERDINANDO DE MEDICI, CARDINAL
    I-502,508
FERNANDES, JEHAN I-155
FÉRNANDEZ, LUCAS I-183,319
FERNANDO DE LAS INFANTAS (see
    Infantas)
FERNANDO ALVAREZ DE TOLEDO, DUKE
    of Alba I-537; II-208
FERRABOSCO (see also Ferabosco)
FERRABOSCO, ALFONSO I I-323,345,
    384,389,409,417,418,429,450,
    495,496,502; II-19,20,82
FERRABOSCO, ALFONSO II I-443,
    459; II-47,86,96,101,102,115,
    117,122,124,130,138,140,142,
    177,232,238,242,243,345
FERRABOSCO ALFONSO III II-199,
    241,243,376
FERRABOSCO, ELIZABETH II-292
FERRABOSCO, HENRY II-217,241,369

FERRABOSCO, JOHN II-231,388,433,
    479,503
FERRADINI, ANTONIO III-203,204,
    312
FERRADINI, GIOVANNI III-203
FERRAND III-438
FERRANDINI, GIOVANNI III-355,
    416,421,432,454,460
FERRANTE I-178
FERRARI, BENEDETTO II-8,14,41,
    265,280,282,283,284,285,288,
    290,292,300,303,305,306,311,
    314,326,341,342,347,350,359,
    367,377,381,388,496
FERRARI, CARLO III-436
FERRARI, GUIDO II-9
FERREL, JEAN FRANÇOIS II-372
FERRETTI, GIOVANNI I-315,410,
    412,418,432,434,438,441,447,
    458,471,486,492,499,503,520;
    II-13
FERRI, BALDASSARE II-126,212,
    224,306,402,423,456,486
FERRI, GASPARO II-506,522
FERRINI III-429,441
FERRO, GIOVANNI I-418
FERTE, DUCHESSE DE LA III-115
FESCHE, WILLEM DE III-18,20,
    374,441,461
FESTA, COSTANZO I-200,235,257,
    262,295,302,303,304,307,308,
    323,325,328,346,371,414
FESTING, MICHAEL C. II-493; III-
    448,488,493
FÉTIS I-67,75,132,197,274,323,
    331,333,341,344,350,377; II-
    4,97,154,162,214,280,339,493,
    511; III-202,375
FEUILLET III-156,169,209,210
FEUSTKING, FRIEDRICH CHRISTIAN
    III-190,197
FÉVIN, DE(?) I-152
FÉVIN, ANTOINE DE I-152,182,
    183,190,246,255,257,258,259,
    266,291,297,371,372

158

FÈVRE, JACQUES LE I-207,303

FEZANDAT I-353

FIAMENGO, MATHIAS I-339

FIAMMA, GABRIEL I-415,491

FIDELI, RUGGERIO III-345

FIEDLER, GOTTLIEB III-62,85,97

FIELD, NATHANIEL II-124

FIELDING, HENRY III-219,444,456,
    480,490

FIESCHI, (Cardinal) OCTOBONI DE'
    I-98

FIESCO, GIULIO I-267,334,360,
    361,362,418,490

FIESOLE, GIOVANNI DI (see An-
    gelico, Fra)

FIGULUS, WOLFGANG I-340

FILIPPI, GASPARE II-281,283,
    314,329,341,349

FILIPPI, PIETRI II-166

FILIPPINI, PIETRO (see Philips,
    Peter)

FILIPPINI, STEFANO II-309,346

FILIPPO, DUKE of Flanders I-422,
    436,486

FILIPPUCCI, AGOSTINO II-321,404,
    420,423,456,485

FILLAGO, CARLO II-214

FILMER II-239

FILTZ, ANTON III-381,436

FINAZZI, FILIPPO III-246,412

FINCH, EDWARD II-397,481; III-
    154,191,228,242,339

FINCK, HEINRICH I-160,203,206,
    209,234,244,250,255,282,301,
    319,368,374

FINCK, HERMANN I-280,282,368,
    369,374

FINE, ARNOLDUS DE I-428

FINE, JOHANN DE (see Enda, Jo-
    hann Vom)

FINGER, GOTTFRIED II-380; III-
    30,48,57,75,95,101,104,111,
    154,156,165,167,169,182,207,
    307,308,309,315

FIOCCO, family II-336
FIOCCO, JEAN-JOSEPH III-13,207,
    215,278
FIOCCO, JOSEPH HECTOR III-182,
    384,391,417,430,440,441,483
FIOCCO, PIETRO ANTONIO II-336,
    497,499,502; III-23,55,57,61,
    102,125,211,276,278
FIORE, ANGELO MARIA II-380; III-
    103,110,118,169,338,352
FIORE, STEFANO ANDREA III-17,
    125,187,214,228,235,244,283,
    452
FIORILLO, IGNAZIO III-284
FIORILLO, SILVIO I-424; II-198
FIORANI, GIOVANNI ANDREA III-
    191
FIRBANK III-302
FIRMIN, ST. I-91
FISCHER(?) II-467
FISCHER, JOHANN (organist) II-
    2,88
FISCHER, JOHANN (violinist and
    composer) II-316; III-177,
    337
FISCHER, JOHANN KASPAR FERDIN-
    AND II-331,380,405,508; III-
    95,104,118,169,177,247,253,
    289,474
FISCHIETTI, DOMENICO III-333,
    381
FISHER, WILLIAM II-497
FITZGERALD OF CLOYNE, (Sir) JOHN
    II-205
FITZJAMES III-13
FITZROY, HENRY (Duke of Richmond)
    I-302
FITZWILLIAM I-377,391,398; II-
    200,203,206,256
FLACCONIO, GIOVANNI PIETRO II-
    24,138,174
FLACKTON (Flacton), WILLIAM III-
    233,493
FLANDRE, GÉRARD DE I-183

160

FLANDRE, JUAN DE   I-215
FLANDRIA, RAYNALDUS ODENOCH DE
   I-187
FLATMAN, THOMAS   II-518
FLAVIAN   I-29
FLECHA, MATEO (the elder)   I-191,
   274,358,463
FLECHA, MATEO (the younger)   I-
   269,397,413,414,463; II-29,
   86
FLEISCHER, FREIDRICH GOTTLOB
   III-343
FLEISCHOR   III-313
FLEMMING, PAUL   II-119,292
FLETCHER, JOHN   I-454; II-127,
   228,235; III-23,28,29,51,81,
   84
FLEURY, NICOLAS   II-377
FLINTOFT, LUKE   III-154,196,287,
   318,319,394
FLIPPA   III-121
FLOOD, VALENTINE   II-238,270,281
FLOR, CHRISTIAN   II-308
FLORENCIA, JOHANNES DA   (see Ca-
   scia)
FLORIANUS, BENEDICTUS   I-426
FLORIDO, R.   II-64,309,320,322,
   397
FLORIMO   III-331
FLORIO   II-26,84,138
FLUDD (Flud), ROBERT   I-437,518;
   II-9,92,120,173,179,210,226,
   248,279
FLUDD, (Sir) THOMAS   I-437
FOGGIA, ANTONIO   III-182,214
FOGGIA, ENRICO RADESCA DI   (see
   Radesca, E.)
FOGGIA, FRANCESCO   II-86,279,
   471; III-26
FOGLIANO, GIACOMO   I-182,286,
   336
FOGLIANO, (Condottiere) GUIDO-
   RICCIO DA   I-115
FOGLIANO, LUDOVICO   I-286

FOGLIAZZI III-354

FOLIOT (Philippe de la Folie)
    I-141,149

FOLQUET, of Marseilles I-93

FOLZ, HANS I-190,379,383

FOND, J.B. DE LA III-377

FONTAINE, JEAN DE LA II-205

FONTAINES, PERRINET DE (Pierre
    Fontaine) I-141,144,147,151,
    155,161

FONTANA, GIOVANNI BATTISTA II-
    251,298,413,429

FONTANA, VINCENZO I-331

FONTANELLI, (Count) ALFONSO II-
    4,68,74,82,88,93,122,169,189,
    201,206

FONTEI, NICCOLÒ II-274,276,287,
    289,294,304,314,321

FONTEIO, GIOVANNI II-102

FONTENELLE, BERNARD LE BOVIER DE
    I-165; III-30,34,331

FONTES, MARQUIS DE III-296

FOQUET, PIERRE CLAUDE III-486

FORBES, JOHN II-360,389,409,
    419,434,455,505; III-215

FORBES, (Sir) SAMUEL (of Foveran)
    II-347; III-301,304

FORCER, FRANCIS II-519;III-115,199

FORD, JOHN II-297

FORD, THOMAS I-459; II-101,107,
    135,157,224,232,323

FORDUN I-88

FORESTIER I-142

FORESTO, MATTEO I-491,518

FORKEL, JOHANN NICOLAUS I-223;
    II-192,328,380,405,492,509;
    III-62,81,304,332,343,351,
    360,361,362,373,401,413,435,
    440,468,478,479,489

FORLI, MELOZZO DA I-156,183,
    190,205

FORMARI III-346

FORMÉ, NICOLAS I-409; II-219,
    231,257,284

FORMOSUS, POPE I-52
FORMSCHNEIDER, HIERONYMUS I-
   297,342,365
FORNACI, GIACOMO II-177
FORNARI, MATTEO III-46,55,242,
   259
FORNSETE, JOHN OF I-91,92
FORQUERAY, ANTOINE II-432; III-
   37,108,191,242
FORQUERAY, JEAN-BAPTISTE-ANTOINE
   III-123,151,454
FORQUERAY, MICHEL II-494
FORQUERAY, NICOLAS GILLES III-
   180
FORREST, EBENEZER III-419
FORRESTIO, MADDALENA ANNA II-
   161
FORSTER, GEORG I-251,258,306,
   308,310,311,313,339,367,370,
   413
FÖRSTER, KASPAR II-174,356,375,
   381,383,442
FORSTER, WILL II-218
FORTINI, PIETRO I-388
FÖRTSCH, JOHANN PHILIPP II-343,
   489,521,522; III-30,39,40,48,
   83,453
FORTUNATUS, VENANTIUS I-36,37,
   39
FOSCARI, FRANCESCO I-148
FOSCARINI (see Caliginoso)
FOSSE, JACQUES LA III-338
FOSSES (Fossa), JEAN DE (Johan-
   nes) II-79
FOSSIS, PIETRO DE I-202,203,
   282
FOSTER, JOHN II-386,466
FOSTER, JOSEPH II-104
FOSTER, OSBORNE I-345
FOSTER, WILLIAM II-230
FOTI, ANNIBALE PIO III-374
FOUCAULT III-172
FOUQUET, JEAN I-147,159,161,
   166,172,173,180,184,191

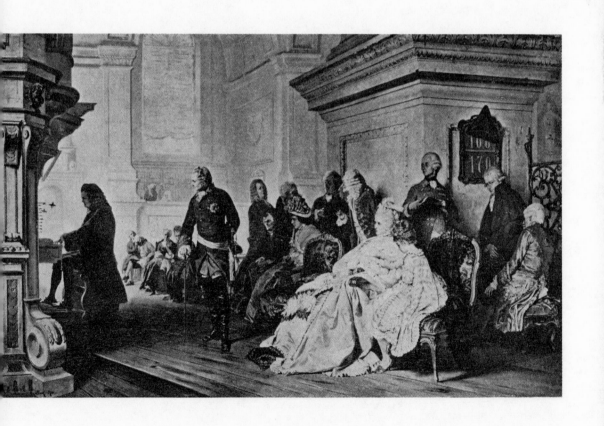

FREDERICK THE GREAT AND JOHANN SEBASTIAN BACH   *165*

FRANCISCI, JURAJ III-234

FRANCISCO II-450,469

FRANCISQUE, ANTOINE I-424; II-
8,59,92

FRANCK, JOHANN II-181,239,244,
248,258,269,276,467

FRANCK, JOHANN WOLFGANG II-301,
405,446,447,457,476,480,483,
484,485,491,499,507,515,522;
III-14,23,48,51,73

FRANCK, MELCHIOR I-431; II-69,
73,75,76,82,84,91,101,115,
128,138,145,150,153,157,164,
170,203,210,215,220

FRANCK, SALOMO III-43,279,284,
286,288,298,307,443

FRANCKE, MASTER (painter) I-
141,149

FRANCO, of Cologne I-61,66,79,
95,96,100

FRANCO, of Dortmund I-81

FRANCO, of Liège I-66,68

FRANCO, FERNANDO I-362,443,479

FRANCO, GIACOMO II-24

FRANCOEUR, FRANÇOIS III-116,242,
384,388,389,490

FRANÇOIS DE FRANCE, DOUNT of
Alencon I-417

FRANÇOIS, DUKE of Guise I-367

FRANCQUART, JACQUES II-216

FRANGIPANE, CORNELIO I-434,437

FRANKLIN, BENJAMIN III-204,237,
414,425,431,434,435,456

FRANKLIN, JAMES III-341

FRANSHAWE, (Sir) HENRY II-168

FRANZONI, AMANTE II-94,107,109,
115,135,138,175,177,189

FRAUENLOB (see Meissen, Heinrich
Von)

FREDDI, AMADIO II-155,261,274

FREDERICI, D. FRANCESCO II-463

FREDERICK, DUKE of Altenburg
II-211

FRIEDRICH III, PRINCE (Gottorf)
   II-266

FRIESE, HEINRICH III-325

FRIESEN, HEINRICH VON I-452

FRITSCH, BARTHOLD III-110,338,
   395

FRIULI, ANTONIO DA CIVIDALE DEL
   (Antonius de Civitate Austrie)
   I-148

FROBERGER, JOHANN JACOB II-167,
   279,283,301,344,350,388,411,
   431,498; III-75,104

FROISSART, JEAN I-115,118,125,
   127

FROMAN, G.H. II-403

FROMENT, NICHOLAS I-155,186,194

FROMM, ANDREAS II-328,329

FROSCHAUER, HANS I-182

FROST I-489

FROUDE I-329

FROVO (Frouvo), JOÃO ALVARES II-
   74,321,332,389,500

FRUEAUF, RUELAND (the elder) I-
   158,180,246

FRUGONI, CARLO INNOCENZIA III-
   64

FRUMENTIUS, ST. I-28

FRUNDSBERG, GEORG VAN I-271

FRUYTIERS, JAN I-169,401,402

FRYE, WALTER (Gualterus Liberti)
   I-151

FUENLLANA, MIGUEL DE I-218,269,
   342,360,361,364,392

FUERTE I-346

FUGGER, GEORG II-15

FUGGER, JOHANN (Jakob) I-358,
   382,491

FUGGER, MARCUS II-16,17

FUGGER, OCTAVIAN II I-478; II-
   15,31

FUHRMANN, LEOPOLD (George) II-
   104,162,164,166; III-208

FULDA, ADAM VON I-160,186,199,
   206,209,212,225

FULLER, THOMAS II-117,304,385,
    388
FULLSACK, ZACHARIAS II-63,107,
    109,122
FURONI III-368
FURSTER, CHRISTOPH III-72
FUST, JOHN I-172
FUX, EGIDIUS I-362
FUX, JOHANN JOSEPH II-375,489;
    III-102,117,158,169,173,174,
    177,200,201,221,222,228,231,
    232,240,251,260,269,275,279,
    283,285,289,293,294,297,298,
    303,307,313,314,317,320,321,
    325,344,346,352,354,355,356,
    357,358,372,377,383,384,392,
    402,439
FUZELIER, LOUIS II-427
FYNER, CONRAD I-182

G

GABLER, JOHANN III-151
GABRIEL (architect) III-121
GABRIELI, brothers I-373
GABRIELI, ANDREA I-250,269,282,
    283,301,345,361,367,368,371,
    374,388,396,397,399,402,405,
    407,416,422,427,429,435,436,
    441,445,454,457,471,475,480,
    481,483,485,491,493,494,499,
    507,529; II-21,109,141,200
GABRIELI, DOMENICO II-336,358,
    462,492,512,513,521; III-7,
    15,23,30,40,44,57,79,95,193
GABRIELI, GIOVANNI I-67,371,
    439,442,444,456,475,478,480,
    484,486,491,493,497,528,529,
    537; II-4,15,16,17,21,29,30,
    34,61,66,78,97,100,109,115,
    120,125,141,143,163,165

FRANCHINO GAFORI 171

GABRIELLI, CATERINA (Cuochetta)
III-426

GABUSSI, GIULIO CESARE II-24,
135

GADDI, TADDEO I-122

GAFFI, BARNARDO III-196

GAFORI, (o), FRANCHINO (Gafur- *See illustration on p. 171*
ius, Franchinus) I-9,170,
182,187,188,189,191,203,207,
208,209,214,236,237,247,254,
264,267,272

GAGLIANO, ALESSANDRO III-100

GAGLIANO, GENNARO III-438

GAGLIANO, GIOVANNI BATTISTA DA
II-234,268,269,307,336

GAGLIANO, MARCO DA I-443,534;
II-75,76,88,94,101,105,107,
110,112,115,117,118,125,130,
135,149,154,158,165,168,170,
177,178,186,195,206,207,210,
215,226,234,241,244,253,301,
302

GAGLIARDI I-504

GAINSBOROUGH, THOMAS III-148,
400

GALATEA I-258

GALE, THOMAS II-230,268

GALEAZZI III-447

GALEAZZO, GIAN I-186

GALENO, GIOVANNI BATTISTA II-
24

GALEOTTO (see Carretto)

GALILEI (architect) III-59

GALILEI, GALILEO I-471

GALILEI, VINCENZO I-88,255,269,
332,348,393,395,414,416,436,
457,462,463,467,471,476,493,
507,517,518; II-7,63

GALL, ST. (Irish hermit) I-39,
40,58,59,66,76

GALLERANO, LEANDRO II-194,219,
263,274

GALLET, FRANÇOIS II-59

GALLI, ANTOINE II-82

GALLI, CATERINA III-401

GALLI, DOMENICO III-57

GALLIA, MARIA MARGHERITA III-
    181,205,212

GALLIARD, JOHANN ERNST II-493;
    III-20,207,261,262,269,307,
    357,367,377,388,408,487

GALLIARD, JOHN III-483

GALLICULUS (see Hähnel, Johann)

GALLICUS, JOHANNES I-158

GALLO, ANTONIO III-313

GALLO, GIOVANNI PIETRO II-17,
    21,59

GALLO, VINCENZO II-10,86,108,
    218

GALLOT(?) II-296; III-60

GALLOT, ANTOINE ANTONI II-320

GALLOT, JACQUES DE II-429,491;
    III-10

GALLUS (organ builder) I-266

GALLUS, JACOBUS (Handl) I-341,
    435,442,457,459,486,489,512,
    516,518,520

GALLUS, JOSEPHUS II-24

GALPIN, CANON II-135; III-126

GALUPPI, BALDASSARE II-412; III-
    206,346,347,350,355,368,408,
    409,419,420,422,434,447,459,
    469,480,490

GAMACHES, ABBE DE III-339

GAMBLE, JOHN II-333,372,389;
    III-20

GANASSI, SILVESTRO DI I-299,
    320,322,324

GANDO, PIERRE FRANÇOIS III-465

GANIERE, HENRI DE I-129

GANJIN I-42

GANTE, PEDRO DE I-190,273,274

GANTEZ II-306,307

GARAAGHER III-220

GARBI III-317

GARCIA, FRANCISCO XAVIER III-
    440

GARDANE ANTONIO (Gardano) I-371

GARDANO, family I-302,304
GARDANO (publishers) I-270,
    302,304,305,307,308,309,318,
    323,324,326,339,343,346,351,
    360,361,366,371,375,376,377,
    386,403,430,441,443,449,452,
    455,463,464,468,471,477,481,
    482,483,488,493,495,499,507,
    508,512,520,521,526,529,535,
    536; II-3,4,11,17,18,24,25,
    31,101,102,106,116,127,138,
    177,216,308,314,515
GARDANO, STAMPA DEL II-515
GARLANDIA, JOHANNES DE I-78,
    82,90,92,93,94,96,97,98
GARNETT, HENRY I-485
GARRO, F. II-213
GARSON I-223
GARTH, JOHN III-345
GARZONI, TOMMASO I-340,503
GASCOIGNE, GEORGE I-280,407,
    408,442,446,449
GASPAR I-152
GASPARDINI, GASPARO II-513,517
GASPARINI, FRANCESCO II-417;
    III-39,81,112,113,158,168,
    175,179,180,186,191,195,198,
    199,201,202,227,228,235,250,
    253,254,257,259,260,269,270,
    316,319,342,353,361,364,372,
    385,392
GASPARINI, MICHEL ANGELO II-
    459; III-97,281,285,315,321,
    367,453
GASPARRI III-276
GASSMANN III-447
GASTANAGA, MARQUIS DE (Governor
    of the Spanish Netherlands)
    III-53
GASTOLDI, GIOVANNI GIACOMO I-
    225,332,368,370,383,467,473,
    518,520,522,523,524,526,535;
    II-4,10,17,22,24,88,103,108,
    115,117,119,208; III-131

GASTONE, GIAN III-187
GATES(?) III-478
GATES, BERNARD III-5,226
GATES, FRANCES III-393
GATTAMELATA I-160
GATTI, TEOBALDO DE II-336,459;
    III-54,104,166,253,331,336,
    394,458
GAU, NIEL III-392
GAUDIO, ANTONIO DAL II-43,458,
    499
GAULLI, G.B. III-238
GAULTIER, DENIS II-14,45,65,
    85,187,294,359,400,424,437,
    439,483,490,491; III-125
GAULTIER, ENNEMOND II-340
GAULTIER, JACQUES II-85,175,180,
    252,320
GAULTIER, PIERRE II-285
GAUTIER, PIERRE II-305; III-
    1,20,109,217
GAVINIES, PIERRE III-136,403,
    478
GAWAIN, SIR I-124
GAWTHORN III-431
GAY, JOHN III-9,10,238,245,266,
    272,281,301,316,322,332,379,
    402,405,408,409,410,411,412,
    419,459,469
GEBEL, GEORG III-232,417,429,
    466,488
GEBEL, GEORG SIGISMUND III-285
GEBEL, JOHANN GEORG III-5,234,
    269,278
GEBLER, TOBIAS PHILLIP VON III-
    390
GEERES, JOHN II-398
GEISSLER II-342
GELASIUS I, POPE I-33
GELASIUS II, POPE I-74
GELLÉE, CLAUDE (see Lorrain,
    Claude)
GELLÉRT, ST. (apostle of Hung-
    ary) I-62

GELLERT, CHRISTIAN FÜRCHTEGOTT
   III-285
GELON I-12
GELOSI, COMICI I-434,502
GEMBLACENSIS, SIGEBERTUS I-74
GEMINIANI, FRANCESCO II-487; *See illustration on p. 175*
   III-19,70,138,220,259,269,
   277,278,286,298,302,390,406,
   431,440,456,466,473,495
GENEST, (Abbe) CHARLES-CLAUDE
   III-217,220
GENEST, ST. I-115
GENET, ELEAZAR (see Carpentras)
GENTILE, GEORGIO III-230,298
GENTILE, ORTENSIO II-170
GENTILESCHI, ORAZIO II-179,297,
   395
GENTILI, FRANCESCO MARIA III-
   114,124,403
GENTILI, MARGARITA III-124
GENTILI, MARIA CATALINA III-
   258,403
GENVINO, FRANCESCO II-94,145,
   158
GEORGE, JOHN III-268
GEORGE I, KING of England (Han-
   over) II-379; III-239,242,
   260,280,281,282,296,400
GEORGE II, KING of England (Han-
   over) II-516; III-186,398,
   401
GEORGE II, LANDGRAVE of Hesse
   II-240
GEORGE, MARY III-197
GEORGE, PRINCE of Denmark II-
   395,509,514; III-207
GEORGE, ST. I-128,145,208,367
GEORGE LOUIS, ELECTOR of Hanover
   (see George I, King of Engl-
   and)
GEORGES, (Sir) ARTHUR II-465
GEORGI, DOROTHEA ELISABETH III-
   337,373
GEORGIUS I-48

GERARDUS, of Lisa I-180
GERBER, HEINRICH NIKOLAUS III-
174,405,406,441
GERBERT I-47; II-45
GERBERT VON HORNAU, MARTIN III-
324
GEREON, ST. I-76
GERHARDI, PAULI II-410
GERHARDT, PAUL II-45,105,151,
462
GERLACH I-410,499,500,507,520
GERLACH, J.B. III-355
GERLANDUS I-77
GERLE, HANS I-215,293,294,303,
330,333,354,421
GERMAIN, ST. I-46
GERMANOS, ST. I-40,42,44
GERMI I-181
GERO, JHAN I-210,266,267,318,
324,386; II-17
GERONIMO DI GHEVARA II-25
GERSON, J. CHARLIER DE I-182,264
GERSON, JOHANNES I-122,151
GERVAIS, CHARLES HUBERT II-431;
III-113,198,231,294,324,403
GERVAIS, LAURENT III-469
GERVAISE, CLAUDE I-342,368,372
GESE, BARTHOLOMÄUS I-499,535;
II-8,17,59,70,82,94,108,128,
138,148,151,165
GESHER, JOHANN MATHIAS III-426,
433,447,476
GESSNER, SOLOMON III-434
GESUALDO, CARLO (Prince of Ven-
osa) I-216,366,367,383,439,
478,479,480,484,486,494,496,
509,510,523,528,531,532,533,
535; II-4,6,9,10,11,55,82,83,
88,108,133,147,148,151,158,
160,170,177,180,189,234
GESUALDO, FABRIZIO I-486
GESUALDO, LUIGI I-479,480
GESUALDO, MRS. (Carlo's wife)
I-509,510

GEUCK, VALENTIN I-421; II-9
GEVAERT III-307
GHENT, JUSTUS OF (see Wassen-
    hove, Joos Van)
GHERARDI (architect) II-312;
    III-17,84,179
GHERARDI, PINELLO DI I-315,490
GHERSEM, GERY (DE) II-22,87,93,
    156,208,250
GHEYN, VAN DEN, family I-262;
    III-310
GHEYN, MATTHIAS VAN DEN III-335
GHEZZI, P.L. III-246
GHIBERT, LORENZO I-125,155,171
GHIBERTI, FLORENZO I-140,149,
    150
GHINI, CAMILLO II-97
GHIRLANDAIO, DOMENICO I-161,
    190,193,194,195,198,203,204
GHISELIN, JOANNES (Verbonnet)
    I-202,238,299
GHIVIZZANI, ALESSANDRO II-186,
    201,260
GHIZEGHEM, HAYNE VAN I-173,178,
    181,200
GHIZZOLO, GIOVANNI II-118,131,
    153,181,189,207,216,229,274
GHUR, BAHRAM I-32
GIACCIO, ORAZIO II-151,161,183,
    194,195,314
GIACHES I-413
GIACOBBI, GIROLAMO II-70,91,
    115,116,122,130,151,165,177,
    178,183,212,215,244,247
GIACOMELLI, GEMINIANO III-69,
    367,401,421,433,446,447,471,
    481,491
GIACOMINI I-393
GIAI, GIOVANNI ANTONIO III-161,
    290,391,428,447,459
GIAMBERTI, GUISEPPE II-215,217,
    247
GIANETTA (see Casanova, Gian-
    etta)

GIANNETTINI, ANTONIO II-323,
    442,458,465; III-15,57,62,
    307,335,336
GIANNINO III-202
GIARDINI, FELICE DI III-293,302
GIATTINO, VINCENZO III-72
GIAZOTTO, R. III-277
GIBBONS, family III-138
GIBBONS, ALICE II-147
GIBBONS, ANN II-180,320,468
GIBBONS, CHRISTOPHER II-162,
    223,285,310,316,346,361,374,
    375,382,387,391,392,396,398,
    402,454,461,467,468,502; III-
    69
GIBBONS, (Rev.) EDWARD I-424,
    523,527; II-27,74,80,105,
    118,119,120,135,161,163,223,
    230,236,237,241,243,268,275,
    313,314,319,336; III-130,138,
    278
GIBBONS, EDUARD (the younger)
    II-260,280
GIBBONS, ELIZABETH (see also
    Dyer, Elizabeth)
GIBBONS, ELIZABETH (mother)
    II-56,104,213,230
GIBBONS, ELIZABETH (daughter
    of Christofer) II-468
GIBBONS, ELIZABETH (daughter
    of Orlando) II-207
GIBBONS, ELLIS I-431,515; II-
    79,80
GIBBONS, FERNANDO II-80
GIBBONS, JAMES II-104
GIBBONS, JANE II-74,230,237,
    241,275
GIBBONS, JANE (daughter of Ed-
    ward and Jane) II-230
GIBBONS, JOAN II-74,236,237
GIBBONS, MARY (daughter of Chris-
    topher) II-468
GIBBONS, MARY (daughter of Or-
    lando) II-200

GIBBONS (Kercher), MARY (wife
of Christopher) II-316,387
GIBBONS, MARY (wife of Murray)
II-260,280
GIBBONS, MARY (wife of William)
II-79
GIBBONS, MURRAY II-260,275,280
GIBBONS, ORLANDO I-269,315,424,
431,444,470; II-9,27,56,74,
75,78,80,84,87,91,97,99,103,
104,105,106,111,125,132,135,
139,142,145,146,147,151,154,
158,161,163,170,177,180,183,
186,187,193,199,200,206,207,
208,212,213,214,223,224,230,
231,243,248,285,299,310,316,
318,320,331,336,341,356,382,
461; III-69,139,278
GIBBONS, ORLANDO (son) II-213,
331
GIBBONS, (Major) ROBERT II-319
GIBBONS, WILLIAM I-315,409,424;
II-1,2,27,56,58,74,75,79,80,
105
GIBBS (architect) II-507; III-
342
GIBBS, JOSEPH III-123
GIBBS, RICHARD II-212,272
GIBERT, PAUL CÉSAR III-304
GIDAYU, TAKEMOTO III-277
GIÉ, JACQUELINE DE ROHAN I-317
GIGAULT, JOACHIM II-461
GIGAULT, NICOLAS II-45,224,346;
III-7,215
GIGLER, ANDREAS I-420
GIGLI, GIROLAMO III-166
GIGLI, INNOCENZO III-223
GILBERT, (Sir) HUMPHREY I-454
GILBERT, JOHN II-279
GILDON III-119
GILES, NATHANIEL I-345,376,385,
448,479; II-1,9,14,57,104,156,
207,225,235,261,263
GILLES III-174

GIUSTI, TOMMASO   III-42,469

GIUSTINIANI, LEONARDO   I-160

GIUSTINIANI, LORENZO   I-177

GIUSTINIANI, OLYMPIA   II-348

GIUSTINIANI, VINCENZO   II-243

GIUSTO, GIOVANNI DI   I-189

GIUSTO, PAOLO   II-218

GIUVO, N.   III-223

GIZEH   I-2

GIZZI, DOMENICO   II-508;   III-64,
    372

GJOE, METTE   II-365

GLAREANUS   (see Févin, Antoine
    De)

GLAREANUS, HENRICUS   I-197,254,
    261,263,310,334,373,392; II-
    24

GLASER   III-72

GLAUKOS, of Reguim   I-15

GLEB, ST.   I-101

GLEIM, JOHANN WILHELM LUDWIG
    III-322

GLETLE, JOHANN MELCHIOR   II-417

GLUCK, ALEXANDER JOHANNES   II-
    496   III-346

GLUCK, JOHANN ADAM   II-331; III-
    345

GLUCK, J. CHRISTOPH WILLIBALD   *See illustration on p. 185*
    I-226; II-263,496   III-15,59,
    136,151,275,276,304,313,315,
    345,346,409,417,422,434,447,
    454,459,482,492

GNOCCHI, GIOVANNI BATTISTA   II-
    21

GOVERT, THOMAS   II-317,319,340,
    436

GOBETTI, FRANCESCO   III-46

GOBIATUS, ADAM   II-97,307,343

GODBID, ANNE   II-481,483,512

GODBID, WILLIAM   II-369,420,480,
    481,512

GODEBRYE, JACOB ("Jacotin")   I-
    188,285,331,335,377

GODEFRIDUS   I-204

GODESCALCUS, PRAETORIUS I-369
GODRIC, ST. (Hermit) I-79
GODUNOV, DZAR BORIS I-353; II-27
GOES, HUGO VAN DER I-158,180, 185,186,190,192
GOFRILLER, MATTEO II-427
GÖHLER, A. I-399
GÓIS, DAMIÃO DE I-236,435
GOLDBERG, JOHANN GOTTLIEB (The-ophilus) III-333,436,448,473
GOLDING I-404
GOLDING, JOHN (see Goldwin, John)
GOLDONI, CARLO III-148,164,219, 459,478,483,492
GOLDSMITH, OLIVER III-411,434
GOLDWIN, JOHN III-47,108,183, 317,318
GOLZIUS, HUBERT I-446
GOMBERT, NICOLAS I-190,238(?), 268,280,282,287,296,303,305, 310,313,318,319,326,330,334, 335,353,368,370,383,384,398; II-129
GOMÓLKA, MICHAL II-118
GOMÓLKA, NICHOLAS I-311,392, 402,457
GOMPERT (Gombert?) I-238
GONCALVES, (Goncalues) NUNO I-163,174,181
GÓNGORA, LUIS DE I-387; II-240
GONTRÁŠEK I-217
GONZAGA, family I-120,183,197, 391,494; II-21,131,212,306
GONZAGA, ALFONSO I I-375,409
GONZAGA, (Duchess) ANNA ISABEL-LA DI II-444
GONZAGO, (Count) CAMILLO, of Novellara II-100
GONZAGA, (Count) CAMILLO (II?) of Novellara II-207
GONZAGA, D. FERRANTE II-22,24
GONZAGA, (Cardinal) ERCOLE I-356

GONZAGA, (Cardinal) FERDINANDO
  II-111,113,134,168,175,208
GONZAGA, FERRANTE I-325,328,
  332,334,336,337,359
GONZAGA, FRANCESCO (son of Vin-
  cenzo I) II-110,141,189
GONZAGA, (Cardinal) FRANCESCO
  III I-181,355
GONZAGA, (Duke) GUGLIELMO, of
  Mantua I-304,379,384,385,
  406,411,413,414,421,423,430,
  450,451,453,465,474,475,491,
  492,494
GONZAGA, IPPOLITA I-337
GONZAGA, ST. LOUIS III-386
GONZAGA, MARGHERITA I-453,454;
  II-1
GONZAGA, SCIPIO I-412,413,478,
  492
GONZAGA, VESPASIANO I-291,517
GONZAGA, VINCENZO I I-400,453,
  474,491,492,494,504,511,513;
  II-3,15,28,29,141,142,143,241
GONZAGA (Duke), WILLIAM, of Man-
  tua (see William V)
GOODGROOME, JOHN II-255,376,396;
  III-189,381
GOODSON, RICHARD (I) II-355,504,
  508; III-118,232,310
GOODSON, RICHARD, (II) III-293,
  313
GOODWIN, JOHN II-502
GÓRA, JASNA (Czestochowa) II-
  260; III-374
GORCZYCKI, GRZEGORZ GERWAZY II-
  400; III-65,84,102,116,117,
  475
GORCZYN, JAN ALEKSANDER II-321,
  385
GORDON, JOHN III-355
GORING III-228
GORIS, FRANCESCO DE I-334
GORIS, LUCREZIA DE I-334
GORLIER, SIMON I-380

GÖRLITZ II-151

GÖRNER, JOHANN GOTTLIEB III-108,
    110,338,351,355,417

GÖRNER, JOHANN VALENTIN III-172

GORZANIS, GIACOMO DE I-385,387

GOSELINI I-493

GOSSAERT, JAN (see Mabuse)

GOSSEC, FRANÇOIS JOSEPH III-474

GOSSON, WILLIAM II-80,247

GOSTERA, (Gostena) GIOVANNI BA-
    TTISTA DALLA II-22,30,93

GOSTLING, JOHN II-336,418,454,
    472,478,482; III-463

GOTHA, DUKE OF III-320

GOTHARDT-NEITHARDT, MATHIS (see
    Grünewald)

GOTTIRE II-488; III-5

GOTTSCHED, JOHANN CHRISTOPH III-
    159,393

GOUDIMEL, CLAUDE I-243,279,311,
    338,339,341,351,352,354,364,
    371,373,374,375,382,384,390,
    397,398,399,401,402,404,407,
    428,429; II-145,457

GOUJON, JEAN I-315,336,337,408

GOULD, ROBERT III-98,155

GOUY II-332

GOWER, JOHN I-125,126,127,129,
    142,193

GOYEN, JAN VAN II-12,300,362

GOZZI, CARLO III-331

GOZZOLI, BENOZZO I-146,173,177,
    178,209

GRABBE, JOHANN I-479

GRABLER, MARIA MAGDALENA, of
    Prettin II-296,382

GRÄBNER, C.H. III-416,463

GRABU, LOUIS II-372,401,402,
    407,408,410,411,412,449,451,
    454,456,472,473,474,481,512,
    521; III-2,3,6,9,18,23,80

GRADENTHALER, HIERONYMUS II-
    280,457,463; III-23,151

GRAF, FRIEDRICH III-395

GRAFE, JOHANN FRIEDRICH III-250

GRÄFF, JOACHIM I-359

GRAFTON, RICHARD I-325,343

GRAMANN, JOHANN I-196,317

GRANCINI, MICHEL ANGELO II-65, 243,279,344,425

GRANCINO, ANGELO II-405

GRANCINO, FRANCESCO III-292

GRANCINO, GIAMBATTISTA III-102, 292

GRANCI, ALLESANDRO II-15,127, 128,151,158,165,170,174,180, 181,189,192,194,195,200,203, 210,220,234,238,244,248,251, 253,281,290; III-217

GRANDI, OTTAVIO II-282

GRANDIS, VINCENZO DE II-88,97, 203,226,316,437,456,509

GRANDVAL, NICOLAS RACOT DE II-466; III-88,330,456

GRANCVAL, PIERRE III-241

GRANGE, LA II-416

GRANJON, ROBERT I-243,273,376, 431,467

GRANOM III-420

GRANVELLE, CARDINAL I-340,475

GRAPHEUS, HIERONYMUS I-308

GRÄSER, HEINRICH II-467

GRASHOF, JOHANNES I-208

GRASSI, PARIDE III-257

GRASSINEAU, JAMES III-292,445, 466

GRASSMANN III-399

GRATI, PAGOL II-171

GRAUN, AUGUST FRIEDRICH III-124,417

GRAUN, JOHANN GOTTLIEB III-121, 182,232,385,386,390,441,454

GRAUN, KARL HEINRICH III-167, 189,269,372,375,380,400,410, 441,446,459,471,488,495

GRAUPHER, CHRISTOPH II-508; III-211,217,219,220,223,228,

236,239,242,249,260,314,321,
323,344,346,347,349,351,388,
408,469
GRAVA, CARL P.   III-342,480
GRAY, THOMAS   III-301,398
GRAZIANI, BONIFAZIO   II-92,328,
396
GRAZIANI, TOMMASO   II-3,29,69,
175
GRAZZINI, ANTON FRANCESCO (see
Lasca Il)
GREAVES, THOMAS   II-88
GREBAN, ARNOUL   I-164
GREBER, JAKOB   III-69,180,181,
189,195,197,202,220,305,307,
308,323,355
GRECO, EL (see ElGreco)
GRECO, GAETANO   II-366,417,456;
III-98,102,107,159,206,231,
255,333,404
GREEN, LUCY   III-487
GREENE, JAMES   III-289,366
GREENE, JOHN   III-289
GREENE, MAURICE   III-92,139,242,
296,305,313,396,406,425,429,
446,457,480,488,493
GREENE, R.L.   I-342
GREENE, ROBERT   I-384,527
GREENHILL, T.   II-485
GREENWOOD, JOHN   III-400
GREETING, THOMAS   II-384,388,
413,417,459,505
GREGORI, ALBERTO   II-273
GREGORI, ANNIBALE   II-273
GREGORI, GIOVANNI LORENZO   II-
392; III-35,118
GREGORY (the illuminator)   I-26
GREGORY (?)   III-36
GREGORY, CHRISTOPHER   II-222
GREGORY I, POPE (the Great) I-
37,50,71,168,458
GREGORY II, POPE   I-43,47
GREGORY III, POPE   I-43,44
GREGORY IV, POPE   I-49

GREGORY V, POPE   I-59
GREGORY VI, POPE   I-64,65
GREGORY VII, POPE   I-68
GREGORY VIII, POPE   I-80
GREGORY IX, POPE   I-92
GREGORY X, POPE   I-98
GREGORY XI, POPE   I-123,124,125
GREGORY XII, POPE   I-141
GREGORY XIII, POPE   I-390,408,
    431,432,434,436,439,444,445,
    447,448,457,463,474,475,477,
    479
GREGORY XIV, POPE   I-513,516,521
GREGORY XV, POPE   II-206
GREGORY, WILLIAM   II-236,364,391
GREINALD   I-49,51
GRENET, FRANÇOIS LUPIN   III-161,
    275,466,479
GRENON   I-129,140,142,143,144,
    146,148,149,151,161
GRENSER, KARL AUGUST   III-326
GRESHAM, LADY   II-8
GRESHAM, (Sir) THOMAS   I-453; II-
    8
GREUENBRUCH   I-535; II-81
GREUZE, JEAN BAPTISTE   III-380
GREW   II-497
GREY, (Lady) JANE   I-304,357,362
GRIEN   (see Baldung)
GRIESETOPFF, ULRICH   I-435
GRIGNAN, MME. DE   III-36
GRIGNANI   II-272,329,333
GRIGNY, LOUIS DE   II-319; III-
    93,233
GRIGNY, NICHOLAS DE   II-432; III-
    78,93,169,181,253
GRILLO, ANGELO   I-493; II-22,24,
    127,159
GRILLO, CARLO   I-183
GRILLO, GIOVANNI BATTISTA   II-177
GRILLS (organist)   II-202
GRIMALD   I-371
GRIMALDI   I-348
GRIMALDI, CATERINA SPERANZA III-166

GROUWELS, family I-528
GRUA, CARLO LUIGI PIETRO II-405;
    III-56,70,77,83,112,113,309,
    311,315
GRUBER, GEORG II-165
GRUBER, GEORG WILHELM III-414
GRUBER, LEWIS II-408
GRUNDMANN, J.F. III-395
GRÜNEWALD, GOTTFRIED II-444;
    III-182,187,191,234,241,264
GRÜNEWALD, MATHIAS (Gothardt-
    Neithardt) I-185,249,255,
    260,265,267,278,284
GRYPHIUS, ANDREAS II-173
GUADAGNI, GAETANO III-381
GUADAGNINI, GIOVANNI BATTISTA
    III-250
GUADAGNINI, LORENZO III-99
GUAITOLI, FRANCESCO MARIA II-
    241
GUALANDI, ANTONIO (see Campioli)
GUALTERI, ALLESANDRO II-170,
    194,195
GUALTERI, ANTONIO II-118
"GUALTIER LE VIEUX" II-350
GUAMI, FRANCESCO I-528; II-27,
    68
GUAMI, GIOSEFFO II-22,134
GUAMI, GIOVANNI I-497
GUARDI, FRANCESCO III-127,259,
    263,342
GUARDI, GIANANTONIO III-127
GUARDUCCI, TOMMASO III-333
GUARINI (architect) II-222,417,
    516
GUARINI, G.F. I-303,450,455,
    458,464,465,470,478,484,486,
    488,493,494,497,507,513,522,
    525,526; II-12,24,29,93,111,
    115,215,382
GUARNECCI, VIRGINIA I-444
GUARNERI, family I-298
GUARNERI, ANDRE III-116

445,447,467,486,487,491,493,
507,523

GUIDICCIONI, LAURA   II-62

GUIDO   (see Arezzo, Guido d')

GUIGHON, JEAN-PIERRE   III-172

GUILAIN, JEAN ADAM GUILLAUME
III-209

GUILLAUME, EDME'   I-511

GUILLEMAIN, (Louis) GABRIEL   III-
198

GUILLET, KAREL   II-129,173,185,
198,333,351

GUILMANT, ALEXANDRE   III-131,457

GUISE, (Cardinal) CHARLES DE   I-
372,474

GUISE, (Cardinal) JEAN DE   I-341

GUISE, (Cardinal) LOUIS   I-495

GUISE, DUKE OF   I-407

GUISE, PRINCESS DE   II-488,492

GUMPELZHAIMER, ADAM   I-376,439,
462; II-4,70,158,189,201,223

GUNDISSALINUS, DOMENICUS   I-56,
77

GUNN, BARNABAS   II-493; III-424
429

GÜNTHER, (Count) ANTON   II-503;
III-114

GÜNTHER, JOHANN CHRISTIAN   III-
92

GÜNTHER, (Count) LUDWIG   II-431;
494

GÜNTHER, MICHAEL   II-513

GUSSAGO, CESARIO   II-131

GUSSANVILLE, PIERRE   II-458

GUSTAV VASA, KING of Sweden   I-
274

GUSTAVIS   II-259

GUSTAVUS ADOLFUS, KING of Sweden
I-532; II-198,262

GUTENBERG   I-172

GUTHRIE   II-431

GUTKNECHT, JOBST   I-275

GUY, HENRY   III-19

GUYOT, JEAN   I-316

GUZZARDI, EMANUELA III-304
GWYNNETH I-290
GYFFARD I-358

H

HAAS, JOHANN WILHELM II-460
HABERL, F.X. I-469
HABERMANN, FRANTIŠEK VÁCLAV
   (Franz Wenzel) III-205,206,
   449
HABSBURG, family II-46,185
HACHBRUCKER, CELESTIN III-395
HACHIMAN I-115
HACK, GEORGE ALEXANDER II-43,
   437; III-95
HACQUART, CHARLES (Carolus) II-
   296,451,453,462,476,481,490;
   III-15,160,436
HADDON, WALTER I-381,384
HADRIAN, EMPEROR I-23
HADRIAN I, POPE (see Adrian I)
HADRIANUS, EMANUEL ADRIANSEN
   (see Adriansen)
HAECKEN, ALEXANDER VAN III-488
HAEMUS, F. I-451
HAFENREFFER, SAMUEL I-490; II-
   375
HAGEN, JOHANN VAN DER III-382
HAGENAUER, of Augsburg I-285
HAGER, MELCHIOR I-352
HAGESANDROS, of Rhodes I-20
HAGIUS II-171
HAHN, ULRICH (see Han, Ulrich)
HÄHNEL, JOHANN (Galliculus and
   Alectorius) I-200,305,308,
   357
HAIDER, HANS CHRISTOPH II-70,
   93,158,169,174; III-298
HAIDER, JORG I-318
HAINLEN, PAUL (see Heinlein)
HÁJJÍ KHALÍFA (see Khalifa)

198

204,207,208,223,224,225,226,
228,229,230,231,232,233,234,
235,236,237,238,239,240,242,
243,245,247,248,251,252,253,
254,255,256,258,259,250,261,
254,265,266,267,270,272,273,
274,278,282,283,284,287,289,
290,291,292,295,296,301,302,
310,313,314,316,319,320,321,
324,326,327,329,331,332,333,
334,335,336,337,338,339,340,
341,346,350,351,355,356,357,
358,361,362,363,364,365,366,
367,371,373,376,377,380,382,
383,384,385,386,387,388,389,
392,394,396,397,398,399,400,
402,403,405,408,409,410,411,
414,415,416,417,419,421,422,
423,424,425,429,430,431,433,
434,435,437,438,439,440,441,
442,444,446,447,449,450,451,
452,453,454,455,457,458,459,
461,462,463,464,465,466,467,
468,469,471,472,473,474,475,
476,479,480,482,483,484,489,
490,495

HANDL (see Gallus, Jacobus)

HANDLO, ROBERT DE I-115

HANFF, JOHANN NICOLAUS II-251;
    III-207

HANOT, FRANÇOIS III-117

HANS (brother of King Christian
    IV, of Denmark)

HANTZSCH, A. II-31

HARANT, KRYSTOF (Christof) I-
    396; II-24,200,201

HARDECANUTE, KING I-63,64

HARDEN, JEAMES (see Harding,
    James)

HARDI, PHILIPPE LE I-99

HARDING, JAMES (Harden, Jeames)
    II-225,231

HARDWOOD, EDWARD III-215

HARE, family III-99

HARE, ELIZABETH   III-380,406,412,
    465,473(?)
HARE, JOHN (I)   III-92,99,212,
    232,247,250,290,330,350,365,
    371,372,406
HARE, JOSEPH (III)   III-99,350,
    380,406,465,473
HARINGTON (Harrington), HENRY
    III-393
HARMODIUS   I-12
HARNISCH, OTTO SIEGFRIED   II-203,
    251
HAROLD I, (Harefoot)   I-63,64
HAROLD II   I-63,67,68
HARPER, THOMAS   II-265,333,335,
    345,349
HARRACH, (Archbishop) FRANZ AN-
    TON VON   III-238
HARRER, JOHANN GOTTLOB   III-182
HARRINGTON(?)   I-522
HARRINGTON, JHON(?)   I-340
HARRINGTON, (Sir) JOHN   II-142
HARRIS, JOHN   III-164,386,417
HARRIS, JOSEPH   III-103,104
HARRIS, RENATUS (I)   II-47,429,
    503,518,519,520; III-12,13,
    14,22,26,27,47,105,242,417
HARRIS, RENATUS (II)   III-242,
    364
HARRIS, THOMAS   II-281,376,408
HARRISON (architect)   III-301
HARSDÖRFFER, GEORG PHILIPP   II-
    105,311,469
HART, "MR." (violinist)   I-349
HART, ANDRO   II-138,158,165,273
HART, JAMES   II-320,427,451,464;
    III-311
HART, PHILIP   III-186,321,364
    365,419
HART, RICHARD   II-444
HARTEL, JOHANN C.   III-467
HARTMANN, HEINRICH   II-151
HARTMANN, JOHAN(N) ERNST   III-
    384

HARWIG, CARL III-463

HARTWIG, (Freiherr) JOSEPH LUD-
     WIG VON III-235

HARUNOBU III-380

HARVARD, JOHN II-278

HARVEY, GABRIEL I-452

HARVEY, MARY (Lady Dering) II-
     247,357

HASELTIN (Heseltine), JAMES III-
     64,251,256

HASSAN IKN-THABIT I-38

HASSE, JOHANN III-122,138,336,
     341,353,355,357,358,364,368,
     375,377,383,385,388,389,391,
     394,396,399,408,409,410,413,
     417,420,422,425,426,428,431,
     433,434,438,439,441,442,445,
     447,448,450,452,454,459,462,
     464,471,474,475,476,480,481,
     482,485,492

HASSLER, CASPAR I-421; II-27,
     60,69,75,141,180

HASSLER, HANS LEO I-396,421,475,
     478,512,520; II-11,15,17,31,
     57,66,67,70,87,108,109,112,
     115,141,143,145,151,165,185,
     282; III-139

HASSLER, ISAAC II-181

HASSLER, JACOB II-59,70,78,185

HATAŠ (Hattasch) ANNA FRANTIŠKA
     III-403

HATAŠ (Hattasch), DISMAS III-362

HATHAWAY, ANNE I-466

HATSHEPSUT I-5

HATTON, (Sir) CHRISTOPHER I-489,
     494,517; II-187

HATTON, LORD CHANCELLOR II-187

HAUDEK, KARL III-337

HAULTIN (firm) II-24

HAULTIN, PIERRE I-279,284,312,
     445,456

HAUMN, NICOLA III-228

HAUSSMAN, VALENTIN II-27,66,76,
     83,88,103

HAUTCOUSTEAUX, A. (see Auxcous-
    teaux)
HAUTIN (see Haultin)
HAVEMANN, J. II-372
HAVERGAL, (Rev.) W.H. I-396,499
HAWARD, C. II-380,417,460
HAWES, WILLIAM I-232
HAWKER, ESSEX III-420
HAWKINS, JAMES (I) II-500; III-
    416
HAWKINS, JAMES (II) III-282,319
HAWKINS, JOHN I-67,107,209,240,
    288,502,520; II-91,265,290,
    327,413,470; III-70,156,162,
    316
HAWKWOOD, SIR JOHN I-156
HAY, (Sir) JAMES II-107,110
HAYDEN, GEORGE III-264,357
HAYDN, CASPAR II-511
HAYDN, FRANZ JOSEPH II-337,511;
    III-121,192,208,213,225,269,
    305,382,406,451,475
HAYDN, MARIA III-406,451
HAYDN, MATHIAS III-121,305,396,
    406,451
HAYE, M. DE LA II-370
HAYES, LORD II-178
HAYES, WILLIAM III-224,417,442,
    479,485,490
HAYM, NICOLA (Francesco) II-485;
    III-125,152,172,200,217,250,
    253,261,265,266,272,289,324,
    350,351,361,362,371,402,414
HAYNE, GILLES II-257,281,306,
    331
HAYNE, GOTTLIEB II-518
HEATH, JOHN II-37,161
HEATHER, WILLIAM (see Heyther,
    William)
HEBENSTREIT, PANTALEON II-422;
    III-110,143,200,211,234,278,
    306,463
HEBRAEUS, BAR (Bar'-Ebhraja) I-
    92,100

HEBRAO (see Rossi, Salomone)

HECKEL, WOLF I-369,390

HECTOR I-10

HEDA II-283

HEDGEMAN, FRANCIS II-219

HEDWIG SOPHIA, PRINCESS II-432

HEEMSKERCK, MARTIN VAN I-209,
286,294,348,437

HEERMAN, JOHANN II-320

HEGESO I-14

HEIDEGGER, JOHANN JAKOT II-406;
III-107,216,242,267,284,327,
479

HEIGHINGTON, MUSGRAVE III-309,
380,473

HEIGHINGTON, WILLIAM II-480

HEINICHEN, JOHANN DAVID II-509;
III-204,234,236,241,244,253,
271,272,276,279,287,315,319,
321,327,389,406,408,414,441,
490

HEINLEIN, PAUL II-230,317,328,
356,361,367; III-12

HEINRICH, DUKE of Merseburg III-
489

HEINRICH, GOTTFRIED III-245

HEINRICH, KAISER (son of Barba-
rossa) I-78

HEINRICH JULIUS, DUKE of Brunswick I-397,509; II-148

HEINRICUS (Wolf Heintz?) I-262

HEITMANN, JOHANN JOACHIM III-
327

HEKTOROVIC, PETAR (of Hvar) I-
217

HELBIG, JOHANN FRIEDRICH III-325

HELDER, BARTHOLOMAEUS II-158,
161,195

HELE (Helle) GEORGE DE LA I-334,
379,426,429,435,445,450,462,
490

HELFER, CHARLES DE II-358

HELLENDAAL, PETRUS III-335,337,
429

206

HELLER, JOHANN II-177
HELLIER, SIR SAMUEL III-488
HELLINCK, LUPUS I-206,245,317, 403

HELLMANN, MAX (Joseph) III-180,
    332,469,480
HELMONT, ADRIEN III-283
HELMONT, CHARLES JOSEPH VON III-
    283,458
HELY, BENJAMIN III-162
HEMBOLD, LUDWIG I-292; II-26
HEMMEL, SIGMUND I-400,418
HEMMERLEIN, ANTON III-427
HEMMERLEIN, JOHANN III-427
HEMONY, FRANCIS II-301,459(?)
HEMONY, PIETER II-301,459(?)
HEMPEL, FRÄULEIN III-402
HEMPSON, CAROLAN DENIS I-230
HEMPSON, CELESTE (Gismondi) III-
    452,453,455,460,461,462,464,
    466,471,472,485
HEMPSON (Hampson) DENIS III-92,
    220,269
HENARES, ALCALÁ DE I-372
HENESTROSA, VENEGAS DE I-372
HENLEY, N. III-82
HENMAN, RICHARD III-111
HENRI, DUC DE GUISE I-495
HENRICI(?) II-89
HENRICI, CHRISTIAN FRIEDRICH
    (see Picander)
HENRIETTA MARIA, QUEEN of France
    II-223,224
HENRIETTE, LOUISE II-237,412
HENRY, DUKE of Brunswick I-330
HENRY IV, of Castile I-171
HENRY III, EMPEROR of Germany
    I-65,66
HENRY I, KING of England (Beau-
    clerc) I-67,69,75
HENRY II, (Canjou) KING of En-
    gland, (Plantagenet) I-75,77,
    78,80
HENRY III, KING of England (Plan-
    tagenet) I-89,90,95,96

HENRY IV, (Bolingbroke) KING of England (Lancaster) I-122, 129

HENRY V KING of England (Lancaster) I-76,127,144

HENRY VI, KING of England (Lancaster) I-147,148,153,159, 179

HENRY VII, KING of England (Tudor) I-173,194,195,204,237, 250; II-123; III-89,343

HENRY VIII, KING of England (Tudor) I-179,195,202,209,250, 259,261,268,281,284,287,289, 290,297,302,306,310,311,312, 314,323,325,329,330,333,336, 337,338,405,456,490,520

HENRY I, KING of France (Capetian) I-62,64

HENRY II, KING of France (Valois) I-266,334,336,353

HENRY III, KING of France (Valois) I-133,352,417,418,433,434,435, 437,438,439,461,465,483,495; II-523

HENRY IV, KING of France (Bourbon) I-357,417,509; II-48, 56,58,91,130,185,212

HENRY VII, KING of Germany (Hohenstaufen) I-111

HENRY, MICHEL I-495

HENRY, PRINCE OF WALES (son of James I) II-86,104,122,130, 133,134,135,136,142,144,146, 150

HENSLOWE II-21

HENSTRIDGE, DANIEL III-128,261

HENTZNER, PAUL II-27

HEPTINSTALL, JOHN II-435,485; III-23,25,48,67,69,83,185

HERA, of Samos I-10,12,13,14

HERACLIDES I-16

HERAKLIOS I-39

HÉRAULT, LOUIS I-334

HERBERGEN, VALERIUS II-151,177
HERBERT, GEORGE II-252,266
HERBING, AUGUST BERNHARD VALENTIN
    III-484,494
HERBST, (Bishop) JOHANNES III-486
HERBST, JOHANN ANDREAS I-495;
    II-151,169,187,195,214,259,
    303,307,349,372,406
HERCULES (God) I-10,12,186
HERCULES I (see Ercole I)
HERCULES II (see Ercole II)
HEREDI (see Eredi)
HEREDIA, PEDRO II-171,255,273,
    318,323
HEREDIA, SEBASTIAN AGUILERA DE
    (see Aguilera)
HEREFORDE, JOHN I-342
HERIBALD I-55
HERLIN, FRIEDRICH I-155,176,185,
    213
HERLITZ, ELIAS I-509
HERMAN, LANDGRAVE of Thuringia
    I-89
HERMAN, NICOLAS I-346,385
HERMES I-16
HERMITE, TRISTAN L' II-73,358
HEROD I-151
HERODIAS I-249
HERODOTOS I-11
HEROLDT, JOHANNES I-535
HERPOL, HOMER I-403
HERRER, MICHAEL I-76,103
HERRERA, JUAN DE I-378
HERRERIUS, M. II-123
HERRICK, ROBERT I-518; II-173,
    252,296,322,326,453
HERRINGMAN, HENRY II-335,429;
    III-30
HERRMANN, JOHANNES I-292
HERSCHEL, FRIEDRICH III-483
HERSCHEL, JACOB III-483
HERT, JOHN I-208
HERTEL, JOHANN CHRISTIAN III-
    124,319

HERTHUM, CHRISTOPH II-340,418;
    III-60,65,241
HERVELOIS, LOUIS DE CAIX D' (see
    Caix D'Hervelois, L. De)
HERVEY, JOHN III-33
HESDIN, JACQUEMART DE I-142
HESELTINE, JAMES (see Haseltine,
    J.)
HESIRE I-2
HESSE, ERNST CHRISTIAN II-462;
    III-188,269,272,282,319
HESSE, (Mrs.) E.C. III-319
HESSE, LUDWIG CHRISTIAN III-
    282
HESSE-DARMSTADT, LANDGRAVE OF
    II-427
HESSEBRUCH, JOHN I-254
HESTIUS, (Magister) ZACHARIUS
    I-509
HEUGEL, HANS I-213,289,300,330,
    334,380,405,407,479,497
HEUSS III-57
HEUSSNER, PAUL II-34
HEWE, JOHN I-194
HEYDEN, HANS CHRISTOPH II-70,
    171
HEYDEN, JOHANN I II-93,94,129,
    148
HEYDEN, MORITZ VON DER I-359
HEYDEN, SEBALD(US) I-242,303,
    313
HEYTHER, WILLIAM II-161,207,208,
    217,232,237,238
HEYTHURYEN, WILLEM VAN II-255
HEYWOOD, JOHN I-209,405,490;
    II-110
HICKES, CAPTAIN II-367,385
HICKFORD, THOMAS III-114
HICKS, (Sir) M. II-141
HIDALGO, JUAN II-264,374,377,
    389,490; III-5
HIERONYMUS DE MORAVIA I-95
HIGDEN, RALPH I-122,126,192,206
HIGGINS, WILLIAM III-461

HIGGONS III-168
HIGHMORE, JOSEPH III-68
HILARY, of Poitiers I-29
HILARY, POPE I-33
HILDEBRAND II-107,122
HILDEBRAND, ZACHARIAS III-52
HILDEBRANDT, LUCAS VON II-421
HILL, JOHN (I) III-363
HILL, JOSEPH III-286
HILL, (Capt.) RICHARD III-62
HILL, ROGER II-383,446,449,457,
    483
HILL AND SONS, W.E. II-376
HILLER (Huller), JOHANN ADAM
    III-404
HILLYARDE, NICHOLAS I-335,502;
    II-191
HILSEY I-308
HILTON, JOHN (I) I-475,533; II-
    17,71,112,248,363
HILTON, JOHN (II) II-29,232,239,
    243,325,327,344,362,363,368,
    414,440
HILVERDING VON WEWEN (see Wewen)
HINDE, HENRY II-297,398
HINDMARSH, JOSEPH II-512
HINE, WILLIAM III-21,87,200,226,
    242,417,425,429,434,485
HINGESTON (Hingston), JOHN II-
    256,354,364,376,391,396,400,
    411,419,443,454,456,482,510,
    511
HINGHAM II-500
HINSCH, HEINRICH III-224
HINTZE, JACOB II-207,408,409;
    III-48,93,96,173
HIPPISLEY, JOHN III-420,457
HIPSHER II-456
HIRSCH, ANDREAS II-389
HITCHCOCK, JOHN II-460
HITCHCOCK, THOMAS II-460; III-
    163
HITZLER, DANIEL I-444; II-244,
    269,272

HO CH'Ü-PING   I-19

HOADLEY, JOHN   III-255

HOBBEMA, MEINDERT   II-287; III-
    238

HOBBES, THOMAS   II-342,484

HOBRECHT   I-152

HOCHBRUCKER, CELESTIN   III-327

HOCHBRUCKER, CHRISTIAN   III-395,
    462

HOCHBRUCKER, SIMON   III-333

HODEMONT, LÉONARD DE   II-1,126,
    186,207,225,226,252,253,288,
    414

HODGES, NATHANIEL   II-399

HOE, JOHANN JOACHIM   III-249

HOE, MATHIAS   (see Hoenegg)

HOECKH, KARL   III-212

HOENEGG, MATHIAS HOE VON   I-537

HOEY, JAMES   III-408

HOF, DOROTHEA VON   III-82

HOFFHAIMER, PAUL   I-135,162,173,
    188,192,193,195,199,200,206,
    255,256,259,266,275,303

HOFFMANN, BARBARA   (see also Bach,
    Barbara)   II-271,275

HOFFMAN, EVA (see also Bach, Eva)
    II-162,480

HOFFMANN, GERHARD   III-44,322,396,
    399,409,467

HOFFMANN, J.C.   III-455

HOFFMANN (Hofman), LEOPOLD   III-
    436

HOFFMASTER, JOHN CHRISTOPHER
    III-488

HOFMANN, PAUL   II-398

HOFMANNSTHAL, HUGO VON   II-300

HOFMANS, MATTHYS   III-38

HOFMEISTER, MICHAEL N.   I-519

HOGARTH, WILLIAM   III-114,422,
    482

HOGON, JOHN   I-304

HOHENLOHE, COUNT   II-149

HOHENRECHBERG, COUNT   II-249

HOLBEIN, HANS (the younger)   I-

209,260,271,274,282,284,285,
289,294,296,307,310,325
HOLBORNE, ANTHONY I-424; II-17,
24,31,74
HOLBORNE, WILLIAM II-16
HOLCOMBE, HENRY III-78,212,216
HOLDER, WILLIAM II-168,393,418,
424,437,450; III-70,85,108,
445
HOLE, ROBERT II-156,158,161
HOLINSHED I-449
HOLLAND, HUGH II-13
HOLLAND, ROBERT II-13
HOLLINGSWORTH, family I-502
HOLLINGSWORTH, LAWRENCE I-468
HOLLINGSWORTH, WILLIAM I-468,528
HOLME, RANDLE II-51; III-29,33,
35
HOLMES, GEORGE III-187,192,337
HOLMES, JOHN II-7,74,283
HOLMES, THOMAS II-257,263,283
HOLOFERNES I-180
HOLSTEIN, DUKE OF II-456; III-
234,319
HOLTZBAUER, IGNAZ (Jakob) III-
249,368,422,447,492
HOLTZNER II-272
HOLZHAMMER, MARGARET II-314
HOMBERGER, PAUL II-69,267
HOMER I-6,7
HOMILIUS, GOTTFRIED AUGUST III-
277,494
HOMMEL, JAN II-179,181,232,242
HONDERIC, RAYNALDUS DE I-203
HONNECOURT, VILLARD DE I-94
HONORIO, ROMUALDO II-285,303,
314
HONORIUS I, POPE I-39
HONORIUS II, POPE I-75
HONORIUS III, POPE I-90
HONORIUS IV, POPE I-100
HONTERUS, JOHANN I-337,390
HOOCH, PIETER DE II-249,369,441,
471,517

HOOKER, RICHARD   I-362; II-62
HOOPER, EDMUND   I-358,469,495,
    525; II-85,98,158,171,200,201
HOPKEN, ARVID NIKLAS   III-240,433
HOPKINS   III-386
HOPKINS, J.   (see also Sternhold
    and Hopkins)   I-339,391
HOPKINSON, FRANCIS   III-136
HOPPER, THOMASINE   II-56
HOPPIN, RICHARD   I-130
HORACE   I-137,247,308
HORMISDAS, POPE   I-34
HORN, JOHANN KASPAR   II-400
HORNAU, MARTIN GERBERT VON   (see
    Gerbert)
HORNER, JOHN   I-438
HORST   I-394
HOSTE   I-337
HOTHBY, JOHN   I-158,166,181,196,
    212
HOTTETERRE, JACQUES   II-459; III-
    203,217,250
HOTTETERRE, JEAN   II-474; III-82
HOTTETERRE, LOUIS   II-400; III-
    125,129,219,318
HOTTETERRE, MARTIN   III-259,318,
    338
HOTTETERRE, NICOLAS   II-408,438;
    III-82,220,259,445
HOUSSU, ANGELIQUE   III-108,242
HOVE, JOACHIM VAN DEN   II-71,144,
    145,211
HOVE, THYSIUS VAN DEN   II-72
HOWARD, family (Ashtead)   III-181
HOWARD, LORD ADMIRAL   I-517,525
HOWARD, (Lady) ELIZABETH   III-
    119
HOWARD, (Lady) FRANCES   II-151,
    152,160
HOWARD, HENRY (poet)   I-264,335
HOWARD, HUGHES (painter)   III-
    115
HOWARD, KATHERINE   III-71,78,79,
    88,89,117

Georges Frideric Schmidt Sculp. à Paris

GEORGE FRIDERIC HANDEL 217

I

IAMBLICHOS   I-28

IBKOWSKY, JAKOB   III-418

IBN (Ikn) -SĪNĀ, BUKHARAN   I-58, 64

ICTINUS   I-13

IDELSOHN   I-9

IGNATIUS   II-124

IGNAZ JOSEPH (Bishop of Brixen)   III-421

IHAN   I-318,319

IKHNATON   I-5

IKN-QUAKISA, IYAS   (see Iyas)

IKN-RIYAH, BILALA   (see Bilal)

IKN-THABIT, HASSAN   (see Hassan)

IKTINOS   I-13

ILDEFONSUS, ST.   I-41

ILEBORGH, ADAM   I-161

IL LASCA (Grazzini) (see Lasca, Il)

IMER   III-487

INDIA, SIGISMONDO D'   II-122,165, 201,203,214,215,218,228,235, 239,255

INFANTAS, FERNANDO DE LAS   I-296, 426,454; II-21,118

INGEGNERI, MARC' ANTONIO   I-329, 396,405,416,420,424,432,443, 445,450,451,454,459,462,466, 487,493,499,511,523

INGELO, (Dr.) NATHANIEL   II-374

INGLOTT, WILLIAM   I-359; II-113, 201; III-259

INNOCENT I, POPE   I-31

INNOCENT II, POPE   I-75; III-341

INNOCENT III, POPE   I-82,90

INNOCENT IV, POPE   I-94

INNOCENT V, POPE   I-99

INNOCENT VI, POPE   I-121

INNOCENT VII, POPE   I-141

INNOCENT VIII, POPE   I-194

INNOCENT IX, POPE I-522

INNOCENT X, POPE II-312

INNOCENT XI, POPE II-465; III-20

INNOCENT XII, POPE III-59,97,113

INNOCENT XIII, POPE III-340,341, 342

INVAGHITO, L' (see Benedetti, Pietro)

IO I-290

IOANNELLI, P. I-415

IRANZO, MIGUEL LUCAS DE I-171

IRELAND, FRANCIS (see Hutcheson, Francis)

IRISHE, THOMAS II-238

ISAAC, HEINRICH I-62,163,178, 188,193,194,197,200,203,205, 206,208,209,244,246,247,248, 255,256,259,262,267,268,308, 309,318,327,342,346,364,370

ISAAC, WILLIAM III-43,212

ISABELLA, ARCHDUCHESS of the Netherlands II-28,38,93,97,143

ISABELLA of Castile, QUEEN of Spain I-157,164,183,184,189, 198,201,204,207,212,236,238, 240,273

ISABELLA of Portugal, (wife of Phillip the Good) I-152

ISABELLA, QUEEN of Portugal I-281

ISABELLA DE VALOIS, QUEEN I-392, 408

ISAIAH (The Prophet) I-128

ISHAM, JOHN III-249,259,267,311, 385,493

ISHTAR I-9

ISIDORE, of Seville I-29,36,37, 40

ISIDORO, SAN I-79

ISIDORUS, of Miletus I-35

ISOUARD III-434

ISRAËL, CARL I-233

ISUM, JOHN (see Isham, John)

222

J

JADRA, MARCUS I-413
JAGIELLO, CARDINAL I-203
JAGIELLO (Kings) I-200
JAGIELLO, WLADISLAUS (II), KING
  of Bohemia I-199,259
JAKOB, HANS III-411
JALÍL, 'ABD AL- II-340
JAMAR, HENRI II-186
JAMES, DUKE of Chandos III-327
JAMES, DUKE of York II-406,501
JAMES I, KING of England (James
  VI of Scotland) I-299,407,
  412,433; II-62,80,81,84,99,
  104,110,140,141,143,147,149,
  163,175,185,199,205,222,224,
  228; III-2
JAMES II, KING of England (House
  of Stuart) II-42,266,406,
  488,500,501,507,517; III-2,
  3,4,5,8,9,10,11,13,16,19,20,
  21,22,24,25,27,28,31,34,35,
  44,63,64,281
JAMES I, KING of Scotland I-128,
  148
JAMES III, KING of Scotland
  I-197
JAMES IV, KING of Scotland II-
  103
JAMES VI, KING of Scotland (see
  James I, King of England)
JAMES EDWARD, PRINCE of England
  (son of James II) III-27,29
JAMES, ST. I-162,171
JAN, of Jenštejn I-126
JAN, of Lublin I-213,304
JANECKI, ADAM II-201,247,375
JANEQUIN (Jannequin), CLEMENT
  I-194,216,225,258,259,267,
  284,285,287,288,292,295,301,
  311,325,330,335,336,339,342,
  351,354,364,367,368,374,376,
  377,379,381,383
JANITSCH, JOHANN GOTTLIEB III-
  222,418

JOHN XXI, POPE · I-99
JOHN XXII, POPE I-113,114
JOHN, PRINCE of Portugal (see
    John IV, King of Portugal)
JOHN, ST. I-24,150,151,165,186,
    372; II-129,405
JOHN, ST. (the Apostle) I-278
JOHN, ST. (the Baptist) I-45,
    64,98,165,195,215,260,282
JOHN, ST. (Chrysostom) I-256
JOHN, ST. (of Damascus) I-44,
    66
JOHN, ST. (the Evangelist) I-
    260,267
JOHNSEN, HENRIK FILIP III-304
JOHNSON, ALICE II-1
JOHNSON, BARTHOLOMEW III-240
JOHNSON, BEN (see Jonson, Ben)
JOHNSON, CHARLES III-288,420
JOHNSON, EDWARD I-345,525,533;
    II-71,203
JOHNSON, JOHN I-532; II-1,2,268
JOHNSON, ROBERT (I), English
    composer I-200,346,383
JOHNSON, ROBERT (II) luteuist
    and composer I-431,438,474;
    II-85,136,140,145,158,177,
    194,203,219,237,243,267,344,
    345,364,372,424
JOHNSON, ROBERT (Scottish com-
    poser) I-180,359
JOHNSON, SAMUEL III-56,238,421,
    492
JOKEI I-87
JOMELLI, NICOLA III-136,147,
    275,313,368,399,409,422,434,
    459
JONAH I-99
JONAS, JUSTUS I-275
JONCKBLOET II-313
JONES (architect) II-191
JONES, EDWARD III-26,34,35,51
JONES, INIGO I-433; II-96,179,
    345

JONES, RICHARD I-467,503,517,
533; II-15
JONES, RICHARD (violinist and
composer) III-429,457
JONES, ROBERT I-424; II-21,59,
63,71,95,10,115,122; II-125,
129,138,158,162,252
JONES, WILLIAM III-384
JONES, WINDET II-108
JONSON, BEN I-433,528; II-20,
26,57,61,85,96,101,102,122,
124,138,140,177,179,205,211,
259,279,281; III-451,459
JORDAN, ABRAHAM (the elder) I-
137; III-260
JORDAN, ABRAHAM (the younger)
III-154,260,327
JORDAN, JOHN II-113
JORDAENS, JACOB I-530; II-200,
230,287,288,477
JOSEPH, CROWN PRINCE of Portugal
III-275,320
JOSEPH I, EMPEROR III-58,169,
200,203,262
JOSEPHO, BENEDICTUS A SAN (see
San Joseph, Bendictus A)
JOSHUA I-39
JOSQUIN (see Pres, Josquin des)
JOY, WILLIAM III-124
JOYE, GILLES I-178,193
JOYEUSE, DUC DE I-461,462
JUAN, COUNT of Urueña I-368
JUAN, DON I-427
JUANA, INFANTA II-243
JUBAL I-9; II-334
JUDENKÜNIG, HANS I-215,262,273,
280
JUDICE, CESARE DE II-104,244,
273,409,486
JUDITH I-180,248
JULIAN, EMPEROR I-29
JULIANE, EMILIE (hymn writer)
II-280; III-207
JULIANUS (Spanish Bishop) I-32

JULIEN (Julian), ST.   I-42,115,
    117,119,127,128,141
JULIERS, PRINCE OF   I-456
JULITA, SANTA   I-70
JULIUS I, POPE   I-28
JULIUS II, POPE   I-159,239,245,
    247,254,255,262,296
JULIUS III, POPE (Cardinal del
    Monte)   I-322,341,344,352,350,
    355,360,361,362
JUMILHAC, (Dom) PIERRE-BENOIT
    DE   II-141,446,501
JUNG, ANTON   I-449
JUNG, CH'EN   I-93
JÜNGER, WOLFGANG   I-302
JUNTA (publisher)   I-281
JUPITER   I-280,290
JUSTIN (philosopher)   I-24
JUSTINIAN (Hymn composer)   I-33,
    35,36
JUSTINIAN, EMPEROR   I-35
JUSTUS OF GHENT   (see Wassenhove,
    Joos van)
JUVARRA, FILIPPO   II-474,477;
    III-226,272,309,322,327,477,
    484
JUXON, GEORGE   II-29

K

KAAPER   I-2
KADIR, ABDUL   I-104
KAEMPFER   III-262,307
KÄFER, JOHANN PHILIPP   III-321,
    338
K'AI-CHIH, KU   (see Ku)
KAISERLING, COUNT   III-333
KALF, WILLEM   II-212,373; III-
    77,98
KAMINSK, MACIEJ   III-476
KANT, EMMANUEL   III-349

KANTZ, KASPAR I-272

KAO K'O-KUNG (see K'O-KUNG)

KAPSBERGER, JOHANN HIERONYMUS
II-89.129,145,171,177,210,
211,215,234,254,294,296,336

KARCZEWSKI, JAN BALTAZAR II-
307,309

KARGEL I-436

KARL JOSEF, ARCHDUKE II-208

KAROL FERDINAND, PRINCE (Bishop
of Plock) II-314

KASPAR, JOHANN III-412

KASTELKORN (see Lichtenstein)

KAUFFMAN, PAUL II-18,21,24

KAUFFMANN, GEORG FREIDRICH II-
478; III-486

KAYSER, JOHANN III-294,327,375,
442

KAYSER, MARGARITE SUSANNE III-
294,423,429

KAYSER, SOPIE III-429,485

KAZIMIERZ, (Prince) OGINSKI MI-
CHEL III-440

KEEKLE, JOHN III-250

KEENE (spinet maker) II-460

KEIMANN, CHRISTIAN II-105,387

KEINSPECK, MICHAEL I-208,212

KEISER, REINHARD III-68,83,86,
88,97,98,106,107,109,112,115,
119,120,127,154,159,169,170,
183,185,186,193,194,195,201,
202,209,210,219,234,238,244,
253,254,261,262,264,280,281,
289,290,300,305,308,323,346,
349,364,378,388,389,406,444,
448,469,475,480,482

KELLER, GODFREY III-217,218

KELLIE, EDWARD II-247,264,272

KELLNER, DAVID II-427; III-324,
457

KELLNER, JOHANN PETER III-198,
375,406

KELLY, JOHN III-490

KELPIUS, JOHANNES II-41; III-86

KELWAY, JOSEPH   III-436
KELWAY, THOMAS   III-386
KELZ, MATTHIAS   II-369
KEMP, WILLIAM   I-483,485,486;II-62
KEMPA, JAN   I-118
KEMPIS, GUILLAUME   III-248
KEMPIS, JEAN FLORENT (Nicolas)
    A'   II-43,219,311,321,329,333,
    337,365
KENNEDY (Sergeant-Major)   II-200
KENNIS, WILLEM   III-302,404
KENSKY, COUNT   III-278
KENT, JAMES   III-151,255,305,442
KENT, WILLIAM   III-10
KEPER, JOHN   I-417,436
KEPLER, JOHANN   I-425; II-73,89,
    124,190,250
KERCHER, MARY   (see Gibbons, Mary)
KERCKHOVEN   II-293
KERLE, GASPARO   III-194
KERLE, JACOBUS DE   I-292,348,364,
    374,386,389,390,393,399,416,
    427,428,441,467,469,518
KERLL, JOHANN CASPAR VON   II-236,
    241,359,363,366,378,385,387,
    404,411,412,420,424,425,436,
    450,451,468,469,471,486,519;
    III-15,70
KERN, GEORG   I-213,255
KETHE   I-352,387
KEUCHENTHAL   I-432
KEUL, BARBARA MARGARETHA   (see
    Bartholomai)
KEVERICH, HEINRICH   III-167
KEYRLEBER, JOHANN GEORG   III-58
KEYSER, LEONHARD   I-283
KEYSERLINGK, HERMANN VON   III-473
KEYSSLER, GEORG   III-433
KHAFRE   I-2
KHALÍFA, HÁJJÍ   II-364,367
KHNUMHOTEP   I-3
KHUEN, JOHANN   II-455
KIESEWETTER (music historian)
    I-81,95,147,238

KILCHEN (Basle) I-197
KILLIGREW II-397
KILWARDY, ROBERT I-99
KINDERMANN, JOHANN ERASMUS II-
    167,272,314,330,355,404
KINDERSLEY, ROBERT II-158,171
KINDLEMARSH, FRANCIS I-424
KING (printer) III-151
KING, CHARLES III-21,213,226,
    379,426
KING, FRANK III-44
KING, MATTHEW (Peter) III-465
KING, ROBERT II-398,485; III-
    37,44,48,51,66,75,102,108,
    250
KING, WILLIAM II-218,323,327,
    344,351,396,420,487
KINGHAM, PHILIP II-125
KINGO III-125
KINSKY, GEORGE III-42,491
KIRBY, CHRISTOPHER II-472
KIRBYE, GEORGE I-405,525; II-
    11,17,20,71,267
KIRCHBACH, HANS CARL VON III-393
KIRCHER, ATHANASIUS II-74,252,
    258,259,264,282,299,333,334,
    346,377,389,446,447,487; III-
    491
KIRCHHAIN, E.H. III-398
KIRCHHOFF, GOTTFRIED III-3,234,
    275
KIRCHMANN, JACOB III-137
KIRCHNER, CHRISTIAN II-393
KIRKHAM, EDWARD II-124
KIRKMAN, JAKOB III-241,434
KIRKPATRICK (historian) III-368,
    423
KIRNBERGER, JOHANN PHILIPP III-
    337
KISL, KARL I-486
KITTEL, JOHANN CHRISTIAN III-
    450
KITTEL, KASPAR II-222,252,263,
    285,304,514

KIYOMASU II-484; III-292

KLEBER, LEONHARD I-200,275,349, 368

KLEIN, VALENTIN I-243

KLEINKNECHT, JACOB FRIEDRICH III-343

KLEINKNECHT, JOHANN WOLFGANG (III) III-284,467

KLEIST, CHRISTIAN EWALD VON III-291

KLEMM, JOHANN GOTTLOB III-46

KLEMME, JOHANN I-528; II-153, 225,258,340

KLENG, GEORGIUS I-206

KLINGENSTEIN, BERNHARD I-329; II-89,106,155

KLOPSTOCK, FRIEDRICH GOTTLIEB III-368

KLOTSCH, MARTIN I-179

KLOTZ, MATTHIAS II-347,430,512

KLUG, JOSEPH I-286,299

KNAPP, WILLIAM III-117

KNAPTON, GEORGE III-487

KNIGHT, (Dr.) RICHARD II-285

KNOLLYS, LORD II-150

KNOLLYS, FRANCES III-4

KNOPKEN, ANDREAS I-299

KNOX I-387

KNUPFER, SEBASTIAN II-260,366, 394,462,463

KOBELIUS, JOHANN AUGUSTIN II-448; III-112,175,183,291,439

KOCHANOWSKI, JAN I-402

KOHATT III-242

K'O-KUNG, KAO I-96

KOLB, KARLMANN III-182,418,469

KOLLER, LORENZ III-192,208,269

KOLLER, MARIA III-213

KOLOF, LORENZ (Christoph) MITSLER VON III-249,479

KONARAK I-87

KÖNIG, ANNA MARGARETHA III-73

KÖNIG, JOHANN BALTHASAR III-55

KÖNIG, JOHANN ULRICH III-253, 335,350,377

235

KRIEGER, JOHANN PHILIPP (Von)
II-327,340; III-371

KRIESSTEIN I-313,330

KROMER, MARTIN I-298

KROTTER, HANS I-195

KROYER I-475

KRUGER, JOHANN (I) III-18

KRZSSICHLEB, PIOTR II-71,195,
284,294,318

KTESIBIOS I-18

KU I-6

KU K'AI-CHI I-26,29,31

K'UAN, FAN I-58

KUEI, HSIA I-82

KUGELMANN, JOHANN I-232,235,313

KÜHNAU, CHRISTOPH III-484

KUHNAU, JOHANN II-374,375,425,
500,504,519; III-29,31,39,41,
43,65,66,96,104,154,156,167,
171,338,340,343,351,391,
428

KÜHNEL, AUGUST II-313,386,402,
519; III-3,4,14,118

KÜHNEL, JOHANN MICHAEL III-
431

KÜHNHAUSEN II-308

KUKUZELES, JOHN I-103

KUNTZEN, JOHANN PAUL III-101,
296,313,319,325,355,455

KUNZEN, ADOLPH KARL III-325

KÜRZINGER, IGNAZ FRANZ XAVER
III-304

KUSSER, JOHANN SIGISMUND II-374,
375,453,505,507; III-45,54,
55,60,62,75,77,78,83,85,87,
113,116,120,121,151,188,204,
249,294,405

KYOL I-536

KYOTO I-129

KYTCH III-322,368

KYTSON, THOMAS I-431

L

LA BARRE (see Barre)
LA BRUERE (see Bruyère)
LA BRUYÈRE (see Bruyère)
LA FAYETTE, MARIE DE (see Fay-
    ette, de la)
LA FOSSE, JACQUES (see Fosse,
    Jacquses La)
LA GRANGE (see Grange, La)
LA GROTTE, NICOLAS DE (see
    Grotte)
LA GUERRE (see Guerre, La)
LA MOTTE (see Motte, La)
LA ROCHEFOUCAULD (see Rochefou-
    cauld, La)
LA TOUR, GEORGES DE (see Tour,
    la)
LA TOUR, M. DE (see Tour, la
LACKLAND, KING JOHN (see John,
    King of England)
LACOSTE II-431; III-74,112,201,
    218,245,261,377,408,455,457
LACROIX, M. III-426
LACY, JOHN II-390
LACY, ROBERT DE I-90
LADERCHI, (Count) FABRIZIO II-
    479
LADISLAS IV, KING of Poland II-
    224,262,266,283
LADISLAUS V, KING of Poland I-
    170
LADRON, COUNT II-191
LAET, J. I-369,375
L'AFFILARD, MICHEL (see Affilard,
    L')
LAGARDE, PIERRE III-302
LAGKHNER, DANIEL II-37,73,111
LAHOUSSAYE, PIERRE III-137,484
LAI'S, of Corinth I-282
LALANDE, MICHEL DE II-363,485,
    510,512,514,519; III-5,15,39,

```
               41,46,98,112,119,128,139,153,
               156,192,251,270,292,329,346,
               384,398,420,456
```

LALANDE, (Mrs.) MICHEL   III-251
LALANDE, RICHARD DE (see La-
    lande, Michel de)
LALLI, DOMENICO III-266,283,294,
    316,342
LALOUETTE, JEAN FRANÇOIS II-340,
    421,469; III-72,93,388,403,
    431
LAMB, BENJAMIN III-129
LAMBARDI, ANDREA II-247
LAMBARDI, CAMILLO II-1,254,268
LAMBARDI, FRANCESCO II-29,108,
    158,167,171,183,219,247,302
LAMBE, WALTER I-164
LAMBERG II-82
LAMBERT, ST. III-218
LAMBERT, MICHEL II-126,131,393;
    III-92,100,107
LAMBRANZI, GREGORIO III-299
LÄMMERHIRT, family II-194
LÄMMERHIRT, ELISABETH II-312,
    417; III-82
LÄMMERHIRT, HEDUIG II-194,455
LÄMMERHIRT, THOMAS III-252
LÄMMERHIRT, TOBIAS III-214,216
LÄMMERHIRT, VALENTIN II-417
LAMPE, C.J.F. III-183
LAMPE, JOHANN FRIEDRICH III-183,
    375,397,424,451,452,457,461,
    464,474,480
LAMPROKLES I-12
LAMPUGNANI, GIOVANNI BATTISTA
    III-207,368,388,409,422,434,
    447,459
LANCIANO, FLAVIO, CARLO II-516;
    III-7,23,31,41,58,59,130,177
LANCRET, NICOLAS III-51
LAND II-313
LANDE (ballet master) III-486
LANDI (publisher) II-322
LANDI, ANTONIO I-307

LANDI, STÉFANO I-31,514; II-186,
    190,194,195,199,219,220,244,
    246,260,261,262,270,334,358;
    III-132
LANDINO (Landini), FRANCESCO I-
    107,114,119,120,122,127,129,
    145
LANDONI, FRANCESCO I-482
LANDUS, ST. I-54
LANFRANCO I-295; II-33
LANG, PAUL HENRY II-236
LANGA, SOTO DE (see Soto de Lan-
    ga)
LANGA, FRANCISCO SOTO DE (see
    Soto de Langa)
LANGBAINE III-28
LANGDON, RICHARD III-423
LANGE, ANNA SIBYLLA III-268
LANGE, GREGOR I-490
LANGE, ULRICH I-314
LANGHANS III-472
LANGHEDUL, MATHIEU II-292
LANGTON, STEPHEN I-92
LANGUEBROEK, CONSTANS DE I-158,
    178,191
LANIERE, JEROME I-426
LANIERE, NICHOLAS I-426,495;
    II-87,149,151,160,174,177,178,
    225,230,252,275,281,313,317,
    349,356,357,364,367,372,384,
    386,394,402,404,407,414,424;
    III-7
LANSDOWNE, LORD III-95
LANTINS, ARNOLD DE I-153,164
LANTINS, HUGHO DE I-147,164
LANZETTI, SALVATORE III-246,435
LAPICIDA, ERASMUS I-244,325
LAPICIDA, GASPAR I-244
LAPIS, SANTO III-420
LAPORTE, JOSEPH DE III-322
L'ARALDO I-243
LARGILLIÈRE, NICOLAS DE II-362
LAROCHE, JAMES III-29,101,109,
    110,254,334

LAROUSSE   I-225
LARVETTE, JEAN LOUIS   III-438
LAS INFANTAS, FERNANDO DE   (see Infantas)
LASAGE   III-289
LASCA, IL (Grazzini, A.F.)   I-376
LASOS, of Hermione   I-11
LASSO, FERDINAND DI   II-89
LASSO (Lassus), ORLANDO DI   I- *See illustration on p. 241*
226,244,252,270,287,292,306,
317,325,326,328,336,350,353,
357,358,359,360,362,364,365
366,367,368,369,370,371,372,
373,374,376,377,380,381,384,
388,389,392,393,398,401,403,
404,409,410,412,413,414,420,
421,422,425,426,429,430,431,
432,433,434,435,438,439,441,
442,444,445,446,449,450,452,
453,459,462,463,465,466,467,
471,476,479,480,481,482,486,
490,491,492,497,499,509,511,
512,518,532,533; II-24,59,89,
96,190,223,226,379
LASSO, (Don) PEDRO DI   I-361
LASSO, RUDOLFO DI   I-497,499;
   II-89,190
LATERE, JEANNE DE   II-502; III-56
LATILLA, GAETANO   III-248,268,
   459,492
LATIO, J.   I-375
LATOUCHE, DAVID   III-137
LAUD, (Archbishop) WILLIAM   II-
   248,271,276,304
LAUFFENBERG, HEINRICH VON   I-134
LAUNAY, SEIGNEUR DE   (see Boes-
   set, Claude Jean Baptiste)
LAURANA   I-177
LAURENCIE, LA   II-397
LAURENTI, BARTOLOMEO GIROLAMO
   II-312; III-57,58,154,383
LAURENZI, FILBERTO   II-305

ORLANDO DI LASSO 241

LAURIE   III-27,28
LAUTENSACH, PAUL   II-171
LAUX   (see Lucas Maler)
LAUXMIN, ZYGMUNT   II-13,414
LAVAT, PÈRE   III-120
LAVEZZOLA, ALBERTO   I-230,323
LAW, ANDREW   III-137,139
LAWES, brothers   II-325,424
LAWES, HENRY   II-1,8,35,208,230,
    231,264,267,269,272,282,286,
    297,317,324,345,349,355,357,
    360,362,368,372,376,383,385,
    387,398,424,429,457; III-138
LAWES, JOHN   II-35,355
LAWES, THOMAS   II-8,292
LAWES, WILLIAM   I-474; II-74,264,
    272,276,314,324,325,345,349,
    372,388,390,424,462,489
LAYAMON   I-89
LAYOLLE, FR. (the younger)   I-
    294,309,313
LAZARI, ALBERTO   II-272,281
LAZARIN   II-348
LAZARINI, SCIPIONE   II-43,318,
    452
LAZARINO   I-252
LAZARUS   I-75,186
LAZZARINI, BENEDETTO DE'   I-410
LE BÈGUE   (see Begue)
LE BEL, FIRMIN   (see Bel, Le)
LE BLANC, DIDIER   (see Blanc,
    Didier le)
LE BRUN, CHARLES   (see Brun,
    Charles le)
LE CÈNE, MICHEL-CHARLES   (see
    Cène, le)
LE CERF   (see Cerf, le)
LE CLERC DE LA BRUÈRE   (see Bru-
    ere)
LE COCQ, JEHAN   (see Cocq
LE COUVREUR, ADRIENNE   (see Cou-
    vreur)
LE FEBURE, JEAN   (see Febure,
    Jean le)

LE FÈVRE, JACQUES (see Fèvre,
Jacques le)

LE JEUNE, CLAUDE (see Jeune,
Claude le)

LE MERCIER (see Mercier, le)

LE NAIN, LOUIS (see Nain, Louis
le)

LE NAIN, MATHIEU (see Nain,
Mathieu le)

LE RICHE DE LA POUPLINIÈRE (see
Riche)

LE ROND, JEAN (see d'Alembert)

LE ROUX, GASPARD (see Roux, G.
le)

LE VAU (see Vau, le)

LEANDER, ARCHBISHOP of Seville
I-37

LECHNER, LEONHARD I-356,454,468,
480,484,535; II-31,99

LECLAIR, JEAN MARIE (l'aine)
III-108,160,181,232,346,355,
357,360,386,406,412,429,437,
461,479,480,488,493

LECLAIR, JEAN MARIE "LE CADET"
III-181,393,467,471

LECLAIR, PIERRE III-232

LEDREDE, RICHARD I-113

LE-DUC, M. VIOLLET I-218

LEDUC, SIMON III-137

LEE, NATHANIEL II-483,484,487,
491,498,513,514; III-62,64,
182

LEENDERS, JAN II-219

LÉGAL, M. DE III-174

LEGATE, CARDINAL III-14

LEGGE, THOMAS I-453,455

LEGRANT, GUILLAUME I-146

LEGRENZI, GIOVANNI II-224,231,
353,357,358,365,377,394,398,
400,404,415,426,438,457,458,
463,466,470,471,497,514,516,
521; III-5,44,66,87,230,286,
345

LEGROS, JOSEPH III-425

LEIBNITZ (philosopher) II-462,
481
LEICESTER, EARL OF I-438,452,
483
LEICHAMSCHNEIDER, MICHAEL III-
239
LEIGH III-68,72,77
LEIGHTON, THOMAS II-93
LEIGHTON, (Sir) WILLIAM I-524;
II-31,34,80,85,93,157,158,
159,160,173,174,394
LEISENTRITT, JOHANN I-411
LEITÃO DE AVILEZ, MANUEL II-
37,225
LEITE, ANTONIO DA SILVA III-199
LEKYTHOS I-13
LELAND I-99
LELANDE II-511
LELY, (Sir) PETER II-185,460,
492
LEMER III-336
LEMLIN, LORENZ I-205,447
L'ENCLOS, SIEUR DE (see Enclos,
Sieur de l')
LENTON, JOHN II-360,509; III-
7,66,67,69,85,156,177,185,
194,201,270,313
LENZ III-304
LEO VI, EMPEROR (Byzantine) I-
52
LEO, LEONARDO III-80,203,234,
238,260,261,266,267,270,280,
281,285,287,299,307,312,314,
321,329,340,347,350,351,355,
357,366,375,377,388,398,399,
408,409,420,431,433,445,457,
459,470,477,481,482,490,491
LEO I, POPE I-32
LEO II, POPE I-42
LEO III, POPE I-46
LEO IV, POPE I-50
LEO V, POPE I-54
LEO VI, POPE I-55
LEO VII, POPE I-55

L'ÉPINE, MARGHERITA DE (see É-
   pine)
LEPORIN, JOHANN CHRISTOPH III-
   110,115
LEPSIUS I-2
LEROY AND BALLARD (publishers)
   I-283,346,350,352,353,358,369,
   371,372,373,374,381,382,398,
   399,410; II-46,49; III-138
LEROY, ADRIEN (see also Leroy
   and Ballard) I-216,312,346,
   350,351,354,365,377,393,402,
   403,414,416,425,426,427,432,
   436,451,466,473,503,535; II-
   18,201
LESAGE III-315,340,348
LESCOT I-252,319,452
LESSING, GOTTHOLD EPHRAIM III-
   422
LESTAINNIER I-337
LESUEUR, EUSTACHE II-179,358
LESZCZYŃSKI, ALEXSANDER WLADY-
   SLAW II-168,260,486
LEVEL, JACOTIN I-262
LEVERETT, JOHN II-444
LEVERIDGE, RICHARD II-431; III-
   92,93,104,112,119,125,126,174,
   185,194,201,209,230,260,289,
   299,357,386,399,455
LEVIS, (Duke) GILBERT DE I-415
LEWES, WILLIAM I-287
LEXHY, GUILLAUME DE II-488
LEUDEN II-290
LEYDEN, LUCAS VAN I-205,271,295
LEYSER, POLYCARP I-537
LHERMITTE, J.B. II-291
L'HERMITE, TRISTAN (see Hermite,
   T.L.')
LIBER, ANTON JOSEPH III-453
LIBERATI, ANTIMO II-384; III-
   5,10
LIBERIUS I-29
LIBERTH, GAULTERIUS (see Frye,
   Walter)

LIBERTI, GAULTERUS (see Frye,
    Walter)
LIBERTI, HENDRIK II-65,203,255,
    261
LIBERTI, VINCENZO II-117
LICHFILD, HENRY II-37,151,159
LICHTENSTEIN-KASTELLKORN, (Prince-
    Bishop) KARL II-218,399,403,
    405; III-90
LICHTENSTEIN, ULRICH VON (see
    Ulrich)
LIEBE, CHRISTIAN II-351,462,519;
    III-47,223
LIEBERT, REGINALD I-124
LIECHTENSTEIN, PETER I-455
LIGHT, EDWARD III-137
LILIUS, FRANCISZEK II-65,250,
    364
LILIUS, SZYMON II-343
LILIUS, V. II-90
LILIUS, WINCENTY II-57,89,120,
    275
LILIYS, JAN II-43
LILLO, GEORGE III-431,445
LIMBOURG, JEAN DE I-143,145
LIMBOURG, POL DE (see Malouel,
    Pol)
LIMENIOS I-19
LIN, MA I-90
LINACRE, THOMAS I-175,275
LINCOLN, EARL OF II-9
LINDAU II-442
LINDELHEIM, JOHANNA MARIA III-
    130,137,180,198,205,213,214,
    221,224,231,266,274
LINDEMANN II-17
LINDNER, FRIEDRICH I-447,518;
    II-14
LING, LUNG I-2
LINIGKE, JOHANN III-243,269,327,
    377
LINNERT, A. WESTERN III-208
LINTERN, JAMES III-137
LINUS, POPE I-21

See illustration on p. 245

MARTIN LUTHER
PAINTED BY CRANACH, THE ELDER   *255*

LOOSEMORE, JOHN   II-403,496
LOPE   II-49
LÓPEZ DE VELASCO SEBASTIÁN   II-
    243,244
LOQUEVILLE, RICHARD   I-106,142,
    144,146
LORENZANI, PAOLO   II-292,493,499;
    III-49,75,267
LORENZETTI, AMBROGIO   I-113,115,
    116,117
LORENZETTI, PIETRO   I-99,113,115,
    117,118,139
LORENZO, THE MAGNIFICENT   I-178
LORETO, VITTORIO   II-321,325
LORIS (Loritus)   (see Glareanus,
    Henricus)
LORRAIN, CLAUDE   (Gellee le)
    II-62,67,291,295,319,322,339,
    507
LORRAINE, CHRISTINA DE   (see
    Medici, Christina)
LORRIS, GUILLAUME DE   I-93
LOSCOS, FRANCISCO MARTINEZ DI
    I-423
LOSENSTEIN, COUNT   II-111
LOSI, ANNA   III-266
LOSSIUS, LUCAS   I-393
LOSSY, JAN WILLEMSZOON   I-332,
    416,449; II-247
LOSSY, WILLEM JANSZOON   II-22
LOSYMTHAL, JOHANN ANTON LOSY
    VON   II-316; III-337
LOTHAIR, KING   I-55,56
LOTTHER   I-303,313
LOTTI, ANTONIO   II-412,516; III-
    36,44,132,189,201,262,271,281,
    294,300,303,307,308,315,317,
    319,406,465
LOTTO, LORENZO   I-189,242,245,
    249,271,280,282,286,292,370
LOUIS, CARDINAL DE GUISE   (see
    Guise)
LOUIS, DUKE of Orleans   I-129
LOUIS, DUKE of Savoy   I-154

257

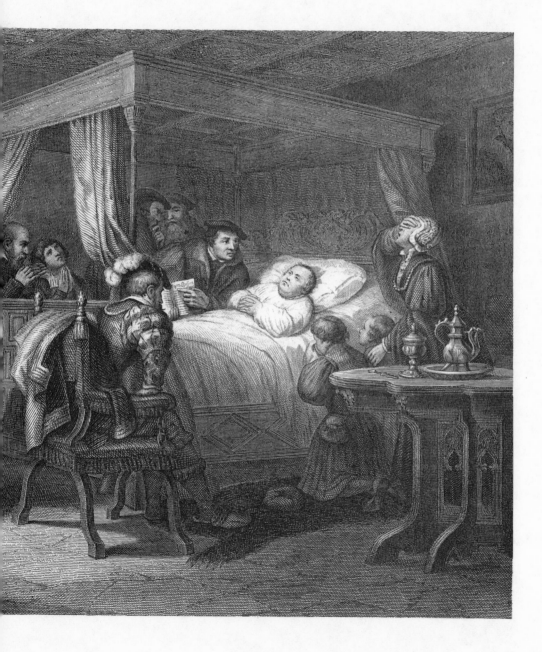

MARTIN LUTHER ON HIS DEATHBED 261

LOULIÉ, ETIENNE II-54; III-104, 105,120

LOUNAY, CARLO DI I-204,210

LOVELACE, RICHARD II-184,296,368

LOVELL I-222

LOW, ANNE III-65

LOW, CHARLES III-281

LOWE, EDWARD II-131,256,376,385, 388,398,501,504,510

LÖWE, JOHANN JAKOB II-242,358, 504; III-182

LOWNDES, HUMPHREY I-340; II-84, 101,103

LOYOLA, ST. IGNATIUS I-297,355, 402

LUBECK, HEINRICH II-26

LÜBECK, VINCENZ II-351; III-175, 179

LUCADELLO, GASPARE II-181

LUCAS, MIGUEL (see Iranzo)

LUCCA, BISHOP OF I-411

LUCCHINI, ANTONIO M. III-308, 390,408

LUCCIO, FRANCESCO II-229,330, 342,350,353,368

LUCIAN I-23

LUCIANO, SEBASTIANO (see Piombo)

LUCIFER II-14

LUCINI III-45

LUCINO II-172,178

LUCIUS I, POPE I-26

LUCIUS II, POPE I-76

LUCIUS III, POPE I-80

LUCREZIA, DUCHESS of Ferrara I-469

LUCREZIA, DUCHESS of Urbino I-464

LUCY, C. III-488

LUDFORD, NICHOLAS I-315

LUDWIG VI, COUNT of Palatinate I-380

LUDWIG, MARGRAVE of Baden II-380

LUDWIG, J. III-366

LUKAČIĆ, IVAN II-132,323
LUKASZEWICZ, MACIEJ III-1
LUKE, ST. I-44,45,49,124,146,
    260,405
LULLY (Lulli), JEAN BAPTISTE *See illustration on p. 251*
    I-350; II-126,193,260,297,316,
    317,320,327,334,337,344,346,
    348,350,351,352,353,354,355,
    356,359,361,363,365,366,369,
    373,374,376,379,381,382,384,
    385,386,391,395,396,397,398,
    400,401,404,406,407,409,411,
    415,417,421,422,425,426,429,
    430,431,432,433,434,436,437,,
    438,439,440,441,442,444,446,
    447,448,452,454,455,457,461,
    466,468,470,472,476,478,485,
    494,498,501,505,506,508,511,
    514,517,519,521,522,523; III-
    1,2,3,7,11,12,14,15,17,18,19,
    25,42,51,92,100,102,127,131,
    162,169,179,189,201,208,215,
    239,337,378,403
LULLY, JEAN BAPTISTE (II) DE II-
    401; III-73,77,90,102,165,166,
    202,300
LULLY,JEAN-LOUIS DE II-412; III-28
LULLY, LOUIS DE II-396
LUMLEY, LORD I-481,516,519
LUNG LING (see Ling, Lung)
LUPACEHINI I-344
LUPACHINO, BERNARDINO I-378
LUPI, DIDIER I-337
LUPI, JOHANNES (choirboy at Cam-
    brai) I-251,264,269,282
LUPI, JOHANNES (the elder-organ-
    ist) I-236
LUPI, JOHANNES, (the younger)
    I-320,324,330,336
"LUPI SECOND" I-377
LUPO, JOSEPH I-533
LUPO, THOMAS I-533; II-243
"LUPUS" (composer) I-255,266,
    294,295,309,313,377

LUSCINIUS, OTTOMARUS (Othmar Na-
     chtigal) I-215,258,302,320
LUSITANO I-301
LUSSIUS, L. I-454
LUTHER, MARTIN I-168,188,192, *See illustrations on pp. 255,*
     193,207,209,242,254,262,266, *260-261*
     268,270,271,272,273,275,276,
     277,278,280,281,283,286,287,
     288,292,296,299,302,312,313,
     317,318,322,324,327,330,332,
     342,353,359,407,486,500,515;
     II-15,45,171,164
LUTHER, WILLIAM I-406
LUTHERO, D. II-329
LUTTRELL II-396,495,518; III-4,
     13,19,60,61,62,71,81,90
LUYNES, CONSTABLE DE II-131,201
LUYTHON, CHARLES (Karel) I-370;
     II-83,89,122,192
LUZARCHES, ROBERT DE I-90
LUZZASCO (Luzzaschi), LUZZASCO
     I-216,329,424,428,446,532; II-
     18,24,71,89,104
LWOWCZYK, MARTIN (Marcin) (see
     Leopolita)
LYDGATE, JOHN I-124,158
LYLY, JOHN I-362,452,458,464,
     477,508,509,510,522; II-102
LYON, CORNEILLE DE (painter)
     I-215,303,317,378,437
LYON, GEORGE M. III-485
LYON, JAMES III-485
LYON, PARSON III-485
LYÓNS, CORNELIUS I-230
LYSICRATES I-17
LYSIPPUS I-16
LYTTICH, JOHANN II-147

M

M.H. I-253
MABUSE (Gossaert) I-188,239,260,
     277,283,296

MAGNI, BARTOLOMEO II-188,216,
    249,261
MAGNUS, ALBERTUS I-99
MAGUIRE (Carolan), MARY III-465
MAHOON II-460
MAHU, STEPHEN I-232
MAICHELBECK, FRANZ ANTON III-173
MAIER, LORD II-8
MAILLARD, JEAN I-354
MAILLARD, PIERRE II-74,125,207
MAILLY, ABBÉ II-318
MAIMONIDES I-75,79,89
MAINE, DUCHESSE DU III-215,216
MAINTENON, MME. DE III-191
MAINZ, ELECTOR OF III-305
MAIO, GIOVAN TOMMASO DI I-263,
    333
MAIO, GIOVANNIE FRANCESCO DI
    III-109,451
MAIO, GIUSEPPE DI III-109,212,
    399,406,409,420
MAIORANO, FRANCESCO III-451
MAIORANO, GAETANO (see Caffar-
    elli)
MAISTRE, MATTHAEUS LE I-360,371,
    393,407,448,449
MAITLAND II-501
MAJER III-460
MAJOR I-88
MALACHOUSKI II-210
MALATESTA, CLEOFE I-146,147,150
MALBECQUE, GUILLAUME I-153
MALCHAIR, JOHANN BAPTIST III-
    401
MALCOLM, ALEXANDER III-21,340,
    431
MALDERG, GUILLAUME VAN III-393,
    394,415
MALDERG, PIERRE VAN III-415
MALEBRANCHE, NICOLAS II-287; III-
    34
MALER, HANS I-213,253
MALER, LUCAS (Laux) I-145,215,
    274,284

MALHERBE, FRANÇOIS DE II-242
MALIN, NICOLAS I-142,144
MALIPIERO, MARIA I-272
MALLAPERT, ROBIN I-307,310
MALLET, A. MANESSON III-105
MALLET, (Sir) CHARLES II-276;
    III-83
MALORY, (Sir) THOMAS I-160,165,
    178,181,194
MALOUEL, JEAN I-129,131
MALOUEL, POL (Pol de Limbourg)
    I-140,143,145
MALTESTE, M. DE II-489
MALVEZZI, CHRISTOFANO I-334,384,
    473,477,502,503,507,510,521;
    II-14
MAMILIANO, FRANCESCO ANTONIO III-
    383
MANCHICOURT, PIERRE DE I-316
MANCINI, FRANCESCO II-480; III-
    214,240,245,313,317,327,366,
    406
MANCINI, GIAMBATTISTA III-295
MANCINUS, THOMAS I-341; II-199
MANDEL II-97
MANDRAGONE, ANTONIO CARAFA DI
    I-337
MANELLI, FRANCESCO II-2,8,97,240,
    254,265,276,280,282,283,284,
    286,288,290,303,316,412
MANELLI, MADDALENA II-265,276
MANENTI, GIOVAMPIER I-487
MANERA III-388
MANESSE, RUEDIGER I-110
MANFREDI III-152
MANFREDINI III-434
MANGOLD, JOHANN HEINRICH III-38
MANGOLT, BURK I-121,148
MANGOT, family III-216
MANGOT (female dancer) III-208,
    234,252,327
MANGOT, JACQUES III-216
MANGOT, MARIE-LOUISE III-215,
    383,479

MANI   I-25

MANICOURT   I-379

MANN, JOHANN CHRISTIAN   III-385

MANNA, GENNARO   III-268,368,406

MANNING   III-157,184

MANS, DU   II-40

MANSART, FRANÇOIS   (architect)
    II-305,316,410

MANSART, JULES HARDOUIN   (archi-
    tect)   II-315,477; III-211,
    229,244

MANSFIELD, COUNT   II-222

MANTEGNA, ANDREA   (painter)   I-
    153,162,171,172,192,194,202,
    208,245

MANTOVA, GIACHETTO DI   I-300

MANTUA, DUKE OF   II-242,360

MANTUA, JAQUET OF   (see Jaquet
    of Mantua)

MANUTIUS, ALDUS   I-163,258

MANZUOLI, GIOVANNI   III-381

MAPES, WALTER   I-85

MARAIS, JEAN-LOUIS   III-464

MARAIS, MARIN   II-54,359; III-
    5,15,17,21,66,73,105,106,149,
    169,186,192,193,202,204,209,
    210,237,254,300,307,308,375,
    377,403

MARAIS, ROLAND   III-254,375,386,
    490

MARAZZOLI, MARCO   II-281,288,290,
    291,348,349,353,362,386

MARBECK, JOHN   (see Merbecke,
    John)

MARCABRO   I-76

MARCELLI   I-226

MARCELLINUS, AMMIANUS   I-31

MARCELLINUS, POPE   I-26

MARCELLO, ALESSANDRO   II-523;
    III-12

MARCELLO, BENEDETTO   III-12,132,
    169,212,214,236,240,252,260,
    307,330,343,366,378,389,399,
    429,470

MARCELLUS I-25
MARCELLUS (Moengal) I-50,51,54
MARCELLUS I, POPE I-27
MARCELLUS II, POPE I-27,363,366, *See ill*
    367,398
MARCHAND DE SAINT MICHEL, ELIZ-
    ABETH II-355
MARCHAND, JEAN III-54
MARCHAND, JEAN-BAPTISTE II-407,
    431; III-54,56,240
MARCHAND, JEAN NOEL II-407; III-
    56,200,240
MARCHAND, LOUIS II-421,512; III-
    125,175,177,183,185,305,450,
    454,457
MARCHESI, (Duke) ANNIBALE III-
    419,420
MARCHETTO, of Padua I-85,98,100,
    111
MARCHI, ANTONIO III-300,308,447,'
    484
MARCHITELLI, PIETRO (Petrillo)
    III-175
MARCOUREAU DE BRÉCOURT, GUILLAUME
    II-407
MARCUS, POPE I-28
MARENZIO, LUCA I-109,123,226,
    256,316,356,366,382,401,403,
    434,449,453,455,456,459,461,
    462,463,464,466,467,468,471,
    472,473,474,475,477,478,479,
    480,481,488,490,491,492,493,
    494,496,497,499,500,502,503,
    504,508,409,512,513,514,519,
    521,522,525,526,528,529,530,
    533,535; II-1,2,3,4,6,11,12,
    18,20,22,24,28,29,31,32,33,
    34,103,109
MAREŠ, JAN ANTONÍN III-319
MARESCHALL, SAMUEL II-99,101,
    171,210,284,288,294,296
MARGARET, of Austria (grand-daugh-
    ter of Charles the Bold) I-
    189,192,244,246,289,320,386

270

CLAUDIO MERULO   271

MARGARET, of York (wife of Charles the Bold) I-179

MARGARET, Regent of Netherlands (see Margaret of Austria)

MARGHERITA, QUEEN of Spain II-96,104,110,117,134,135,381

MARGUERITE, of France I-378

MARIA, EMPRESS (wife of Holy Roman Emperor Maximilian II) I-476; II-79,96,136

MARIA, of Portugal I-403,404

MARIA ANNA, QUEEN of Portugal (daughter of Leopold I) III-229

MARIA ANTONIA, ARCHDUCHESS of Munich III-9,17

MARIA CASIMIRA, QUEEN of Poland III-229,239,274,281,300

MARIA JOSEPHA, ARCHDUCHESS of Austria III-317

MARIA THERESA, EMPRESS of Austria III-308,318,336

MARIA THERESA, QUEEN (?) II-379

MARIA, G. (?) II-9

MARIA, GALEAZZO (see Sforza)

MARIA, GAUDE (Okegus, Johannes) I-305

MARIANA I-300; II-213,217

MARIANI, TOMMASO III-476,483

MARIANNA, QUEEN of Portugal III-324

MARIE, ARCHDUCHESS of Austria II-134

MARIGLIANI, ERCOLE II-138,177'

MARIN, ELEONORA III-66

MARIN, JEAN-BAPTISTE III-209

MARIN, JOSÉ II-187,310,361; III-121

MARINE, B. II-319

MARINI, BIAGIO II-6,14,52,65, 175,177,178,180,183,184,193, 194,195,198,208,210,215,232, 234,248,249,256,269,273,299, 311,329,348,349,352,353,356, 357,375,401,402,413,429

MARINI, GIAMBATTISTA I-417; II-224

MARINO, CANON I-475

MARINO, CARLO III-21

MARINUS I, POPE (Martin II, Pope) I-51,99

MARINUS II, POPE (Martin III, Pope) I-56,99

MARISCOTTI II-215

MARIUS III-296

MARIVAUX III-448

MARK, ST. I-337,391

MARKHAM, FRANCIS II-208,210

MARLBOROUGH, GENERAL III-195, 211,343

MARLOWE, CHRISTOPHER I-399,465, 477,494,502,509,513,528,530, 531; II-34,173

MARMION, SIMON I-162

MARMONTEL, JEAN FRANÇOIS III-352

MARONCELLI, PIERO II-430

MAROT, CLÉMENT I-208,258,295,303, 309,317,318,319,320,322,325, 335,339,350,351,352,355,365, 374,390,394,398,399,402,403

MAROT, JEAN I-208,325

MAROTTA, ERASMO II-297

MARPUNG, FRIEDRICY WILHELM III-149,312

MARS I-195

MARSCHALL, SAMUEL I-371,535

MARSH, ALPHONSO (I) II-241,376, 390,420,424,430,447,464,495; III-61

MARSH, ALPHONSO (II) II-461; III-10,34,61

MARSHALL I-300

MARSOLO, PIETRO MARIA II-143

MARSON, GEORGE II-3,22,29,71,85, 106,183,260

MARSTON, JOHN II-95,101,184

MARSUPPINI, CARLO I-172

MARTELLI, ERNESTA MUCENNI III-327

MARTELLI, PIETRO JACOPO III-122, 289

MARTIAL, ST. I-74

MARTIN I, of Aragon I-142

MARTIN I, POPE (St.) I-40,99, 172

MARTIN II, POPE (see Marinus I, Pope)

MARTIN III, POPE (see Marinus II, Pope)

MARTIN IV, POPE I-99

MARTIN V, POPE I-145

MARTIN, JONATHON III-286

MARTINELLI, CATERINA II-111

MARTINENGO, (Rev.) GIULIO CESARE I-479,513; II-95,97,119,129, 148,226

MARTINEZ DI LOSCOS, FRANCISCO (see Loscos)

MARTINI (?) I-142

MARTINI, GIOVANNI BATTISTA ("Padre") III-146,205,344,375, 467,481

MARTINI, JOHANNES I-183,184,198, 199,203,256

MARTINI, SIMONE (painter) I-100, 112,113,114,115,116,117,118, 139

MARTORETTA, GIANDOMENICO I-328, 354,360,361

MARULIĆ, MARKO I-168

MARVELL, ANDREW II-205

MARWOOD, RICHARD II-225

MARX III-83

MARY(S) (Three Biblical) I-53

MARY I-70,106,111; II-505; III-230

MARY, of Burgundy (Daughter of Charles the Bold) I-187,192, 253

MARY, of Modena (wife of James II) III-4,19,21

MARY, QUEEN of England (wife of Edward II) I-112

MARY II QUEEN of England (Stuart)
II-42,390,469; III-34,36,37,
43,44,47,50,54,55,61,63,66,
67,69,70,71,73,76,77,79,81,
85,88,89,91,92,93,94,96,281

MARY, QUEEN of England (Tudor)
I-259,261,311,340,355,357,358,
359,362,368,370,380,433

MARY, QUEEN of Hungary I-264,
269,281,291,300,337

MARY, QUEEN of Scots I-489,494

MARY MAGDALEN(E) I-65,170,171,
202,208,237,260,291; II-155,
393

MARZIO, GALEOTTO I-194

MASACCIO, TOMASO I-131,140,147,
149,150,151

MASACONI I-308

MASAMI, KATO III-373

MASANIELLO (see Massaniello)

MASCARDI II-255,469

MASCHERA, FLORENZIO I-477,529;
II-66

MASCITTI III-399

MASO (see Banco, di)

MASOLINO I-150

MASON, JOHN I-247,249,278,328,334

MASON, MATTHIAS II-129

MASON, WILLIAM III-361

MASOTTI II-238

MASSAINO, TIBURZIO I-341,454,
533; II-3

MASSANIELLO II-326; III-127

MASSARD DE LA TOUR, CHARLOTTE
(see Tour)

MASSINGER, PHILIP II-203; III-
28,29,44

MASSOTTI, PAOLO II-273

MASSYS, QUENTIN I-176,203,258,
260,270,289

MASTER OF MOULINS (see Moulins,
Master of)

MASTROLUCO, PAOLO MASSONIO III-
11,101

MASUMI, KATO III-11
MATELART, JEAN I-377; II-65
MATEO, MASTER I-80
MATHER, COTTON II-392; III-340
MATHEW, RICHARD II-345
MATHIAS I-258,319,377
MATHO III-280
MATSYE, QUINTEN (see Massys)
MATTEI III-341
MATTEIS, NICOLA II-438,442,449,
    456,485; III-7,31,51,100,102,
    104,126,160,412
MATTEO I-104
MATTHESIUS I-312
MATTHESON, JOHANN II-495; III-
    47,102,127,128,177,178,184,
    188,190,192,195,200,205,208,
    249,261,264,269,270,287,291,
    297,303,307,316,319,321,340,
    350,355,377,406,409,429,442,
    445,490
MATTHEW, ST. I-45,47,49,186,240;
    II-129,405
MATTHEW, of Austria II-139,146
MATTIAS I-199
MATTHIAS, ARCHDUKE (King of Bo-
    hemia and Hungary) II-113
MATTHIJSZ, P. II-521
MAUBURNUS, JOHANNES I-205,236
MAUDIT, JACQUES I-370,462,515;
    II-132,237
MAUGARS, ANDRÉ II-199,222,288,
    289,290,314
MAURICE, ST. I-278
MAURICE, CARDINAL of Savoy II-
    218
MAURO, O III-51,178,248
MAURO, (Rev.) PADRE MATTIA I-427
MAURUS, HRABANUS I-50
MAUSOLUS I-16
MAWGRIDGE, JOHN II-376,433,451,
    461; III-28,37,123,359
MAXEY, ANTHONY (Dean of Windsor)
    II-183

MAXIMILIAN, ARCHDUKE of Austria
II-127

MAXIMILIAN I, EMPEROR of Bavaria
I-433; II-342

MAXIMILIAN I, HOLY ROMAN EMPEROR
I-172,187,192,196,199,203,205,
206,208,209,246,255,259,260,
265,266

MAXIMILIAN II, HOLY ROMAN EMPER-
OR I-396,409,412,414,421,438,
445,476

MAXIMILIAN EMANUEL, ELECTOR of
Munich (Bavaria) II-486; III-
9,14,83,90,190,281,282

MAXIMILIAN FRIEDRICH, ELECTOR of
Cologne III-222

MAXLEWICZ, WINCENTY III-5

MAYER, E. DE II-163

MAYNARD, JOHN II-34,69,138

MAYNE, CUTHBERT I-447

MAYONE II-197

MAYR, RUPERT II-317

MAZARIN, CARDINAL II-77,191,309,
375,378,381,384,385,438,516

MAZIANI III-12

MAZZAFERRATA, GIOVANNI BATTISTA
II-420,452,464,470,476,490,
522; III-53,54

MAZZELLA, SALVATORE III-39

MAZZOCCHI, DOMENICO I-523; II-
232,234,235,252,258,282,288,
290,316,334,400,401

MAZZOCCHI, VIRGILIO II-13,245,
286,294,316,325

MAZZOLA, FRANCESCO (see Parmigianino)

MAZZONE I-419

MAZZONI, ANTONIO MARIA III-312,
492

MCGIBBON III-93

MEARES, RICHARD (I) II-423; III-
29,329,350

MEARES, RICHARD (II) III-310

MECKENEM, ISRAEL VAN I-249

MEDER, JOHANN VALENTIN II-308,
    327,328,451; III-21,92,120,318
MEDICI, family I-205,254,256,283,
    478,497; II-21,87,186,332,335,
    500
MEDICI, CARDINAL(?) DE' II-170,
    207
MEDICI, (Don) ANTONIO DE II-131
MEDICI, CATERINA DE' I-448,478;
    II-175
MEDICI, CHRISTINA DE' (Lorraine)
    I-503
MEDICI, CLAUDIA DE' II-200
MEDICI, COSIMO (I) DE' I-307,
    308,309,335,411
MEDICI, COSIMO (II) DE' II-87
MEDICI, FERDINANDO (I) DE' I-
    334,391,502,503,504; II-87
MEDICI, FERDINANDO (II) DE'
    (Grand Duke of Tuscany) I-
    532; II-37,243,268,459
MEDICI (Prince), FERDINANDO DE'
    III-187,197,198,200,205,213,
    214,226
MEDICI, FRANCESCO DE' I-334,400,
    453,454
MEDICI, GIULIANO DE' I-107,278
MEDICI, ISABELLA DE' I-321,374,
    393
MEDICI, LEONORA DE' I-410
MEDICI, LORENZO DE' I-162,179,
    181,197,198,202,203,256,271,
    278
MEDICI, MARCO DE' I-471
MEDICI, MARGHERITA DE' II-241
MEDICI, MARIA DE' II-56,58,60,
    137,205,212,306
MEDICI, PIETRO DE' I-178,204
MEDICI, VIRGINIA DE' I-486,488
MEDINA (painter) II-460
MEDIOLANESIS, ANNIBALIS I-342,
    418
MEDIOLANI I-271
MEDUSA I-10

MEGLI, DOMENICO MARIA   II-78

MEI, LENG   III-148

MEIBOOM, MARCUS   II-236,344,345;
   III-239

MEILAND, JACOB   I-322,381,448

MEISSEN, HEINRICH VON   I-96,112,
   113

MEL, RENÉ DE   I-362,389,456,469,
   490,492,510,519; II-27

MELANCHTHON   I-337

MELANI, ALESSANDRO   II-413,421,
   438; III-182

MELANI, ANTONIO   III-41

MELANI, ATTO   II-230,241,319,
   371; III-182,277

MELANI, BARTOLOMEO   II-267,366

MELANI, DOMENICO   II-352,354,
   489; III-72

MELANI, FRANCESCO MARIA   II-241,
   376

MELANI, JACOPO   II-212,230,241,
   352,354,360,365,382,425,462,
   499; III-182,277

MELANI, NICOLA   II-352

MELANUZII,C.   II-190,273,302

MELCHISEDEK   I-81

MELE, GIOVANNI BATTISTA   III-
   494

MELII, PIETRO PAOLO   II-145,159,
   171

MELL, DAVIS   II-86,360,379,382,
   384,522

MELONE   (see Bottrigari, Ercole)

MELTIADES, POPE   I-28

MELVILLE, ANDREW   II-279

MEMLINC, HANS   I-153,177,179,
   185,188,189,197,198,201,205

MEMMI, LIPPO   I-116,118

MEMMO, DIONISIO   I-247,259

MENANTE   III-261

MENCKEN, THOMAS   II-129,193

MENDELSSOHN, FELIX   I-226

MENDELSSOHN, MOSES   III-414

MENDÈS, MANUEL   I-383; II-92,127

MICHELE DE MONTAIGNE   285

MERULO, GIOVANNI, ANTONIO I-
   492(?); II-215
MÉSANGEAU, RENÉ (see Mézangeau)
MESENETZ, ALEXANDER II-421
MESOMEDES I-23
MESSAUS, GULIELMUS A II-244
MESSINA, ANTONELLO DA I-153,184,
   188
METALLO II-222
METASTASIO, PIETRO II-418; III-
   115,137,138,164,308,316,319,
   340,355,357,361,368,372,379,
   388,394,399,400,402,407,409,
   410,411,421,422,426,430,433,
   434,438,439,445,447,450,452,
   459,464,472,474,476,482,484,
   485,492
METHODIUS (missionary) I-46
MEUNG, JEAN DE I-98
MEUSEL III-395
MEYER (Burgomaster) I-285
MEYER, FRANZ JOSEPH LEONTI III-
   324
MEYER, GREGOR I-444
MEYERBEER, GIACOMO III-422
MEYERE, JACQUES DE I-291,292
MÉZANGEAU, RENÉ II-288,291
MEZZAGORRI, GIOVANNI NICOLO II-
   141,143
MIČA (father) III-252
MIČA, FRATIŠEK VÁCLAU III-80,252,
   420,421,431,435,457,491
MICHAEL, ST. II-14
MICHAËL, ARCHANGEL I-111
MICHAEL, BISHOP of Bulgaria I-
   58
MICHAEL, BROTHER I-64
MICHAEL, CHRISTIAN II-216
MICHAEL, DANIEL II-216
MICHAEL, ROGER I-529; II-4,77,
   83,89,108,129,151,192,216,363
MICHAEL, TOBIAS II-188.216,258,
   270,282,363,366
MICHAELIS I-187,307,354

Cernimus excelsum mente, arte, et nomine MONTEM,
Quo Musæ, et Charites constituére domum.

ADMODV̄ R.ᵈᵒ C̄ ᵗ PRÆCLAR.ᵐᶜ VIRO, DÑO PHILIPPO
DE MONTE, BELGÆ, DD. MAX.ᵐⁱ II. & RVDOL. II.
ROM. IMPP. CHORI MVSICI PRÆFECTO,
Metropol: ecciæ Cameracen. Can.ᶜᵒ et Thesaurario. et c: Raphael
Sadeler observant. ergò scalpsit, et dedicavit   Monachij.
Cum privilegio Sar. Cæs. M.

MICHAILOVITCH, (Czar) ALEXIS II-356,421

MICHEL I-317; II-183

MICHELANGELO(?) II-189

MICHELANGELO (Buonarotti) I-184, 185,206,210,239,247,248,255, 256,262,264,277,278,302,314, 322,335,399,458,515; II-91

MICHELI, DOMENICO I-443

MICHELI, ROMANO II-37,127,165, 169,171,202,203,204,225,286, 329,333,368; III-40,48

MICHELOZZO I-129,159,182

MICHIEL I-279

MICHNA, ADAM VÁCLAV II-65,140, 265,321,325,349,353,385,462

MICHON (see Bourdelot, Pierre)

MICO, RICHARD II-337,402

MIDDLETON, THOMAS I-423; II-166, 237

MIELCZEWSKI, MARCIN II-285,307, 314,340,341,362,372,498; III-31

MIELECKI, MARCIN II-222

MIELICH, HANS I-374,403,405

MIGNARD, PIERRE II-130,146; III-98

MIGNATTA (see Musi, Maddalena)

MÍLAN, LUIS I-213,214,290,299, 385,386

MILANI, DORALICE (Stradivarius) II-56

MILANO, FRANCESCO CANOVA DA I-180,200,250,287,290,299,301, 304,305,323,351,408

MILANUZII (Milanuzzi), CARLO II-183,190,192,204,208,210,216, 217,220,221,226,240,244,245, 249,250,253,261,276,277,303, 308,309,316,321

MILEHAM, DOROTHY II-300

MILES, JAMES III-115,363

MILLAR, EDWARD II-219,230,238, 272,273

MILLAR, ROBERT II-230
MILLARD II-26
MILLER, EDWARD III-440
MILLERAN, RENÉ III-382
MILLEVILLE, FRANCESCO II-156,177,
    179,208,238
MILTON, CHRISTOPHER II-280,295
MILTON, JOHN II-6,56,71,117,160,
    205,249,263,267,269,280,282,
    285,287,291,295,304,309,312,
    315,317,320,362,379,385,416,
    435,453; III-390,408,419
MILTON, SARAH II-280
MINATO, CHICCOLÒ II-374,429,435,
    508; III-335,433
MINDEN, EBERHARD VON I-140
MING, DYNASTY I-122; II-312
MINGOTTI, ANGELO III-161
MINGOTTI, PIETRO III-180,343
MINGOTTI, REGINA III-343
MINISCALCHI, GUGLIELMO II-208,
    210,221,227,240,253
MINUGLIAIO, GIOVANNI DEL I-509
MIO, ASCANIO II-113,115
MIRANDOLA, DUKE OF II-474
MIREPOIX, MARQUIS DE III-467
MIRZA, (Sultan) HUSSEIN I-198
MISINTA DE PAPIA, BERNADINUS I-
    236
MISKIEWICZ, MACIEJ ARNULF II-
    348,417; III-11
MITCHELL III-340
MIZZLER, L.C. III-493
MNESICLES I-13
MOCENIGO, GIROLAMO II-221
MOCENIGO, TOMMASO I-144
MODENA, DUKE OF II-481; III-39
MODENA, LEO DI II-216
MODENESE, ALESSANDRO PASI I-199
MODERNE, JACQUES (publisher) I-
    294,306,309,310,313
MOENGAL (see Marcellus)
MOHAMMED II, Sultan I-189
MOJIDAYU, TOKIWAZU III-233

FIORI POETICI
Raccolti nel Funerale
DEL MOLTO ILLVSTRE:

MOLIÈRE, (Poquelin) II-211,376, *See illustration on pp. 278-279*
379,384,395,397,398,400,401,
425,426,430,431,433,436,437,
439,445,446,447,448,452,457;
III-71,389,394,456

MOLINARO, SIMONE II-32,93,151

MOLINET (poet) I-155

MOLINO, ANTONIO (Burchiella) I-415,419,422,427

MOLLE, HENRY II-211,274,277,290,
394

MÖLLER, (Müller) JOHANN (see
Burgk, Joachim)

MOLTENI, BENEDETTA EMILIA III-345

MOLTER, JOHANN III-319,338,433,
467

MOLZA, TARQUINIA I-319,379,428,
450,460,469,474,502,503,520

MONA LISA I-256

MONACHUS, GUIELMUS I-132

MONDONVILLE, JEAN DE III-250

MONDONVILLE, JEAN JOSEPH DE III-250,293,470,479,483

MONETARIUS, STEPHANUS I-264,267

MONFERRATO, NATALE II-480

MONIGLIA, ANDREA II-365

MONK OF MONTAUDON, THE I-85

MONMOUTH II-486,495,500,510; III-2,6,16

MONN, GEORG MATTHIAS III-304

MONREALE, ARCHBISHOP OF II-371

MONRO, GEORGE II-282; III-412,
423,448,472

MONSART II-27

MONSIGNY, PIERRE ALEXANDRE III-415

MONSON, (Sir) THOMAS II-180

MONT, DU (see Dumont)

MONTAGNANA, ANTONIO III-440,450,
455,467,482,493

MONTAGNANA, DOMENICO II-511; III-160

MONTAGU, LADY MARY WORTLEY III-38,297

MONTAIGNE, MICHELE DE I-456,461; *See illustration on p. 285*
II-84

MONTANARI, FRANCESCO III-154,
427

MONTANARI, G.B. II-201

MONTAÑES, JUAN I-460; II-330

MONTANOS, FRANCISCO DE I-336,
492; III-139

MONTANUS, J. I-339,362,377,398

MONTAUDON, MONK OF (see Monk)

MONTDORGE III-220

MONTE (publisher) II-447

MONTE, COLO NARDO DI I-457

MONTE, (Cardinal) GIAMMARIA CI-
OCCHI DEL (see Jucius III,
POPE)

MONTE, PHILIPPE DE (Filippo da *See illustration on p. 289*
Monte) I-270,314,316,342,
360,361,362,363,364,370,372,
374,388,389,406,409,411,412,
413,416,417,419,421,422,441,
445,446,455,456,457,459,461,
462,468,472,473,476,486,488,
490,492,500,510,512; II-25,79,
83

MONTECLAIR, MICHEL II-412; III-
216,235,242,254,294,297,347,
348,413,415,450,455,457,459,
463

MONTECUCOLI, (Count) ALVISE II-
13

MONTEFELTRO, FEDERIGO DA I-177

MONTELLA, GIAN DOMENICO I-421,
519; II-4,105,108

MONTESARCHIO, ANTONIELLODI III-
47

MONTESARDO(?) II-99,101,113,115,
145

MONTESQUIEU, CHARLES LOUIS III-
42

MONTEVERDI, BALDESAR I-445; II-
28

MONTEVERDI, CLARA MASSIMILIA
I-453

MONTEVERDI, CLAUDIA (Cattaneo)
I-536; II-3,28,104

MONTEVERDI(E), CLAUDIO I-383, *See illustration on p. 293*
400,408,412,445,450,459,466,
468,469,470,472,473,477,478,
479,492,493,494,495,496,509,
510,511,512,513,514,515,518,
523,525,526,527,535,536; II-
3,6,7,10,13,14,18,28,29,32,
34,37,41,58,67,68,69,78,79,
80,83,86,93,95,97,104,106,
108,109,110,111,112,113,114,
115,116,117,119,120,121,122,
124,126,127,129,133,134,141,
143,145,147,148,149,152,154,
159,162,163,165,168,173,174,
177,180,185,190,192,194,196,
199,204,210,212,216,218,221,
222,226,227,236,237,238,241,
242,243,245,249,254,255,258,
260,261,262,264,269,279,284,
286,288,289,290,291,293,299,
300,301,302,303,304,305,307,
314,327,333,341,342,370,401,
461; III-132

MONTEVERDI, GIULIO CESARE I-
431; II-37,109,115,117,138,
141,143,195

MONTEVERDI, LUCA I-461

MONTEVERDI, MARIA DOMITILLA I-
425

MONTEVERDI, MASSIMILIANO II-
237,241

MONTEZUMA I-73

MONTFLEURY III-400

MONTFORT, COUNT HUGO VON I-121,
148

MONTI, GIACOMO II-415,420,470,
476,491,515; III-6

MONTICELLI, ANGELO MARIA III-
246,429,442,455

MONTIER III-451

MONTREUIL, PIERRE DE I-97

MONTROSE II-394

MOORE, JOHN (Lord Mayor of London) II-501
MOORE, THOMAS III-23,25,31
MOORS, HIERONYMUS II-22,85
MOORS, JACOB II-85
MOQUÉ, ANTOINE II-370,468,486;
    III-39,56,62,194,244,252,263,
    289,315,346,352
MORAGO, ESTÉVÃO LOPES II-35
MORALES, CHRISTOBAL I-213,257,
    281,282,299,301,305,311,312,
    316,318,327,329,330,335,354,
    356,503
MORALES, LUIS DE (painter) I-
    215,425,489
MORANDI, BERNARDO II-300
MORATELLI, SEBASTIANO II-296,
    482; III-18,19,33,59,80,88,
    206
MORAVIA, HIERONYMUS DE (see Hier-
    onymus)
MORE, (Sir) THOMAS I-187,263,284,
    299
MOREAU, JEAN-BAPTISTE II-347,
    360; III-18,20,41,58,59,83,
    96,104,112,157,177,209,378,
    463
MORELL, DAVID II-225,247
MORELL, JOHN II-225,247
MORETUS, BALTHASAR II-203,290,297
MORETUS, JAN II-76,95,126,297
MORGAN, ("Mr.") II-391,416,458;
    III-82,97,105,106,112,114
MORGAN, JOHN III-255
MORGAN, NICHOLAS I-409; II-3,93,
    117,147
MORI, JACAPO II-32
MORIGI, ANGELO III-373
MORIN, JEAN BAPTISTE II-471; III-
    194,218,235,261
MORITZ OF HESSE-CASSEL, LANDGRAVE
    I-405,430,500,525,529,536; II-
    5,10,15,22,23,30,71,77,93,139,
    145,188,238,260

MOSER, LUCAS I-153
MOSER, WILLIAM II-218
MOSES I-26,81,256
MOSS, JOHN II-394,424,434,446,
    473,474,519
MOSTO I-217,449; II-5
MOTOKIYO, SEAMI I-122,159
MOTTE, BENJAMIN III-21
MOTTE, HAUDART DE LA III-113,
    155,197,204,237,393,397
MOTTEUX, PETER III-55,61,63,64,
    73,81,104,106,125,126,127,
    188,195,202,212,221
MOTTLEY, JOHN III-409
MOULINS, MASTER OF I-190,191,
    201,202,207,210
MOULU, PIERRE I-200,256,309
MOUNTFORT, WILLIAM III-30,62,
    63,68,72,77
MOURET, JEAN JOSEPH II-501; III-
    137,216,275,276,278,280,281,
    302,394,406,455,459
MOUTON, CHARLES II-231,236; III-
    121,246
MOUTON, JEAN (Joannis) I-185,
    187,210,212,234,248,249,256,
    257,258,259,263,268,271,272,
    297,301,365,430
MOYNE, FRANÇOIS LE III-34
MOZART, ANNA MARIA III-325
MOZART, LEOPOLD (Wolfgang's fa- *See illustration on pp. 304-305*
    ther) II-54,55; III-24,317,
    406
MOZART, LEOPOLD JOSEPH (Wolfgang's
    uncle) III-101
MOZART, WOLFGANG AMADEUS I-226; *See illustration on pp. 304-305*
    III-115,205,317,318,325,382,
    465,492
MOZZACCHI, V. II-250
MUDARRA, ALONSO I-245,333,455
MUDD, family II-388
MUDD, JOHN II-258,259,394(?)
MUDD, THOMAS II-259,263,394(?)
MUFFAT, GEORG II-54,314,456,478,

504,505; III-44,47,49,93,96,
97,98,119,149,169,188,191

MUFFAT, GOTTLIEB THEOPHIL II-
54; III-44,46,49,50,149,305,
388,389

MUGLING, HEINRICH VON I-121

MUHAMMAD (Ridhavi, Jalàl) II-
187

MÜLICH, of Prague I-111,135

MÜLLER, (Doctor) AUGUST FRIED-
RICH III-371

MÜLLER, HEINRICH II-257,372,400,
448,454

MÜLLER, JOHANN SAMUEL III-403

MULLERSTEDT, ELIAS I-322

MULLINER, THOMAS I-332,377

MU'MIN, SAFĪ AL-DĪN 'ABD AL-
II-41,405

MUNCH VON SALZBURG I-119,123,
129

MUNCHHAUSEN, LUCIE ELISABETH
(wife of J.C.F. Bach) III-
453

MÜNCHHAUSEN, LUDOLF A. III-114

MUNDY, JOHN I-405,484,485,518,
519,533,535; II-71,219,251

MUNDY, WILLIAM I-289,320,322,
336,376,392,397,518,519,523

MUNRO, ALEXANDER III-457

MÜNSTER, JOHANN VON I-535

MÜNZER, THOMAS I-274

MUONI I-496

MURAD IV, (Sultan) II-283,285

MURE, (Sir) WILLIAM of Rowallen
II-364

MUREAU, GILLES I-176,182,254

MURER, BERNARDO DI STEFANINO
I-160

MURET I-354

MURILLO, BARTOLOMÉ ESTEBAN II-
179,315,339,405,477,507

MURIS, JOANNES DE I-88,101,104,
112,114,116,117,118,120,144,
364

MURPHY, DAVID   III-307
MURRIE, E.B.   II-343
MURSCHHAUSER, FRANZ XAVIER ANTON
    II-391,392; III-104,157,218,
    261,280,340
MUSAGETES, VOLUPIUS (see Scho-
    ensleder, Wolfgang)
MUSCATBLUT   I-145
MUSCETTOLA, ANTONIA   III-296
MUSCETTOLA, TERESA   III-296
MUSCULUS, WOLFGANG   I-302
MUSI, MADDALENA   III-187
MUSKIEWICZ, M.A.   II-340
MÜTHEL, JOHANN GOTTFRIED   III-
    310,326
MUTII   II-32
MYLLER   II-116
MYRIELL, THOMAS   II-170,171,172
MYRON   I-11,13
MYSZKOWSKI, (Bishop) PETER   I-
    402

N

N.C.   I-253
NACHTIGAL, OTHMAR (see
    Luscinius, Ottomarus)
NAGGARA, ISRAEL   II-198
NAGOYA (architect)   II-140
NAIN, LOUIS LE   I-531;   II-274,
    297,300,304,309,326
NAIN, MATHIEU LE   II-111,326,
    471
NAKHT   I-5
NALDI, ANTONIO   I-37
NALDI, ROMULO   II-37,67
NALDINI, (Bishop) PAOLO   III-235
NELSON, VALENTINE   III-345
NAMIEYSKI   III-137
NANINO, GIOVANNI, BERNARDINO
    I-345,383,447,504; II-32,213

NANINO, GIOVANNI, MARIA I-323,
    329,338,345,383,416,426,428,
    439,442,451,452,455,458,468,
    477,484,486,488,494,500,530;
    II-20,25,87,93,95,104,201,
    214,352
NANNI (see Bianco, Nanni di)
NAPLES, VICEROY OF II-517
NARAM-SIN I-2,3
NARDINI, PIETRO III-343
NARDO, BENEDETTO SERAFICO DI
    I-424
NARES, JAMES III-286
NARVAEZ, LUIS DE I-305
NASARRE, PABLO II-397; III-363
NASCIMBENI, MARIA FRANCESA
    II-43
NASCIMBENI, STEFANO II-37
NASCO, GIOVANNI I-324,337,344,
    353,360,386
NASH, THOMAS I-411,531,536;
    II-73
NATALE, POMPEO II-388; III-128
NATTIER, JEAN-MARC III-10,460
NAUDOT, JEAN-JACQUES III-137,
    391
NAUFRAGANTE, IL (Vacchelli,
    G.B.) II-44,318,364,398,
    399,414,415
NAUMANN III-422
NAUWACH, JOHANN II-2,37,216,
    240,304
NAVAGELO, BERNARDO I-392
NAVARRO, JUAN I-290,360,456;
    II-89,131
NAWRAT, A.T. III-294,351
NAZIANZEN, (St.) GREGORY I-28,
    51,458
NEALE, JOHN III-164,355,392,
    424,477
NEALE, WILLIAM III-164,392,
    424,477
NEANDER, ALEXIS II-37,93,96
NEANDER, JOACHIM II-331,488

NEBRA, JOSÉ DE III-35,364,
    380,477
NEEDLER, HENRY III-5,243
NEFERSESHEMPTAH I-5
NEFERT (?) I-2
NEFERTITI I-5
NEGRI, CESARE II-37,77,78,89
NEGRI, MARC' ANTONIO II-37,
    115,116,136,138,143,152,194,
    199
NEGRO (Negri) GIULIO SANO
    PIETRO DEL II-38,87,109,
    152,159,171,196
NEIDHARDT, (Baron) VON III-94
NEIDHARDT, JOHANN GEORG III-366
NEIDT, F. III-340
NEL, JOHANN I-432
NEMESIS I-23
NEMORARIUS, JORDANUS I-93
NENCHEFTKAI I-2
NENNA, POMPONIO I-367,436,439,
    467,468; II-37,109,125,180,
    204,210
NEPOMUK, (Count) SPAUR JOHANN
    III-368
NERI, GIOVANNI BATTISTA III-
    113,195,268,347
NERI, MASSIMILIANO II-43,198,
    310,311,340,341,397,399
NERI, PHILIP (St. Philip Romolo
    de Neri) I-111,226,258,343,
    350,353,360,374,376,394,397,
    438,439,465; II-1,5,30,62
NERICI, L. III-487
NERITI DE SALO, V. II-32
NERO I-21
NERUDA, JOHANNA BAPTIST (see
    Neruda, J.C.)
NERUDA, JOHANN CHRYSOSTOM III-
    198,230,386,467
NESLES, BLONDEL DES I-72,77,
    81,85
NESTOR I-52
NEUBAUER II-328

NEUBER, A.   I-339,362,377,398,
    415 (?)
NEUBER, ULRICH   I-345,415 (?)
NEUBURG-WITTELSBACH (Elector)
    JOHANN WILHELM VON   III-221
NEUKIRCH, BANJAMIN   III-340
NEUKOMM   III-422
NEUMANN   III-25
NEUMARK, GOERG   II-200,201,304,
    340,365,495
NEUMEISTER, ERDMANN   II-432;
    III-154,157,194,228,255,279,
    299
NEUSCHEL, HANS   I-295
NEUSIEDLER, CONRAD   II-232
NEVERS, GUILLAUME   II-174;III-
    183
NEVILL, MARY   I-362,439,473,523
NEWARK, WILLIAM   I-164,204,249
NEWEY, (Rev.) JOHN   III-102
NEWSIDLER, HANS   I-186,247,327,
    369,392
NEWSIDLER, MELCHIOR   I-245,301,
    314,407,435,436,510
NEWTON, (Sir) ISAAC   II-304,410;
    III-17,400
NIBBIO, STEFANO VENTURI DEL
    (see Venturi,S.)
NICETA of REMESIANA   I-28
NICHELMANN, CHRISTOPH   III-303
NICHOLAS (Byron character)
    I-149
NICHOLAS of Bari, ST.   I-116
NICHOLAS III of FERRARA   I-154
NICHOLAS of Radom   I-109
NICHOLAS I, POPE (St.)   I-50,
    75,286
NICHOLAS II, POPE   I-66
NICHOLAS III, POPE   I-99
NICHOLAS IV, POPE   I-100
NICHOLAS V, POPE   I-161-162,239
NICHOLSON, RICHARD (see Nicolson)
NICOLAI, CHRISTOPH FRIEDRICH
    III-465

NICOLAI, JOHANN MICHAEL   II-43,
    423,424,457
NICOLAI, PHILIPP   I-32,73,111,
    112
NICOLETTI, FILIPPO   II-37,89,
    93,95
NICOLINI (Grimaldi, Nicola)
    II-443;   III-5,47,56,166,167,
    198,199,224,226,232,233,243,
    249,250,257,258,260,269,275,
    278,280,283,293,297,302,305,
    312,313,320,372,440,449
NICOLL   III-27,28
NICOLSON, RICHARD   II-1,8,71,238,
    288,289
NICOTERA, MARCELLO FOSCATARO DI
    I-508
NIEDT, FRIEDRICH   II-450;   III-
    157,210,228,244,307,310
NIELSEN, HANS   II-34,37,78,99,
    102,103,136,214,219
NIETRAWSKI   III-137
NIEUCOMBE, THOMAS   II-451
NIEUWENHOVE, MARTIN VAN   I-197
NIGER, FRANCISCUS   I-189
NIJEVELT, WILHELM VAN ZUYLEN VAN
    I-314
NIKANDRA   I-7
NIKE of Delos   I-10
NIKKO   II-56
NIKOMACHOS   I-25
NIPREDI (see Pedrini, Theodorio)
NITHART   I-85
NIVERS, GUILLAUME GABRIEL   II-
    293,319,413;   III-74,277
NIZANKOWSKI, ANDRZEJ   II-167,354
NOAH   I-72;   II-399
NOAILLES, DUC DE   III-479
NOBLE, J. CAMPBELL   III-97
NOÉ   I-335
NOEL, HENRY   I-524
NOLA, GIOVANE DOMENICO DA   I-
    318,410
NOORDT, family   II-187,293

See illustration on p. 315

TITUS OATES

OKER, JOHN II-132,191,296,379,
392,393
OLAF I-55
OLDENBERG III-234
OLDFIELD, THOMAS II-37
OLDMIXON, GEORGE III-184,475
OLDYS, VALENTINE II-357
OLEARIUS, JOHANNES II-134,518
OLIVIERI, GIUSEPPE II-37,178,
209,214
OLTHOFF, STATIUS II-156,190,
246,362
OPITIIS (Opicijs) BENEDICTUS DE
I-258,260,261,272,293
OPITZ, MARTIN II-12,240,291
OPMEERE, PETER I-519; II-319
ORCAGNA I-118,119
ORDELLAFI, GIORGIO I-148
ORDONEZ, PEDRO I-213,307,341
OREFICE III-236
O'REILLY, MYLES II-274
ORESTES I-20
ORGAS, (Father) ANNIBAL II-194,
241,243,246,247
ORIGEN I-24
ORIO, GIROLAMO I-427
ORISTAGNO, GIULIO II-77,213
ORLANDI, CAMILLO II-37,170,171
ORLANDI, LUIGI III-18
ORLANDI, SANTI II-78,113,141,
174,186
ORLANDINI, GIUSEPPE MARIA III-
26,230,290,303,312,336,346
ORLEANS, (Mlle.) D' II-317
ORLEANS, DUKE of (see Philip)
ORLEANS, GIRARD of I-117,121
ORLEY, BERNARD VAN (van) I-204,
230,266,321
ORNÉVAL, D' III-315,340
ORNITHOPARCUS (Ornitoparchus),
ANDREAS I-260,261,262,263,
295,298; II-101,122,123
OROLOGIO, ALLESSANDRO I-533,
536; II-19,37,80

ORSINI, (Cardinal) FLAVIO I-413
ORSINI, PAOLO GIORDANO I-374,
　393,446
ORSINI, VIRGINIO I-521
ORTIZ, DIEGO I-356,357,367,408
ORTO, MARBRIANO DE I-194-196,
　198,241,242,244,259,285
ORVIETO, UGOLINO D' I-130
OS, ALBERT VAN I-74
OS, PETRUS I-205
OSBORNE, (Sir) THOMAS III-262
OSIANDER, LUCAS I-296,486,488;
　II-86
OSIRIS I-5
OSSUNA I-364
OSTADE, ADRIAEN VAN II-48,130,
　522
OSTERMAYER, GEORG I-419
OSTERMAYER, HIERONYMUS I-326
OSWALD, JAMES III-477,480
OSWY, KING of Northumbria I-40
OTHMAYR, CASPAR I-258,335,356,
　433
OTT, JOHANN I-297,308,326,327
OTTAVIO II-282
OTTEY, SARAH III-99,137,342
OTTO I, HOLY ROMAN EMPEROR
　I-54,55,72,181
OTTO II, HOLY ROMAN EMPEROR
　I-57
OTTO III, HOLY ROMAN EMPEROR
　I-58
OTTO, GEORGIUS I-325, 345,397,
　421,436,457,472,497,500,521;
　II-90,138(?),181,188
OTTO, JOHANNES I-305
OTTO, STEPHAN II-37,262,306,
　324,325
OTTO, VALENTEN I-399
OTTO, VALERIUS II-37,106,136,
　138(?)
OTTOBI, FRA ANGELICO I-120
OTTOBONE, (Prince) ANTONIO
　III-87,187

OTTOBONI, (Cardinal) PIETRO
  I-223; II-51,413,485; III-
  37,45,47,56,58,65,68,74,123,
  151,154,170,182,184,203,210,
  211,213,216,224,226,229,231,
  239,251,285,397
OTWAY, THOMAS II-469,490,492,
  507,514; II-185
OULIBISCHEFF III-140
OUSELEY II-46
OUVRARD, (Canon) RENÉ II-393,
  409,413
OXENFORD, EARL of I-434

P

PA-ATEN-MHEB I-5
PABLOS, JUAN I-376
PACACEO, CARDINAL I-401
PACCHIEROTTO I-439
PACCHIONI(e), ANTONIO MARIA
  II-351; III-467
PACE, PIETRO II-19,75,141,152,
  153,178,200,207
PACELLI, ASPRILLIO I-424; II-
  32,72,80,113,116,139,159,204,
  212
PACHECO, FABIÁN GARCÍA III-381
PACHELBEL, CHARLES THEODORE
  III-46,467
PACHELBEL, JOHANN I-214; II-
  347,419,432,433,451,468,471,
  474,514; III-5,51,58,65,68,
  75,93,126,205,467
PACHELBEL, WILHELM HIERONYMOUS
  III-5,126,208,378
PACHER, MICHAEL I-155,193,209
PACHOMIUS I-26
PACHYMERES, GEORGE I-94,99,112
PACINI III-374
PACIOTTI, PIETRO PAOLO II-37,72

PANFILI, CARDINAL II-312; III-18

PANG-CHI, HAN I-188,363

PANNONE, (Baron) III-123

PANORINO, VINCENZO III-476

PAOLO, CIOVANNI (composer) II-441

PAOLO, GIOVANNI DI (painter) I-140,158,192

PAOLO, MESSER (organist) I-197,198

PAOLUCCI, GUISEPPE III-383

PAPA, CLEMENS NON (see Clemens, Jacobus)'

PAPIA, BERNADINUS MISINTA DE (see Misinta)

PAPIS III-275,469

PARABOSCO, GIROLAMO I-333,343,351,374,397

PARADISI, PIETRO DOMENICO III-215,241

PARDINE, (Signoe) III-275

PAREDES, SANCHO DE I-189,212

PAREJA, BARTOLOMÉ RAMOS DE I-134,139,158,173,182,185,192,202,203,286

PARIATI, PIETRO III-202,214,244,254,262,275,290,336,349,351,474

PARIO II-129

PARIS (Greek God) I-286

PARIS, ARCHBISHOP (see Ladron, Count)

PARIS, MATTHEW I-96,97

PARISINA I-149

PARKER, (Archbishop) MATTHEW I-372,381,411,412

PARLER, PETER (the younger) I-125

PARMA, DUKE of (see Farnese)

PARMA, HORATIO DA II-68,288

PARMA, NICOLA II-37,102,136

PARMIGIANINO (Mazzola, Francesco) I-239,298,314

PARNASSO, FELICE II-486
PARRAN II-318
PARRY II-41
PARSLEY, OSBERT I-253,479
PARSON, THEOPHILUS III-75
PARSONS, JOHN II-169,201,214
PARSONS, ROBERT I-341,392,417
PARTENIO, GIOVANNI DOMENICO
    II-424,435
PAS, CHARLES DE (Abbot of Saint-
    Armond) II-172,322
PASCAL II-64,390
PASCHAL I, POPE I-48
PASCHAL II, POPE I-69
PASCHE, WILLIAM I-202,222
PASI, ALESSANDRO (see Modenese)
PASINO, GHIZZOLA STEFFANO II-
    43,302,303,341
PASQUALATI, JOSEPH III-465
PASQUALI, FRANCESCO II-37,167
PASQUALIGO, BENEDETTO III-312,
    419
PASQUINI, BERNARDO II-279,280,
    358,397,433,461,465,478,484;
    III-24,49,194,205,240
PASSARINI, FRANCESCO II-438;
    III-107,117
PASSETTO, GIORDANO I-318
PASTA, GIOVANNI II-87,234,236,
    269,397
PASTERWITZ, GEORG III-425
PASZKIEWICA, ANDRZEJ II-43,424
PATAVINI, ANTONI I-342
PATER, JEAN BAPTISTE III-98
PATINIR, JOACHIM I-185,260,270,
    277
PATIÑO, CARLOS II-261,265,511
PATRICIO, ANDREA I-343
PATRICK, ST. I-30,33
PATRICK, NATHANIEL I-514;
    II-1,19
PATRIZZI, FRANCESCO I-287
PATTA, SERAFINO II-37,102,123,
    139,152,159,190

PATTEN, ELIZABETH II-104,111,
    468
PATTEN, JOHN II-104,106,111,
    206,214
PATTI, ANGELO II-152
PAUER, EMIL III-130
PAUL, BISHOP of Edessa I-39,41
PAUL I, POPE I-44
PAUL II, POPE I-176
PAUL III, POPE I-281,297,298,
    299,305,310,316,331,333,338
PAUL IV, POPE I-366,376,380
PAUL V, POPE II-97,124
PAUL, ST. I-21,29,32,38,77
PARRLATI, ANDREA III-269
PAULINA, (Mrs.) III-266
PAULIRINUS, PAULUS I-174
PAUMANN, CONRAD I-142,170,182
PAUSANIAS I-23
PAWLOWSKI, STANISLAS I-459
PAXTON, STEPHEN III-486
PAYEN I-337
PAYNTER I-408
PEACHAM, HENRY II-145,208,238
PEARCE, EDWARD II-37,156
PEARSON, ALICE III-488,493
PEARSON, WILLIAM III-124,125,
    126,128,130,137,154,157,364,
    488
PEASABLE, JACQUES (James)(see
    Paisible, James)
PEBLIS, DAVID I-288
PECCI, DESIDERIO II-38,103,178,
    226,234
PECCI, TOMMASO II-34,38,99,103
PECPROMA. :A O-329
PEDERSON, MOGENS II-29,30,80,
    97,116,120,136,181,196,214
PEDERZUOLI II-425
PEDRELL II-26
PEDRINI, THEODORIC II-427
PEDRO, FRAY I-277,283
PEELE, GEORGE I-376,449,477;
    II-6,26,34

PEERSON, AMY II-120,264

PEERSON, MARTIN I-431,444;
    II-85,120,123,147,154,159,
    194,196,204,230,253,264,265,
    331

PEETRINO, JACOPO (see Pietro,
    Jacob)

PEISISTRATUS I-10

PEKIEL, BARTOMIE(j) II-44,266,
    294,298,307,328,356,364,381,
    385,387,399,421,423,427

PELAGIUS I, POPE I-36

PELAGIUS II,POPE I-36

PELE, ROBERT LE (see Magdalain,
    Robinet de la)

PELESTINO I-504

PELAHM (Mr.) III-439,440

PELLEGRIN, ABBE II-394; III-
    153,192,252,280,282,455,463,
    465,470,471

PELLEGRINI I-27

PELLEGRINI, VALERIANO III-130,
    260

PELLEGRINI, VINCENZO I-522;
    II-38,85,141,178

PEMBROKE, EARL of II-15

PEÑALOSA, FRANCISCO DE I-180,
    209,262,263,278,284

PENDA, KING OF THE MERCIANS I-40

PENET I-257

PENN, JOHN III-421

PENNA, LORENZO II-148,361,423,
    425,439,446; III-49,71

PENNLLYN, WILLIAM II-154

PEPERARA, LAURA I-454,462,470,
    473

PEPIL THE SHORT I-43,44,45

PEPUSCH, JOHN CHRISTOPHER II-
    413; III-86,155,212,218,219,
    243,260,267,278,289,293,299,
    304,313,327,357,362,364,388,
    408,409,410,420,431,434,438,
    445

PEPYS, SAMUEL I-236; II-263,
    355,369,373,374,376,379,382,
    388,391,392,396,401,407,411,
    412,417; III-123,181,186
PERANDA, MARCO GIUSEPPE II-435,
    439,445
PERCY, THOMAS III-422
PEREGRINE, CHARLES III-21
PEREZ, DAVID III-251,313,422,
    459
PÉREZ, JUAN GINÉS I-336; II-80,
    142
PEREZ, PIETRO I-235
PERFETTI III-379
PERGOLESI, family III-242
PERGOLESI, ANTONIO III-361
PERGOLESI, BARTOLOMEO III-223
PERGOLESI, CRUCIANO DRAGHI II-
    393
PERGOLESI, DONNA ANNA III-394
PERGOLESI, FRANCESCO ANDREA
    II-393; III-451
PERGOLESI, GIOVANNI BATTISTA
    II-274,393,502,570; III-
    200,206,223,239,249,386,408,
    422,427,434,440,442,445,446,
    447,453,455,459,460,463,467,
    470,471,475,476,477,479,481,
    482,483,484,486,488,489,491
PERGOLESI, ROSA III-206
PERI, JACOPO I-33r,345,385,470,
    533,534,537; II-7,12,15,19,20,
    56,57,60,62,68,69,72,90,106,
    111,112,113,115,116,119,122,
    123,125,136,139,140,167,171,
    173,178,181,186,190,198,212,
    227,240,241,263,301
PERICLES I-12,13,14
PERLUIGI, GIOVANNI (see
    Palestrina, Giovanni)
PEROTIN I-78,80,81,82,85,89
PEROTTO, NICCOLO I-189,198
PEROZ I I-33
PERPOINT, SAMUEL III-414,418

PERRAULT, CHARLES II-153,417;
  III-34,186
PERRIN, (Abbé) PIERRE II-193,
  224,246,335,370,371,372,422,
  423,425,426,427,432,435,449,
  455,470
PERRINE II-43,483,490,491
PERRONI, ANNA (Ambrevil Anna)
  III-28,52,252,268,269,278,
  338,355,386,406
PERRONI, GIOVANNI III-28,335,
  340,348,378,420,431
PERRY, (Rev. WILLIAM II-497
PERS, DIRK PIETERSZON II-167
PERSAPEGI, OVIDIO III-5
PERSEUS I-10
PERSONS, FATHER I-531
PERTI, GIACOMO ANTONIO II-382,
  433,483,492,494,498,512,514;
  III-6,9,17,23,25,31,42,47,49,
  58,59,66,76,87,96,102,104,106,
  114,120,126,229,244,245,300,
  308,491
PERTI, LORENZO II-433
PERUGIA, MATTEO DA I-130
PERUGIA, NICOLÒ DA I-123
PERUGINO (Pietro Vannucci) I-
  160,182,191,202,208,213,242,
  248,274
PERUZZI I-191,250,300,302
PERWICH, SUSANNA II-383
PESARO, family I-267,282
PESARO, DOMENICO DI I-511
PESARO, FRANCESCO DA I-117,419
PESCETTI, GIOVANNI BATTISTA
  II-196,378,408,409,419,420,459
PESCIOLINI, BIAGIO II-19,38
PESENTI, MARTINO II-65,322,429
PESENTI, MICHELE I-212
PESORI, STEFANO II-326
PESSTAIN, CHAILLOU DE I-112
PESTEL, T. II-370
PETER, ST. I-21,29,32,71,111,
  150,155,160,188,245

PETER OF CHELČIC   I-217

PETER, COUNT of Savoy   I-95,126

PETER I, CZAR OF RUSSIA (the
   great)   II-441,507,508

PETER II,CZAR OF RUSSIA   III-291

PETER, DEACON   I-71

PETER THE GREAT, KING of Cyprus
   I-122

PETER, ANNA DOROTHEA   II-479

PETERHOUSE   I-316

(?)PETERS, FRANCES   II-500

PETITPAS, (Mlle.)   III-351

PETRARCH   I-113,117,119,165,211,
   261,263,268,296,321,344,358,
   375,379,393,427,429,446,464,
   481,493,501,513

PETRE, LORD of Writtle   I-445;
   II-94

PETRE, (SIR) WILLIAM   I-429

PETREIUS, JOHANN   I-281,303,308,
   309,310,313,318,321,327,341

PETRI, THEODORICUS   I-468

PETROBELLI, FRANCESCO   II-43,
   309,343

PETRONILLA   I-188

PETRUCCI, OCTAVIANO DEI   I-177,
   209,234,235,236,237,238,239,
   240,241,242,243,244,246,247,
   248,249,251,253,255,256,257,
   258,259,260,261,265,266,268,
   272,273,274,307,313,325

PETRUS   I-45

PETTY, (SIR) W.   II-332

PETY   III-7

PETZ, JOHANN CHRISTOPH   II-396,
   425,465;   III-87,93,104,170,
   187,200,204,218,295,297

PETZOLD, JOHANN CHRISTOPH   II-
   288,386,424,425,438,457,576;
   III-7,15,80

PEUERL, PAUL   II-38,139,152,196,
   227,229

PEUTINGER, CONRAD   I-177,204,
   267,271,334

PEVERNAGE, ANDRIES (Bevernage)
   I-323,392,418,434,451,472,
   476,509,515,518; II-249
PEYRO, JOSÉ II-38,67,248,249
PFEILSCHMIDT II-114
PFLEGER II-308
PHAER I-375
PHALÈSE (publishers) I-329,333,
   354,357,361,374,393,415,422,
   427,430,453,471,472,482,484,
   512,521,526,529,535; II-8,11,
   16,18,22,72,100,102,143,146,
   152,172,204,227,242,248,249,
   255,266,307,333,410; III-49
PHALÈSE (wife of Pierre, II)
   II-187
PHALÈSE, ANNE II-81,143
PHALÈSE, BARBARA II-127
PHALÈSE, CORNEILLE (Cornelis)
   II-81,113,143
PHALÈSE, MADELEINE II-247,343,
   444
PHALÈSE, MARIE II-113,163,247,
   444
PHALÈSE, PIERRE (I) I-251,434
PHALÈSE, PIERRE (II) II-102,
   127,187,246,247,331,432
PHALÈSE, PIERRE (III) II-388,
   420,432,452
PHALÈSE, ROBERT II-143
PHEIDIAS I-12
PHEREKRATES I-14
PHIDIAS I-11,13,14
PHILADELPHUS, PTOLEMY I-18
PHILIBERT II-427
PHILIDOR, family II-374,459,
   479; III-48
PHILIDOR, ALEXANDRE II-380,485
PHILIDOR, ANDRÉ II-320,363,371,
   495,510,523; III-18,20,31,
   33,36,151,176,201,222,304,425
PHILIDOR, ANNE II-483,484,495;
   III-119,120,170,176,191,192,
   380,403,439

PALESTRINA PLAYING FOR POPE MARCELLUS II   *333*

PHILIDOR, FRANÇOIS   III-35,88,
    122,226,297,299,304,314,425
PHILIDOR, FRANÇOIS ANDRÉ   III-
    455
PHILIDOR, JACQUES (I) ("Le
    Cadet")   II-363,380,423,427,
    495,512;   III-12,47,88,222,
    225,226,384,403,439
PHILIDOR, JACQUES (II)   III-12,
    36,226,304,384
PHILIDOR, JEAN   II-193,199,320,
    371,423,479;   II-425
PHILIDOR, MICHAEL   II-193,341,
    371,374,509;   II-12
PHILIDOR, MICHEL III   III-364
PHILIDOR, NICOLAS   III-122
PHILIDOR, PIERRE   II-495; III-
    114,260,297,309,439
PHILIP, (the bold) DUKE of
    Burgundy   I-122,126,127,141
PHILIP, (the good) DUKE of
    Burgundy   I-130,141,146,149,
    152,155,158,161,177,178,191,
    277
PHILIP, DUKE of Orleans (Regent
    of France)   II-449;   III-198,
    226,231,249,291
PHILIP, DUKE of Rouvre   I-121
PHILIP of Luxemburg   I-151
PHILIP, KING (Indian leaver)
    II-456
PHILIP I, KING of France
    (Capetian)   I-66
PHILIP II, (Philip Augustus)
    KING of France (Capetian)
    I-78,79
PHILIP III, (The Bold) KING of
    France (Capetian)   I-94,98
PHILIP OV (The Fiar) KING of
    France (Capetian)   I-98,100
PHILIP V (The Tall) KING of
    France (Capetian)   I-101,113
PHILIP VI, KING of France
    (Valois)   I-101,115

PHILIP II, KING of Macedonia
   I-16
PHILIP I, (The handsome), KING
   of Spain   I-192,205,208,212,
   240,242,244,295
PHILIP II, KING of Spain   I-250,
   338,340,358,359,361,362,362,
   368,369,373,392,401,402,411,
   415,419,420,426,455,458,472,
   476,504,524,528; II-22,27,77
PHILIP III, KING of Spain   II-
   22,26,92,213,278
PHILIP OV, KING of Spain   II-73,
   409,416,478
PHILIP V, KING of Spain (Bour-
   bon)   III-154,160,177,181
PHILIP JULIUS, DUKE of Wolgast
PHILIP LUDWIG II, COUNT of
   Hanau-Münzenberg   I-534
PHILIPON   I-239
PHILIPP, GERARD   II-143
PHILIPP, PRINCE of Hessen-
   Darmstadt   III-219,238,282,
   316,323
PHILIPP WILHELM, Elector of
   Neuberg on Danube   II-481,482
PHILIPPE (Chancellor of Paris)
   I-94
PHILIPS, KATHERINE   II-393
PHILIPS, PETER   I-290,383,457,
   460,468,511,522,526,528,529,
   530,531,536; II-5,8,11,22,25,
   27,32,40,72,77,79,83,90,95,96
   109,123,125,127,132,134,136,
   139,143,146,152,154,166,172,
   200,202,204,206,209,211,216,
   219,227,238,242,245,246,249,
   251,252,258,264,265,266,322,
   329,368; III-138
PHILLIPE, PIERRE   III-427
PHILLIPS, ARTHUR   II-92,209,284,
   289,292,299,329; III-89
PHILLIPS, CHARLES (Claudius)
   III-453

PHILLIPS, EDWARD III-211,431,470

PHILO OF ALEXANDRIA I-21

PHILOLAUS I-9

PHINOT, DOMINIQUE I-269,337

PHLY, DU III-312

PHOEBUS, GASTON I-141

PHRYNIS I-15

PIACENZA, DOMENICO of I-162

PIAZZETTA, GIAMBATTISTA II-471,
   III-382

PICANDER III-159,363,371,379,
   384,411,418,422,443,445,447,
   449,460,473,479

PICCHI, GIOVANNI II-38,194,196

PICCINNI (Piccini) NICCOLO
   III-368,388,399,402,422,434,
   459

PICCIOLI, G. MARIA II-479,491

PICCIONI, GIOVANNI II-38,75,169

PICINNI (see Piccinni)

PICITONO, ANGELO DA I-335

PICKERING, JANE II-170,172,173

PICKHAVER II-396

PICO, RANUCCIO II-303

PICQUIGNY, DUKE of III-421

PIERAZZO D'ASSISSI, FRA (see
   Assissi d')

PIERCE, DR. II-329

PIERLUIGI, GIOVANNI (see
   Belardino)

PIERIE (see Bréhy, Hercule)

"PIERRE, MAITRE" I-385

PIERS, (Sir) HENRY II-506

PIETER (see Sweelinck)

PIETEREZ, ADRIAN I-143,171

PIETERS, JACOPO (see Pietro,
   Jacob)

PIETERSZON, DIRK II-356

PIETKIN, LAMBERT II-252

PIETRO, JACOB I-488

PIETRO, SANI DI I-141,156,159,
   160,172,188,191

PIETROPAULO DA SAN CHIRICO
   I-298

PIPELAKE, MATTHAEUS   I-209
PIPPARD, LUKE   III-238
PIPPIN (Pepin, the short, KING
   of France   I-44
PIPPO, SIGR. (see Amadei)
PIRANESI, GIAMBATTISTA   III-332
PIRCKHEIMER   I-245
PIRON   III-320,351,375,388,481
PISADOR, DIEGO   I-249,354,371
PISAN   I-281
PISANELLO ANTONIO   I-128,142,148,
   149,152,153,156,157,158,172
PISANO, ANDREA   I-114,115,116,
   117
PISANO, BERNARDO   I-268
PISANO, GIOVANNI   I-96,101
PISANO, NICOLA   I-95,96
PISANUS, F. BARTHOLOMAEUS   I-140
PISARI, PASQUALE   III-137,373
PISENDEL, GEORG JOHANN   III-20,
   176,234,256,260,278,287,297,
   301,313,429,442
PISING, WILLIAM (see Pysing)
PISTOCCHI, FRANCESCO ANTONIO
   MAMILIANO   II-370,384,415,
   425,428,451,456,484,507;
   III-26,59,109,114,119,126,
   152,168,192,218,245,287,307,
   385
PISTOIA, GIUSTINI DI   III-458
PITONI, GIUSEPPE OTTAVIO   II-92,
   156,363,388,424,444,463,468;
   III-14,41,226,317,320
PIUS I, POPE   I-23
PIUS II, POPE   I-173
PIUS III, POPE   I-239
PIUS IV, POPE   I-378,381,394,
   400,401
PIUS V, POPE   I-400,408,411,
   428,528
PIX, MARY   III-104
PIZAN, CHRISTINE DE   I-152
PIZARRO, DIEGO   II-43
PIZZOLA, NICCOLO   I-147,162,171

ANDREA PALLADIO　　*341*

THE PALLAVICINI FAMILY MADE CITIZENS OF ANTWERP   *347*

POURBUS, FRANS II-185,212
POUSSIN, GASPARD II-148
POUSSIN, NICOLAS I-536; II-64,
    212,222,256,287,295,304,315,
    326,330,339,379,405
POUVOYEUR, N. III-481
POWELL, GEORGE III-64,72,106,
    114
POWELL, MARY II-304
POWER I-130
POYNET, JOHN I-356
PRAETORIUS, BARTHOLOMAEUS II-
    172
PRAETORIUS, FRIEDRICH EMANUEL
    II-214; III-92
PRAETORIUS, GODESCALCUS (Schulz)
    I-284,408,431
PRAETORIUS, HIERONYMUS I-227,
    379,408; II-33,35,66,77,90,
    97,108,109,146,161,172,246
PRAETORIUS, JACOB II-90,281,340
PRAETORIUS, MICHAEL (Schulz)
    I-121,425; II-97,111,129,139,
    159,166,181,182,184,185,188,
    190,191,194,196,197,200
PRAISSAC, DE II-290,291
PRANDTAUER, JAKOB II-379; III-
    171,390
PRATICHISTA, F. II-441
PRATO, GIOVANNI DA I-127
PRATT, ROGER II-198; III-10
PRAXITELES I-15,16
PREDIERI, LÚC ANTONIO II-459;
    III-29,492
PRELLEUR III-445,446
PREMAZONE, ELISABETTA III-270
PRÉS, JOSQUIN DES I-133,160,163,
    167,173,180,181,183,185,188,
    189,190,193,194,195,197,199,
    200,204,205,206,209,210,212,
    213,214,215,216,222,224,226,
    234,235,236,237,238,239,240,
    241,245,248,252,256,257,258,
    259,260,261,262,266,267,270,

350

HENRY PURCELL   *351*

285,291,305,306,308,313,326,
330,335,336,345,354,357,381,
382,390,392,393,398,410,414,
430,519; II-90,139
PRESTON OF YORK II-489
PRESTON, ELEANOR I-396
PRESTON, THOMAS (II) II-387;
   III-52,427
PREUNEN, CORNELIS II-27
PFÈVOST III-287
PRÈVOST, ABBÉ III-472
PRICE, GERVASE II-374; III-21
PRICE, JOHN (I) II-93,132,225,
   247,260,268,280,297
PRICE, JOHN (II) II-297,343
PRIEST, JOSIAH II-475,473,489;
   III-37,38
PRIMATICCIO, FRANCESCO I-240,
   317,423
PRIMAVERA I0403,407,410,419,434,
   436,480
PRIMROSE II-43,318
PRIN, JEAN BAPTISTE II-336
PRINTZ, WOLFGANG KASPAR (von
   Waldthurn) II-297,403,489;
   III-49,104,303
PRIOLI, GIOVANNI (see Priuli)
PRIORIS, JOHANNES I-194,199,
   246,254,293
PRITCHARD, (Sir) WILLIAM II-502
PRIULI, family I-480
PRIULI, GIOVANNI II-91,188,211,
   247
PROCLUS I-31,33
PRODOSCIMUS (see Beldemandis)
PROTE (Profius), AMBROSIUS II-
   247,265,299,301,318,329,364,
   382
PROMNITZ, PRINCE III-192,227
PROSKE, (Dr.) KARL I-223,224
"PROTICO" (see Pasquini)
PROVENZALE, FRANCESCO II-237,
   335,350,395,434,448,476,483;
   III-5,17,191

PYTHAGORAS *355*

370,386,397,411,412,415,422,
423,426,428,429,432,436,438,
442,443,445,449,450,456,458,
463,464,466,468,470,472,473,
476,477,478,479,482,483,484,
485,486,487,488,489,491,492,
493,494,495,496,497,499,500,
501,502,504,506,507,508,509,
510,511,512,513,514,515,516,
517,518,519,520,521,522; III-
2,3,4,6,7,8,10,11,12,13,14,15,
16,17,18,19,20; III-22,23,24,
27,28,29,30,21,33,35,36,38,39,
41,43,44,45,47,49,51,53,54,55,
57,58,59,61,62,63,64,65,66,67,
68,70,71,72,73,74,75,76,77,78,
79,80,81,82,83,84,85,87,88,89,
90,91,92,93,94,95,96,97,103,
104,105,106,108,110,112,117,
118,119,121,122,124,128,134,
141,152,153,157,177,181,204,
211,223,264,363,491

PURCELL, HENRY, JR. III-18,20

PURCELL, JOHN BAPTISTA II-501,
502,504

PURCELL, JOSEPH II-392

PURCELL, KATHERINE II-386;
III-54,122

PURCELL, MARY PETERS III-72

PURCELL, MATTHEW II-495; III-
13

PURCELL, THOMAS II-369,376,384,
386,387,398,406,436,438,441,
445,451,454,472,478,494,495,
501,513; III-12

PUSCHMANN, ADAM ZACHARIAS I-293,
434,459; II-56,57

PUTTA, BISHOP I-41

PUTTEN, ERICH VAN DER II-33,77

PYAMOR, JOHN I-146

PYGOTT, RICHARD I-260,290m358

PYNSON I-224

PYPER, JOHN II-161

PYRA, JACOB IMMANUEL III-291

PYRAMUS   I-275
PYSING, WILLIAM   II-44,274
PYTHAGORAS   I-9,10,17,21   *See illustration on p. 355*

Q

QAKISA, IYAS IKN-(see Iyas)
QUADRIO, FRANCESCO SAVERIO   I-344; III-97,98
QUADRIS, JOHANNES DE   I-244
QUAGLIATI, PAOLO   I-384; II-19, 33,69,72,100,102,103,109,116, 118,139,146,178,196,204,206, 216,242,251
QUANTZ, JOHANN, JOACHIM   III-108,149,313,323,362,364,375, 386,387,390,397,406
QUARLES   III-35,117
QUERCIA, JACOPO DELLA   I-124, 149,156
QUESNEL, FRANÇOIS   I-328,443; II-173
QUESTENBECK, (Count) JAN   III-242
QUICKELBERG, SAMUEL VAN   I-285, 401
QUINAULT, JEAN BAPTISTE MAURICE   II-368
QUINAULT, PHILIPPE   II-271,274, 334,400,439,441,446,448,452, 492,517; III-15,28
QUINOÑES, CRISTOBAL DE   II-120
QUINTIANI   II-20
QUINTILIANUS, ARISTIDES   I-24
QUIRCE DE PEDRET, ST.   I-71
QUIRICO, ST.   I-70
QUITSCHREIBER, GEORG   I-417; II-116,284
QULI, SHÁH   II-283,285
QUSANQUINE   III-368,447
QUTHE, PIERRE   I-391

R

RA, AMON   I-3,5

RABAN, EDWARD   II-194,216,227,
228,266,328,367

RABELAIS   I-354,483

RACINE, JEAN   II-291,400; III-
39,41,43,58,112,127

RACOT DE GRANDVAL, NICOLAS (see
Grandval)

RADESCA, ENRICO   II-15,94,97,109,
163,178,224

RADINO, GIOVANNI MARIA   I-526;
II-25

RAFTOR, CATHERINE   (see Clive,
Catherine)

RAHMAN, 'ABD AL-   (see Jalíl)

RAGUENET, (Abbé) FRANÇOIS   III-
114,176,177,191,192,194,201

RAHOTEP   I-2

RAICK, DIEUDONNÉ DE   III-174,
338,372

RAINALDUS, MAGISTER   I-181

RAISON, ANDRÉ   II-331; III-24,
29,30,130,326

RÁKOCZY, (Prince) FRANZ LEOPOLD
II-465; III-486

RALEIGH, (Sir) WALTER   I-356,
454,477,501,513; II-185

RALPH, JAMES   III-121,431,433

RAMANDON, LEWIS   III-197

RAMBACHIUS   I-61

RAMEAU, CLAUDE (I)   III-283,285,
287

RAMEAU, CLAUDE (II)   III-362,393

RAMEAU, JEAN   II-252; III-39,47,
78(?),277

RAMEAU, JEAN-FRANCOIS   III-295

RAMEAU, JEAN-PHILIPPE   II-510; *See illustration on p. 369*
III-39,47,78(?),138,139,149,
158,161,168,171,174,176,177,
206,208,210,212,214,216,218,

RASI, FRANCESCO   II-38,116,146
RASTENBERG, GERHARD HOFFMANN OF
    (see Hoffmann, Gerhard)
RATDOLT   I-203
RATHGEBER   III-470
RATISPONAE   I-417
RATOERT   I-51
RATTI, LORENZO   II-250
RATTI, P. BARTOLOMEO   II-274
RATZEBERGER   I-342
RAUCH   III-324
RAUGEL   I-475
RAUPACH, CHRISTOPH   III-12,388,
    405
RAUPACH, HERMANN FREIDRICH   III-
    405
RAVAL, SABASTIAN   I-384,530; II-
    58
RAVENSCROFT, JOHN   III-96,101,
    162
RAVENSCROFT, THOMAS   I-469,524;
    II-121,123,125,139,156,157,
    159,201,202,204,205,245,256,
    265,439,471; III-232
RAVERI   II-116
RAWLINGS, THOMAS   III-188
RAYMAN, JACOB   II-199
RAYNALDINO   I-181,187,198,203
RAYNALUS DE ODENA   (see Odena)
RAZZI, SERAFINO   I-394; II-123
READE, CHARLES   I-349
READING, JOHN (II)   II-453; III-
    64
READING, JOHN (III)   II-467; III-
    328
REALES, DESCALZAS   I-476
REALI, GIOVANNI   III-234,236
REASON, JOHN   I-461; II-30
RÉBEL, ANNE-RENÉE   II-388,519
RÉBEL, FRANÇOIS   III-166,397
RÉBEL, JEAN-FÉRY   II-383,388;
    III-97,98,137,166,193,389,
    397,477
REBELLO, JOÃO SOARES   II-119,219

RECIBERGA, QUEEN of Spain I-40

REDFORD, JOHN I-195,214,290,306,
    325,329

REDI, TOMMASO II-458; III-467

REENE, RALPH II-125

REGGIO, L'HOSTE DA I-359

REGGIO, PIETRO II-449,450,470,
    486,491; III-2,65

REGHIUS, G.B. II-298

REGINO, of Prüm I-52,54

REGIS, JOHANNES I-153,173,176,
    183,191

REGNARD III-80

REGNART, FRANÇOIS I-441

REGNART, JACOB I-315,325,367,
    423,436,446,449,454,472,510;
    II-28,65

REICHBRODT, CHRISTIAN II-344

REICHE, JOHANN GOTTFRIED II-411;
    III-429

REID, BISHOP I-326

REID, JOHN III-335

REINA, SISTO II-44

REINAGLE, JOSEPH III-137

REINER, AMBROSIUS II-86

REINER, JACOB II-99

REINHARD, ANDREAS II-38

REINHARD, JOHANN GEORG II-471

REINHARDT, (Dr.) E I-152

REINKEN, JOHANN (Jan) ADAM II-
    212,354,453,472,475; III-24,
    345

REISSIGER III-368

REKHMERE I-4

REMBRANDT (Harmensz van Rijn)
    II-102,211,262,271,304,339,
    354,358,359,362,365,373,379,
    406,421,425

RENATA, PRINCESS of Lorraine
    I-413

RÉNÉ, KING (Provence) I-182

RENÉE (daughter of Louis XII)
    I-249,284

RENÉE, of Lorainne I-413,418

RENER, ADAM   I-195,209,246,267,
    319,327
RENI, GUIDO   II-304
RESINARIUS, BALTHASAR   I-251,324
RESSONS, JEAN LEFEVRE DE   I-124
REUENTHAL, NEIDART VON   I-79,92,
    94
REUSNER, ESAIAS (I)   II-275
REUSNER, ESAJAS (Esaias II)   II-
    275,356,415,480
REUSS, COUNT OF   II-477
REUSS, HEINRICH POSTHUMUS VON
    I-470
REUTLINGEN, HUGO SPECHTSHART
    VON   I-100,121
REUTTER, GEORG (von)   II-360
REUTTER, JOHANN ADAM KARL GEORGE
    III-225,446,492
REY, JEAN-BAPTISTE II   III-477
REYMERSWAEL, MARINUS VAN   I-207,
    411
REYNART, JAC   (see Regnart, Ja-
    cob)
REYNEAU, GACIAN   I-142,145,151
REYNOLDS, (Sir) JOSHUA   III-148,
    359
REYSER, JÖRG   I-191
RHAMES, AARON   III-424
RHAW, GEORG   I-197,266,274,277,
    278,281,284,287,293,305,306,
    309,318,319,320,321,324,326,
    327,330,331,336
RIANS, MADAME DE   II-473
RIBAYAZ, LUCAS RUIZ DE   II-44,
    440
RIBERA (architect)   II-517
RIBERA, ANTONIO DE   I-257
RIBERA, BERNARDINO DE   I-393
RIBERA, JOSÉ DE (Lo Spagnoletto)
    I-522; II-292,346
RICCATI, GIORDANO   I-378
RICCATI, (Count) GIORDANO   III-
    231
RICCI, A.   II-171

RICCI, ANTONIO III-76
RICCI, MARCO III-230
RICCI, PASQUALE III-473
RICCI, SEBASTIANO II-373; III-
   482
RICCIARDI II-401
RICCIO(?) II-282
RICCIO, GIOVANNI BATTISTA I-508;
   II-87,196
RICCIO, TEODORO I-499
RICCIOTTI, CARLO II-496
RICCOBONI, LUIGI III-255,308
RICH, BARNABY II-184
RICH, JOHN III-216,306,402,452,
   455
RICH, LADY I-458
RICHAFORT, JEAN I-190,222,246,
   249,291,311,316,322,336
RICHARD (artist) II-199
RICHARD I, (Cover de Lion), KING
   of England I-72,78,80,81,82,
   90
RICHARD II KING of England (Plau-
   tageuet) I-122,125,128,130;
   II-499
RICHARD III, KING of England
   (York) I-170,193
RICHARD, LEWIS II-38
RICHARDSON, FERDINAND I-439
RICHARDSON, SAMUEL III-42,448,
   472
RICHARDSON, VAUGHAN III-255,416
RICHARDSON, WILLIAM III-461
RICHARDUS, ANTONIUS (see Divi-
   tis)
RICHE DE LA POUPLINIÈRE, LE (see
   Pouplenière)
RICHE, ANTOINE LE (see Divitis)
RICHÉE, PHILIPP FRANZ LE SAGE
   DE III-94,97,128
RICHELIEU, CARDINAL I-483,501;
   II-77,274,304,309
RICHOMME II-218
RICHTER, CHRISTOPH II-477

RIVINUS, (Professor) FLORENS
    III-473
RIYAH, BILAL IKN-   (see Bilal)
RIZZIO   I-385,400
ROBART   III-126
ROBARTT, of Crewkerne   I-351
ROBBIA, LUCA DELLA   I-108,130,
    153,192
ROBERDAY, FRANÇOIS   II-199,378;
    II1-52
ROBERT II (Comte d'Artois)   I-
    99
ROBERT (Dauphin of Auvergne)
    I-79,93
ROBERT, DUKE of Bar I-142
ROBERT, HUBERT   III-472
ROBERT I, KING of France (Carol-
    ingiau)   I-50,54,59
ROBERT II (The Pious) KING of
    France   I-57,59,276
ROBERTI (librettist)   III-194,
    219
ROBERTI, ERCOLE DE   I-172,179,
    190,191,208
ROBERTO   I-311
ROBERTS, HENRY   III-137
ROBINSON, ANASTASIA   III-99,161,
    284,328,364
ROBINSON, ELIZABETH   III-161
ROBINSON (Robinso), JOHN   II-503;
    III-393
ROBINSON (Robinso), RICHARD   II-
    494
ROBINSON, THOMAS   II-38,83,121,123
ROBLECTUM, J.B.   II-129
ROBLEDO, MELCHOR   I-415,418,490
ROBLES, MARIA LORENA DE   III-414
ROBLETTI, G.B.   II-184,190,220,
    226,233,238,243,262
ROBSARD DES FONTAINES   (see Bros-
    sard)
ROBUSTI, JACOPO   (see Tintoretto)
ROCHE-GUILHEN, MADAME DE LA   II-
    466,470

ROCHEFOUCAULD, LA II-405
ROCHESTER, EARL OF II-472
RODE III-256
RODERICK II-46
RODIER III-14
RODIO, ROCCO II-123
ROGER, of Amsterdam III-169,194,
   242
ROGER, ESTIENNE III-14,94,130,
   155,162,250,296,297,298,301,
   329,345,373
ROGERS, BENJAMIN II-155,289,310,
   349,374; III-115
ROGERS, ELIZABETH II-359,362
ROGERS, H. II-510
ROGERS, JOHN II-395
ROGIER(?) III-274
ROGIER, PHILIPPE I-391,429,504;
   II-9,23,120
ROGIER, PIERRE I-72
ROGNIONO, RICHARDO I-527
ROGNONI, R. II-196
ROGONE-TAEGIO, FRANCESCO II-131,
   138
ROGONE-TAEGIO, GIOVANNI DOMEN-
   ICO II-97,221
ROIERI, CLAUDIO (I) III-266
ROLIN, (chancellor) I-154
ROLIN, (Cardinal) JEAN I-190
ROLLE, JOHANN HEINRICH III-312,
   455
ROLLE, RICHARD I-103,118
ROLLI, PAOLO A. III-324,335,
   336,383,394
ROMAIN, JACQUES H. LE (see
   Hotteterre, Jacques)
ROMAINE, WILLIAM III-281
ROMAN, JOHAN HELMICH III-80,
   278,327,418
ROMANO (see also Capece)
ROMANO (see also Viola, Della)
ROMANO, ANTONIO I-144
ROMANO, BATTISTA I-420
ROMANO, GIULIO (see Caccini,G.)

ROMANO, REMIGIO II-222

ROMANUS I-45

ROMANUS, POPE I-52

ROMANOV, (Czar) MICHAEL II-12,
235

ROMERO, MATEO I-487,534; II-
23,120,265,319

ROMNEY, GEORGE III-482

RONCAGLIA III-48

ROND(E), JEAN LE (see Alembert,
d')

RONDELET, MARGUERITE III-287

RONER, A. III-340

RONG, WILHELM FERDINAND III-333

RONSARD, CHARLES DE I-336

RONSARD, PIERRE DE I-190,272,
292,350,381,404,418,430,441,
445,451,461,503; II-220,277

RONTANI, RAFFAELLO II-131,169,
208

ROOME, VAN I-230

ROOSE, JOHN I-172

RORE, CIPRIANO DE I-226,244,
261,262,284,298,314,321,322,
326,327,331,334,336,339,344,
346,361,365,366,370,372,374,
376,383,386,392,395,398,400,
401,402,405,407,415,422,432,
433,449,450,492; II-5,23,104,
109

ROSA, SALVATORE II-296,332,344,
383,401,418,421

ROSATI, F. III-170

ROSE, JOHN II-26,265,413

ROSEINGRAVE, DANIEL II-336,485,
507; III-46,69,99,116,117

ROSEINGRAVE, RALPH III-99,316,
387

ROSEINGRAVE, THOMAS III-46,243,
311,328,375,399

ROSELLI I-311

ROSENBERGER (organ-builder) I-
204

ROSENBLUT, HANS I-141

JEAN-PHILIPPE RAMEAU   *369*

ROSENKRON, NIKOL   II-482

ROSENMÜLLER, JOHANN   II-187,192,
    193,229,293,302,315,325,341,
    355,415,429,444,518; III-6

ROSER, VALENTIN   III-137

ROSETTER, J.A.   III-278

ROSIDOR   III-127

ROSIERS, CHARLES   III-32,58,126

ROSINI, FRANCESCO   II-15

ROSPIGLIOSI, GUILIO   II-288,303,
    319,348,349,353,359

ROSS (viol maker)   I-231

ROSSELLI, FRANCESCO   I-365

ROSSELLINO, ANTONIO   I-151,188

ROSSETER, PHILIP   I-443; II-34,
    69,70,72,123,125,214

ROSSETTI, MARGARITA   III-403

ROSSETTI, STEFANO   I-381,408,411

ROSSI (librettist)   III-475,476

ROSSI, (Abbate) LORENZO DE   III-
    326

ROSSI, BERNARDO DE   I-242

ROSSI, FRANCESCO   II-44,116

ROSSI, GIACOMO   III-249,258

ROSSI, GIOVANNI BATTISTA   II-38

ROSSI, GIUSEPPE (I)   III-323

ROSSI, GIUSEPPE (II)   III-130

ROSSI, LUIGI   I-514; II-14,299,
    303,304,319,320,322,348,386,
    474,475,476

ROSSI, MICHEL ANGELO   II-65,215,
    229,266,282,286

ROSSI, PIETRO   III-333

ROSSI, ROCCO MARIA   III-210

ROSSI, SALOMONE (Ebreo)   I-424,
    490; II-60,77,109,115,117,211,
    216,217,242

ROSSIGNOL(?)   I-466

ROSSINI, GIUSEPPE   III-128

ROSSO, GIOVANNI BATTISTA   I-206,
    314

ROSSO, HANNIBAL   I-342,364,366,
    448; II-5

ROST, SECRETARY   I-354

ROSTH, JOHANN KASPAR NIKOLAUS
II-38
ROSTHIUS, NIKOLAUS II-33
ROSZKOWICZ, PAWEL II-38
ROTROU II-329
ROTTA I-333
ROTTENBURGH, ANNE CAROLINE III-426
ROUSSEAU, JEAN II-44; III-24, 25,58
ROUSSEAU, JEAN-JACQUES III-139, 258,401,426,433,473,493
ROUSSEL (publisher) III-193
ROUSSEL, FRANÇOIS I-338
ROUSSEL, LOUISE III-429
ROUTROV II-270
ROUX, GASPARD LE II-375,380; III-10,50,65,93,165,169,220
ROVELLI, GIOVANNI BATTISTA III-436
ROVERE, FEDERICO FELTRIO DELLA II-200
ROVERE, GIULIANO DELLA II-75
ROVERO, (Cardinal) GIULIO FELTRIO DELLA I-415,418,448
ROVETTA, GIOVANNI II-220,249, 290,418,444
ROVIGO, FRANCESCO I-338,494, 522; II-14
ROW (Minister of Carnock) II-302
ROWALLAN II-200,256
ROWE(?) III-156,185
ROWE, WALTER (I) II-155,232,432
ROWE, WALTER (II) II-432
ROWLEY II-96
ROU(?) I-481,514,532
ROY, ADRIAN LE (see LeRoy and LeRoy and Ballard)
ROY, PIERRE-CHARLES III-399
ROYER, JOSEPH III-161,375,388, 435
ROZMITAL, LEO VON I-177
ROZYCKI, HYACINTHUS (Jacek) II-44,364

RUBENIAN   I-68

RUBENS, PETER PAUL   I-449; II-
    63,124,140,147,167,173,180,198,
    200,205,206,212,240,254,255,
    256,270,274,278,295

RUBINI, NICCOLO   II-38,111

RUBINO   I-307,311,350

RUBLEV, ANDREI   I-121,152

RUBY, GUILLAUME   I-129,144,152

RUCIŃSKI, CHRYSTIAN   III-137

RUCKERS, family   II-44

RUCKERS, ANDRIES   I-453

RUCKERS, HANS   I-367,438,450,453,
    511,519,528,534; II-27,302(?)

RUCKERS, HANS (the younger)   II-
    27,302(?)

RUDE   II-59

RUDEL, JAUFRÉ   I-75

RUDENIUS, J.   II-60

RÜDIGER, J.F.   III-398

RUDOLF, ARCHDUKE of Bavaria   I-
    395

RUDOLF II, EMPEROR   I-397,445,
    462,469,520; II-6,73,87,146

RUDOLF, JAKOB   I-406

RUDOLF, KING of the Francs (Duke
    of Burgundy)   I-55

RUE, PIERRE DE LA   I-133,164,187,
    203,208,222,235,238,244,250,
    263,264,267,297,371

RUFFO, VINCENZO   I-309,321,324,
    331,344,352,360,361,369,372,
    393,396,416,436,437,440,456,
    457,490,527

RUFILLUS, FRATER   I-92

RUFILO   I-337

RÜGEN, WITZLAU VON   I-114

RUGERIIS, UGO DE   I-196

RUGGIERI (librettist)   III-236,
    379

RUGGIERI, FRANCESCO   II-421

RUGGLES, GEORGE   II-159

RUIMONTE   (see Rimonte)

RUIS, GIROLAMO   I-474

RUISDAEL, JACOB VAN   II-246,381,
    405,507
RUISDAEL, SALOMON VAN   II-67,312
RUIZ, JUAN   I-99,119
RULLIG, JOHANN GEORG   III-241
RUNGE, CHRISTOPH   II-187,497
RUPERT, PRINCE   II-362
RUPHINUS   I-200
RUPSCH, CONRAD   I-185,280,287
RUSSELL, LORD   I-357
RUSSELL, WRIOTHESLEY (Duke of
    Bedford)   III-172
RUSSIGNOL   I-315
RUST, MARIA JOHANNA   III-465
RUST, SAMUEL   III-256
RUTEBEUF   I-93,99
RUTINI, FERDINANDO   III-351
RUTINI, GIOVANNI MARIO (Marco)
    PLACIDO   III-351,427
RUTLAND, COUNTESS OF   III-1,4
RUYCKERS, HANS   (see Ruckers,
    Hans)
RYAN, LUCY   III-420
RYKEL, C.   III-164

S

SABATINI(?)   II-308
SABBATINI, PIETRO PAOLO   II-65,
    243,246,255,332
SABBATINO, NICCOLO   III-486
SABBIO (publisher)   I-499
SABINIANUS, POPE   I-39
SABLONARA, CLAUDIO DE LA   II-64
SACCHETTI, FRANCO   I-123,403
SACCHI(?)   II-324
SACCHI, GIOVENALE   III-384
SACCHINI, ANTONIO MARIA GASPERE
    III-425,477; III-368,422,425,
    477

SACER, GOTTFRIED WILHELM II-272;
   III-124
SACHS, CURT III-163
SACHS, HANS I-205,229,293,388,
   434,444,459; II-57
SACKVILLE, THOMAS I-302,387,391,
   395,517; II-117
SACRATI, FRANCESCO II-291,299,
   300,304,308,312,313,326,327,
   331
SACRATI, PAOLO II-290
SADELER, JOHANNES I-476
SADLER II-515
SADLER, JOHN I-176,178
SAENREDAM, PIETER JANSZ II-21,
   405
SAFÍ AL-DÍN 'ABD AL-MU'MIN (see
   Mu'Min)
SAFÍ, SHÁH II-250
SAGAN, PRINCE III-345
SAGE, LE (see Le Sage)
SAGGIONE, JOSEPH III-205
SAINT-COLOMBE II-44
SAINT-CYR III-43
SAINT-ÉVREMOND III-16
SAINTHILL, SAMUEL II-373
SAINT-LAMBER II-491
SAINT MICHEL, ELIZABETH MARCHAND
   DE (see Marchand)
SAINTWIX, THOMAS I-176
SAKADAS I-9
SALA, NICOLA III-266,453
SALA, (Dom) PIER PAOLO III-265
SALABUE, (Count) CORZIO DI II-
   371
SALAVERDE, BARTOLOMÉ DE (see
   Selma)
SALE, FRANÇOIS I-504; II-5,11,
   19,25,28
SALE, JOHN III-475
SALE, WILLIAM III-122
SALES, PIETRO POMPEO III-312
SALICOLA, MARGHERITA III-6,74
SALIERI III-422,434

SALIMBENI III-442
SALINAS, BERNHARD I-235
SALINAS, FRANCISCO DE I-255,305,
358,372,386,406,449,450,510,
527
SALISBURY, LORD II-28,111,135
SALIX III-400
SALLÉ III-479
SALMON(?) I-461
SALMON, THOMAS II-323,395,439,
440,444; III-29,32,199,205,
206
SALÒ, GASPARO DA I-298,319,349,
461,462,516; II-5,6,30,119,
134,260
SALO, V. NERITI DE (see Neriti
de Salo, V.)
SALTER, HUMPHRY II-515
SALTORIO, A. II-416,437
SALVADORI, ANDREA II-168
SALVI, ANTONIO III-114,182,207,
290,300,312,315,358,389,425,
484,492,493
SALZILLI, CRESCENZO II-109,127,
139,172,202,204
SAMBETHA, SIBYL I-189
SAMMARTINI, GIOVANNI BATTISTA
III-117,161,167,368,394,397,
435,460,481
SAMMARTINI, GIUSEPPE III-78
SAMMARUCO II-227
SAMPSON, RICHARD I-261,264,362
SANCES, GIOVANNI FELICE II-65,
220,266,281,327,422,425,426,
480
SANCHEZ DIEGO (see Badajos, de)
SANCHO DE PAREDES (see Paredes)
SANCTA MARIA, TOMÁS DE I-366,
403,415,421
SANDAM, HENRY II-69
SANDBERGER I-365
SANDBY, PAUL III-380
SANDFORD III-64
SANDYS, GEORGE II-286,399

RENOUNCING THE VANITIES BY ORDER OF SAVONAROLA   *379*

SAN GALLO, ANTONIO DA (the elder) I-171,265

SANGALLO, ANTONIO DA (the younger) I-185,194,298,333

SANGUIN, LOUIS (Comte de Livre) II-479 III-447

SANGUSKO, (Polish Prince)III-468

SAN JOSEPHO, BENEDICTUS A II-305,407

SANMICHELI I-193,290,378

SANNAZARO (Sannazard) I-236, 240,296,501,513

SANQUIN, LOUIS (see Sanguin, Louis)

SANSEVERINO, BARBARA I-433

SANSONE I-361

SANSONI II-243

SANSOVINO, JACOPO I-196,302, 404,423

SANTA CRUZ, ANTONIO DE II-45

SANTA MARIA, TOMAS DE (see Sancta Maria)

SANTARINI, FRANCESCO II-451

SANTINI III-278

SANUDO, family I-480

SANUDO, LEONARDO I-525

SANUTUS, MARINUS I-112

SAN VITALE, LEONORA I-433

SANZ, GASPAR II-64,452,521; III-112

SANZIO (see Raphael)

SARA (Biblical) I-368

SARACINELLI, FERDINANDO II-118, 157

SARACINI, CLAUDIO II-156,159, 196,221

SARGON I-7

SARINI, NICOLA III-105,170,195

SARNGADEVA I-85

SARRO, DOMENICO II-480; III-34,260,357,361,368,385,388, 400,433,475

SARTI, GIOVANNI VINCENZO II-309,324; III-388,447

SARTO, ANDREA DEL I-196,279,
  290,292
SARTORIO, ANTONIO II-199,406,
  410,430,435,438,440,465,503;
  III-11,45,72,97,114,210
SARTORIUS, PAUL II-30,60,72,
  77
SASSETTA I-152
SAUGUS II-342
SAUVAL III-364
SAUVEUR, JOSEPH III-170
SAVAGE, WILLIAM III-326,489
SAVANAROLA I-209
SAVETTA ANTONIO II-277
SAVILE, HENRY (see Carey, Henry)
SAVIONI, MARIO II-306,374,378,
  420,440,464
SAVONAROLA, family I-205 *See illustration on pp. 378-379*
SAVORGNANO, (Bishop) GIROLAMO
  I-222,373,394,398
SAVOY, DUCHESS OF (wife of Duke
  Charles Emanuel) I-492
SAVOY, DUKE OF III-187,338
SAVOYE, RENÉ II-127,130
SAXE, GOTHA, DUKE OF II-375
SAXE-WEISSENFELS, DUKE OF III-
  183
SAXONY, ELECTOR OF (see Johann
  Georg I)
SAXONY, PRINCESS OF II-268
SAYRE, ARNOLD DE II-180
SAYRE, ERASMUS DE II-159,169
SAYRE, MATTHAIS DE II-5,84
SAYVE, LAMBERT DE II-90,93,113,
  139,143,146,147,155
SBARRA, FRANCESCO II-307,342,
  348,352,364,416
SCACCHI, MARCO II-6,44,78,217,
  243,269,282,286,293,294,307,
  308,322,328,334; III-24
SCALABRINI, PAOLO III-268
SCALETTA, ORAZIO II-73,89,251
SCALIGER I-193,239,269,341
SCANDELLO, ANTONIO I-262,367,

Etched by Albert Rosenthal, Philad[...]

DOMENICO SCARLATTI   *387*

SCARLATTI, GASPARE   III-183
SCARLATTI, GIOVANNI FRANCESCO
    DIODATO   III-89
SCARLATTI, GIUSEPPE (composer)
    III-316
SCARLATTI, GIUSEPPE (son of Tom-
    maso)   III-352
SCARLATTI, GIUSEPPE NICOLA ROBER-
    TO DOMENICO ANTONIO   III-35
SCARLATTI, ISIDORO FRANCESCO   III-
    268
SCARLATTI, JUAN ANTONIO   III-416,
    418,484
SCARLATTI, MARIA CATALINA   III-
    403,484
SCARLATTI, MARIANA   III-460,484
SCARLATTI, MATTEO   III-45
SCARLATTI, MELCHIORRA BRIGIDA
    II-437; III-26,344
SCARLATTI, NICOLETTA   III-174
SCARLATTI, PIETRO (father of Al-
    lessandro)   II-366
SCARLATTI, PIETRO FILIPPO   II-
    478; III-197,199,223,227,255,
    258,260,314,410
SCARLATTI, RAIMONDO   III-306
SCARLATTI, ROSA   III-295
SCARLATTI, TERESA   III-199
SCARLATTI, TERESA ELEONORA SA-
    VERIA ANNA   III-275
SCARLATTI, TOMMASO   II-471; III-
    165,192,245,352
SCARLATTI, VIOLONTE   III-337
SCARLETT, ARTHUR   II-3
SCELLERY, CHARLES BORJON DE'
    (see Borjon)
SCHACCHI, MARCO   (see Scacchi)
SCHACHT, M.H.   II-375; III-24,
    153
SCHADAEUS   II-137,138,139,150
SCHADE, ABRAHAM   II-153,175
SCHADENSEE, FRANZ JOSEPH   (see
    Meyer, Franz Joseph)
SCHAEFFER, PAUL   II-179,202,211

SCHÄFFLER, J. I-208

SCHAFFRATH, CHRISTOPH III-233,
    468,489

SCHALE, CHRISTIAN FRIEDRICH III-
    266

SCHEDEL, HARTMANN I-157,174,256

SCHEFFLER, JOHANNES (see Siles-
    ius, Angelus)

SCHEIBE, JOHANN ADOLPH III-222,
    418,489

SCHEIDEMANN, family I-231

SCHEIDEMANN, DAVID I-481

SCHEIDEMANN, HEINRICH II-13,154,
    212,392,475

SCHEIDT, SAMUEL I-214,227,490;
    II-93,118,132,196,199,204,
    205,206,211,218,221,228,256,
    258,267,273,301,311,333,339,
    351,464

SCHEIFFELHUT, JAKOB II-319,320,
    508,521; III-8,218,232

SCHEIN, JOHANN HERMANN I-227,
    485; II-30,81,106,123,149,
    162,166,167,178,184,204,205,
    206,216,221,234,240,245,250,
    258,259,275,304,311,315,328,
    506

SCHELLE, JOHANN II-323,438,463;
    III-165,428

SCHEMELLI, GEORG CHRISTIAN II-
    478; III-94

SCHENK, JOHANN III-24,67,76,
    105

SCHERER, SEBASTIAN II-257,348,
    398,419,433,518; III-258

SCHIASSI, GAETANO MARIA III-487

SCHIAVETTO, GIULIO I-222,394,398

SCHICKHARD, JOHANN CHRISTIAN
    III-436

SCHIEDEMANN, HEINRICH II-298

SCHIEFERDECKER III-177

SCHILD, MELCHIOR II-217,235,
    247,411

SCHIO I-381

SCHWEIZELSPERG, KASPAR KASIMIR
II-418; III-208,227,280,282,
320

SCHWEMMER, HEINRICH II-200,298,
328,332; III-100

SCIVOLI, GREGORIO III-372

SCOLARI, GIUSEPPE III-326

SCOREL, JAN VAN I-207,292,294,
391

SCOT, CAPTAIN WALTER III-34

SCOTT III-97

SCOTT, DARBY II-206

SCOTT, HARRY I-230

SCOTT, JOHN I-230

SCOTTI, MARQUIS III-322

SCOTTO, OTTAVIO (publisher) I-
191,269,303,304,321,324,327,
346,380,390,394,416,419,441,
443,452,454,457,458,464,468,
476,477,482,489,493,500,508,
536; II-4,11

SCOTUS, DUNS I-111

SCOTUS, JOHANNES I-48

SCRIBANO, GIOVANNI I-235

SCRIPTOR, HENRICUS I-257

SCROPE II-465

SCUDAMORE, (Sir) JOHN II-99

SCUDÉRY, MADELEINE DE II-110;
III-171

SEAGAR, FRANCYS I-357

SEBASTIAN, ST. I-179,185,194

SEBASTIANI, CANDIUS I-393

SEBASTIANI, JOHANN II-207,308,
337,384,393,440,441,458,482,
510

SEDLEY, (Sir) CHARLES II-419;
III-63,108

SEDULIUS, COELIUS I-31,32,317

SEEBACH, JOHANN GEORG III-280

"SEEDO" II-409,435

SEEGR, JOSEPH III-293,489

SEGHERS, HERCULES I-509; II-
287

SEIFERT III-83

SEIKILOS   I-18
SEIYAS, CARLOS   III-189,328
SELD, DR.   I-362,363
SELDEN   III-41
SELESSES, JACOPIN   I-124
SELEUCIDES   I-25
SELEUCUS   I-17
SELLE, THOMAS   II-28,29,220,225,
    268,269,277,281,298,303,308,
    391
SELMA, DE   II-286
SELMA Y SALAVERDE, BARTOLOMÉ
    II-286
SELNECCER, NICOLAUS   I-307,371,
    483,494
SELVAGGI, GASPARE   III-372
SELVE, GEORGES DE   I-296
SELVIUS   I-402
SEMPILL, HUGH   II-9,163,351;
    III-97
SENAILLÉ, JEAN BAPTISTE   III-
    19,244,261,299,328,340,399,
    425,426
SENARDI, CATERINA   II-351
SENDYE, ELIZABETH   II-154
SENECA   I-20,21,22
SENESINO (Francesco Bernardi)
    III-320,325,327,356,365,376,
    387,397,407,416,438,442,451,
    452,455,465,466,468,482,489,
    493
SENFL, LUDWIG   I-200,227,244,
    255,259,265,267,268,274,279,
    281,285,288,297,304,306,312,
    319,327,363,367,370
SERAPHIN, SANTO   III-124
SERES, WYLLYAM   I-357
SERGIOS, PATRIARCH OF CONSTAN-
    TINOPLE   I-39
SERGIUS I, POPE   I-42
SERGIUS II, POPE   I-50
SERGIUS III, POPE   I-54
SERGIUS IV, POPE   I-62
SERLIO   I-184,307,362

SIDNEY, (Sir) PHILIP   I-362,431,
    452,454,458,473,489,513,522;
    II-6
SIEBENHAAR, MALACHIAS   II-167,
    310,361; III-1
SIEBER, JEAN GEORGES   III-478
SIEFER, JOHANNA SOPHIA (wife
    of J.B. BACH)   III-454
SIEFERT, PAUL   I-485; II-215,315,
    406
SIENA, GUIDO DA   I-97
SIETZ   II-370
"SIFACE"   (see Grossi, Giovanni
    Francesco)
SIGISMUND, ARCHDUKE of Austria
    I-197,199
SIGISMUND, JOHANN   II-111,143
SIGISMUND, KING of Bohemia (Ro-
    man Emperor)   I-145,150,154
SIGISMUND III, (Bathori) KING
    of Hungary   II-3,5,12,57,80,
    103,125
SIGISMUND (Zapolya), KING of
    Hungary   I-315,401,409
SIGISMUND (the elder), KING of
    Poland   I-245,324,337
SIGISMUND I (Augustus), KING of
    Poland   I-264,337
SIGISMUND II, KING of Poland
    I-402
SIGISMUND III, KING of Poland
    I-495; II-262
SIGISMUND, PRINCE of Poland   I-
    537
SIGMUND, ARCHBISHOP   I-188
SIGNORELLI, LUCA   I-158,186,191,
    194,202,209,210,213,215,274
SIGNORINI, GIOVANNI BATTISTA   II-
    142,171
SIGNORUCCI, POMPEO   II-113
SILBER, MARCELLO   I-250
SILBERMANN, brothers   III-248
SILBERMANN, ANDREAS   II-472; III-
    155,184,196,272,278,475

SILBERMANN, GOTTFRIED II-508;
    III-216,235,278,339,376
SILBERMANN, JOHANN ANDREAS III-
    258
SILBERMANN, JOHANN DANIEL III-
    302
SILBERMANN, JOHANN HEINRICH III-
    393
SILENO I-309
SILESIUS, ANGELUS II-218,467
SILÍCEO, CARDINAL I-201,329
SILVA, ANDREAS DE I-256,266,272
SILVA, ANTONIO JOSE DA III-199
SILVA, JOÃO VIERA DA III-165
SILVANI, FRANCESCO II-514; III-
    59,266,293,294,353,358,368,
    389,390,410,419
SILVANI, GIUSEPPE ANTONIO II-
    436; III-178,179,194,202,218,
    228,254,271,299,329,330,367,
    368,378
SILVANI, MARCO II-429
SILVANI, MARINO II-434
SILVERI, FRANCESCO III-259
SILVERIUS, POPE I-36
SILVESTRIS A BARBARINO, FLORIDE
    DE II-318
SIMARD III-406
SIMCOCK, JOHN III-265
SIMON, COUNT of Lippe II-15
SIMON, SIMON III-333
SIMONETTI, LEONARDO II-226,227,
    253
SIMONIS, GUILHELMI II-92
SIMPLICIUS, POPE I-33
SIMPSON, CHRISTOPHER I-444; II-
    307,356,357,371,373,398,404,
    415,422,476,521; III-210,261,
    280,348,399
SIMPSON, JOHN III-412,479
SIMPSON, THOMAS II-128,129,132,
    139,175,178,185,203,204,205
SINIBALDI III-237
SINKLER, MARGARET III-244

SIRENA, GALEAZZO II-119,235
SIRET III-242,321
SIRICIUS, POPE I-30
SIRMEN, MADDALENA III-494
SISINNIUS, POPE I-43
SISSA, COUNT of Parma II-447
SIXDENIERS, CHRISTIAN I-300
SIXTUS I, POPE I-23
SIXTUS II, POPE I-26
SIXTUS III, POPE I-32
SIXTUS IV, POPE I-181,182,189,
    254
SIXTUS V, POPE I-479,480,483,
    484,485,486,487,491,494,503,
    525
SKENE, JOHN II-19,46
SLATKONIA, BISHOP I-172
SLESVIG, DUKE OF II-403
SLOANE, (Sir) HANS III-32,218
SLOBACI, JOHANNIS II-322
SLUTER, CLAUS I-126,127,128,141
SLYE, THOMAS II-62
SMALLEY, JANE II-231
SMEGERGILL, WILLIAM (Caesar)
    II-45,163,348
SMITH, BERNHARD II-47,256,377,
    456,463,503,513,515,518,519,
    520; III-12,18,22,27,29,30,
    50,80,81,87,100,109,124,221,
    265
SMITH, CHRISTOPHER III-329
SMITH, (Dr.) COOPER, RECTOR of
    Basingstoke II-269
SMITH, HENRY I-232; II-265,413
SMITH, JOHN CHRISTOPHER (Johann
    Christoph Schmid) III-259,
    452,470
SMITH, ROBERT II-326,436,444,
    455
SMITH, ROBERT (Mathematiciau)
    III-43,132,302
SMITH, THOMAS II-368
SMITH, WILLIAM III-332,333,340,
    341,366,390,391,448

SMITHFIELD II-262

SMOLLETT, TOBIAS III-342

SMOUT, ADRIAAN JORISZOON II-66

SMYTH, EDWARD II-134

SMYTH, WILLIAM II-30

SNETZLER, JOHN III-246

SNODHAM, THOMAS II-118,120,137,
138,166,183,220

SNOEK, C. III-163

SNOW, MOSES II-509; III-43,174

SNYDERS, FRANZ I-455; II-77,365

SO-AMI I-140

SOBIESKI (Prince) ALEXANDER (Poland) III-227,279

SOBIESKI (King), JAN (Poland)
II-453; III-223,261

SODOMA, of Siena I-248

SOHIER, PIERRE I-265

SOHREN, PETER III-64

SOLARIO, ANDREA I-175 215,268

SOLDI II-185,188,202

SOLER, (Padre) ANTONIO III-489

SOLERTI I-360

SOLIR, ANTONIO III-371

SOLOFRA, GIOVANNI CAMILLO MAFFEI
DA I-390

SOLOMON I-6,170,300

SOLT, SUZANNE VAN II-33

SOMAIZE II-385

SOMIS, CHRISTINE (see Loo, Mme
Van)

SOMIS, GIOVANNI, BATTISTA II-
462; III-13,184,348,378,389,
481

SOMIS, LORENZO III-28

SONNECK, OSCAR G.T. III-146

SONNLEITHNER, CHRISTOPH III-475

SOPHIA, DUCHESS of Hanover II-
462

SOPHIA, DUCHESS of Saxony II-25,
216

SOPHIA, ELECTRESS of Hanover
III-296

SPARCK, COUNT VON   III-117

SPARENBURG   I-394

SPATARO, GIOVANNI   I-139,173,202,
    271,294,317

SPECHTSHART VON REUTLINGEN, HUGO
    (see Reutlingen)

SPEE, FRIEDRICH VON   II-229,271,
    315,329

SPEER, DANIEL   II-490; III-3,24,
    34,65,67,112,229

SPENCE, F.   III-16

SPENCER (?)   II-136

SPENCER, (Sir) EDWARD   II-310

SPENSER, EDMUND   I-88,355,419,
    433,446,452,454,489,513,536;
    II-6,12,26,28

SPENER, PHILIPP JAKOB   II-272,
    274,458; III-199

SPERATUS   I-278

SPERVOGEL   I-85

SPIESS, MEINRAD   II-509; III-263

SPINACCINO, FRANCESCO   I-246

SPINETTI   I-239

SPIRA, FORTUNIO   I-372

SPIRIDO, BERTHOLD   II-428,429,
    435,515

SPITTA, PHILIPP   II-509; III-36,
    216,309,359,361,430

SPONGA, FRANCESCO   (see Usper)

SPONTONE, BARTOLOMMEO   I-399,411,
    415,472,483,536

SPORCK, COUNT   III-363

SPORER   I-279

SPÖRL   I-128

SPRETUS, POMPONIUS   I-456

SPROGEL, LOD C.   III-403

SQUARCIALUPI, ANTONIO   I-133,130,
    145,178,188

SQUIRE, LAURENCE   I-196

STABILE, ANNIBALE   I-315,504;II-6

STADEN, JOHANN   I-462; II-84,102,
    123,129,169,172,184,205,216,
    217,227,235,245,253,266,267,
    268,282,308,318,355

STADEN, SIGMUND GOTTLIEB (Theo-
    phil) II-105,232,238,268,282,
    311,325,355
STADLMANN, D. III-290
STADLMAYER, JOHANN I-529; II-
    81,83,116,127,129,160,172,184,
    225,227,245,259,276,286,294,
    299,303,308,318,323,326
STAFFORD, VISCOUNT (see Howard,
    William)
STAGGINS, family II-44
STAGGINS, CHARLES II-44; III-
    165
STAGGINS, ISSAC II-44,360,384,
    398,406,455,518; III-1
STAGGINS, JAMES II-44
STAGGINS, MARY III-165
STAGGINS, NICHOLAS II-44,430,
    435,441,451,453,454,455,461,
    465,472,478,505,517,520; III-
    2,14,36,47,55,72,74,108,109,
    151,165,176
STÄHLIN, JAKOB VON III-246,492
STAINER, JACOB II-200,298,314,
    324,368,423,430,468,511
STAMITZ, ANTONÍN III-243
STAMITZ, JOHANN WENZEL ANTON
    III-137,243,304
STAMPIGLIA, SILVIO III-109,152,
    179,191,194,198,199,213,424
STANDISH, family II-38
STANDISH, DAVID II-386,471
STANDISH, ROGER III-52
STANDISH, WILLIAM II-471
STANESBY, THOMAS (I) III-164,
    208,397,477,488
STANESBY, THOMAS (II) III-64,
    164,208
STANICZEWSKI (Stanicze), ANDRZEJ
    II-90
STANIHURST I-88
STANLEY, (Charles) JOHN III-
    265,287,328,365,387,414,479
STANLEY, EDWARD I-236

STEPHEN, (St.), KING of Hungary
   I-62
STEPHAN, KING of Poland I-470,
   477
STEPHEN, MASTER I-163
STEPHEN I, POPE I-26
STEPHEN II, (III) POPE I-44
STEPHEN III, (IV) POPE I-44,45
STEPHEN IV, (V) POPE I-48
STEPHEN V, (VI) POPE I-52
STEPHEN VI, (VII) POPE I-52
STEPHEN VII, (VIII) POPE I-55
STEPHEN VIII, (IX) POPE I-55
STEPHEN IX, (X) POPE I-66
STEPHEN, ST. I-166,254
STEPHEN, WILLIAM FITZ I-81
STERNE, LAURENCE III-262,272
STERNHOLD AND HOPKINS (psalmists)
   I-338,340,349,357,391; II-111
STERNHOLD(E), T. (see also Stern-
   hold and Hopkins) I-338,339,
   340,369,381,387,391
STEWART, NEIL III-137
STIVORI, FRANCESCO II-38,72,73,
   78,95
STOBAEUS, JOHANN I-455; II-3,
   30,58,69,75,221,235,269,303,
   305,311,316,349
STOCK, JEAN BAPTISTE III-236,
   331
STOCKE, WILLIAM II-320
STOKHEM, JOHANNES I-196
STOKROCKI, SAMUEL II-44,308
STOLTZER, THOMAS I-134,164,180,
   206,217,280,281,293,346
STÖLZEL, GOTTFRIED HEINRICH III-
   43,254,260,270,282,314,320
STONARD, WILLIAM II-113,251
STONE, ROBERT I-382; II-81,147,
   149
STORACE, BERNARD II-399
STORL, JOHANN GEORG CHRISTIAN
   III-188
STOSS, VEIT I-158,187,295

STRUTIUS, THOMAS   II-81,361,368,
    399,419,474
STRYPE   I-380
STRZYZEWSKI, JAN   II-44,199
STUART(?)   III-392
STUART, (Lady) ARABELLA   II-105
STUBBS, SIMON   II-38,172,205
STUCK, JEAN BAPTISTE   II-493; III-
    176,212,228,254,282,291,308,
    349,421
STUYKERS, MARY LOUISE   III-215
SUARD, JEAN BAPTISTE   III-471
SUBIRA, JOSÉ   III-203
SUCCENTOR, PETRUS   I-89
SUCKLING, (Sir) JOHN   II-124
SUEUR, EUSTACHE LE   II-319
SUEVUS, FELICIANUS   (Schwab, F.)
    II-270,288,361
SUGER, ABBOT   I-68,75,77
SÚILLEABHÁIN TADHG GAEDHLACH Ó
    III-292
SULLA   I-19
SUMAYA, M. DE   III-254
SUNDERLAND, LORD   III-1
SUPPIG, FRIEDRICH   III-348
SUSANNA (Biblical)   I-385
SUSATO, TYLMAN   I-190,285,287,
    291,293,311,323,324,325,330,
    331,333,338,351,358,365,370,
    375,386,387
SUTTERMANS, JUSTUS   II-21,500
SUZANNE, ST.   III-121
SWART, WILLEM   I-443; II-296
SWAYNE, W.   I-520
"SWEDE"   (see Baltzar)
SWEELINCK, family   I-414
SWEELINCK, father   (see Swybert-
    szoon)
SWEELINCK, DIRCK JANSZOON   II-
    202,311,343
SWEELINCK, JAN PIETRSZOON   I-163,
    382,388,406,431,448,450,457,
    461,477,485,487,511,527,528,
    529,530,531,534,563; II-22,

T

TAG, CHRISTIAN GOTTHILF III-484

TAGLIA, PIETRO I-366

TAGLIACOZZO, DUKE OF (see Colonna, Fabrizio)

TAGLIAVIA, PALAZOTTO II-95,178, 196

TAGLIETTI, GIULO II-380,488; III-154

TAI, CHIN (see Chin, Tai)

TAILER, DANIEL (see Taylor, Daniel)

TAILLE, DE LA I-389

TAILOUR, ROBERT II-38,166,182

TALBOT, GENERAL III-24

TALBOT, JAMES III-99,100

TALLARD, COUNT DE III-123

TALLIS, THOMAS I-227,242,253, 269,292,303,312,314,316,336, 343,354,358,370,376,379,381, 384,390,391,394,398,428,429, 433,438,439,440,441,479,480, 481,500,502; II-23,91,200,423

TAMBURINA, GALLIARDA I-227

TANG DYNASTY I-39

T'ANG, LI I-72

TANNER, ROBERT II-509

TANNHAUSER I-89,97

TANSILLO, LUIGI I-377,415,449, 483

TANSUR, WILLIAM III-159,207, 257,491

TANZUR, EDWARD III-257

TAO-SHENG, KUAN I-108,111

TAPISSIER I-130,142,145

TARANTINO, IL (see Fago, Nicola)

TARDITTI, ORAZIO II-321,324,431

TARIQ I-43

TARONI, GIOVANNI BATTISTA III-84

TARRI III-408

TARTAGLINI, IPPOLITO I-439

TARTINI, GIUSEPPE III-61,235, *See illustration on p. 417* 270,271,294,298,335,337,343, 356,359,387,407,429,430,479

TASKIN, PASCAL   I-367; III-354
TASSO, JOAN MARIA   I-379
TASSO, TORQUATO   I-296,328,372,
 400,404,405,418,433,442,450,
 451,454,455,464,465,470,478,
 481,485,490,492,493,496,512,
 519,520,523,531,534; II-2,
 145,221,237,245; III-15,17,
 249
TASSONI   I-400
TATE, NAHUM   II-475,477,487,521;
 III-2,8,71,92,104,105,157,159,
 469
TATHAM, JOHN   II-389
TATTENBACH, COUNT VON   II-413
TAULER, JOHANNES   I-209
TAURINI   I-271
TAUS, ANDREW   II-205
TAVERNER, JOHN (of Norfolk)   I-
 474; II-127,284
TAVERNER, JOHN (Tudor composer)
 I-206,212,222,261,277,279,
 281,282,287,288,289,290,291,
 306,328
TAVERNIER   I-175
TAVOLA, ANTONIO DELLA   II-274
TAYLOR, DANIEL   II-225,306
TAYLOR, JEREMY   II-153,335,342,
 416
TAYLOR, JOHN   III-186
TAYLOR, SILAS   II-218,473
TEDDER, ROBERT   II-248
TEIBER, MATTHÄUS   III-251
TELEMANN, GEORG PHILIPP   II-494;
 III-74,94,119,155,167,168,
 172,175,176,192,196,227,229,
 235,238,260,261,264,270,328,
 335,339,341,343,344,347,348,
 362,378,400,403,407,409,410,
 415,421,429,481,482,491
TELESPHORUS, POPE   I-23
TELLER   (see Deller)
TEMPEST, MICHAEL   I-423,461
TEMPO, ANTONIO DA   I-116

421

TING I-5
TINGHI, CESARE II-182
TINI, PIETRO I-474
TINÓDI, SEBASTIAN I-219,243,356,
    361,368; III-135
TINTORETTO I-265,332,335,337,
    367,385,391,395,399,404,405,
    452,473,501,527,536
TIRABOSCHI, GIROLAMO III-439
TISON, JOSEPH II-402
TISSU, CLAUDE II-413
TITELOUZE, JEAN I-392; II-216,
    235,263,265
TITIAN (Vecellio, Tiziano) I- *See illustration on p. 423*
    195,248,253,258,265,267,272,
    280,282,291,300,303,306,317,
    322,331,333,348,355,385,395,
    405,412,446; II-63,205
TITON DE TILLET (see Tillet)
TITUS I-21
TODI, ANTONIO BRACCINO DA (see
    Braccino)
TODI, FACOPONE DA I-110; III-
    400
TODI, G.F. II-483
TOESCHI, ALESSANDRO III-430
TOESCHI, CARLO GUISEPPE III-345
TOESCHI, GIOVANNI BATTISTA III-
    395
TOFTS, CATHERINE III-182,188,
    192,200,216,230,235
TOLEDO, JUAN BAUTISTA I-378
TOLLET, THOMAS II-421; III-40
    66,67,226
TOLLIUS, JAN II-19,85
TOLOMEI I-307
TOLSTAGO, PETR ANDREEVIČ III-
    117
TOMASI, BIAGIO II-44,136,163,
    272
TOMASI, BIAGIO II-44,136,163,
    272
TOMEK I-217
TOMKINS, ALICE II-302

422

TOMKINS, BRIDGET II-472
TOMKINS, GILES II-220,252,418
TOMKINS, GILES (II) II-264,384;
    III-371
TOMKINS, JOHN II-100,113,188,
    225,265,284
TOMKINS, NATHANIEL (chorister)
    I-474; II-13
TOMKINS, NATHANIEL (organist)
    II-29,233,248,421,495
TOMKINS, NICHOLAS II-268
TOMKINS, ROBERT II-265,298,388
TOMKINS, THOMAS (I) I-519; II-
    131,225,241,268,360,513(?)
TOMKINS, THOMAS (II) II-268
TOMKINS, THOMAS (III) I-428,444,
    519,534; II-13,46,81,106,175,
    191,194,202,205,209,211,220,
    225,227,233,243,262,282,300,
    302,318,322,327,328,329,351,
    360,361,399,420
TOMKINS, THOMAS (IV) (III) II-
    284
TOMKINS, WILLIAM II-424
TONELLI, ANTONIO III-12,367,386,
    424
TONGE, ISRAEL II-473
TONTO, ISABELLA I-525
TOPHAM, WILLIAM III-232
TORCHI II-76,193,194
TORELLI(?) I-531; II-15,25
TORELLI, GIUSEPPI II-39,339,364,
    366,466,488; III-14,16,68,86,
    119,154,159,168,231,236
TORINO, ILLUMINATO DA III-470
TORRE, FRANCISCO DE LA I-213
TORRE, PIETRO PAOLO II-38,211
TORRENTES, ANDRES I-329,456
TORRI, PIETRO II-359,406; III-
    40,103,184,212,287,317,325,
    352,416,427,455
TORRIAN, JEHAN I-211,240
TOSI, GIUSEPPE FELICE II-256,
    482,513

TOSI, PIER FRANCESCO   II-317,336;
    III-72,74,358,427
TOTIS (librettist)   II-499,510;
    III-3,18
TOTTEL   I-373
TOUCHEMOULIN, JOSEPH   III-395
TOULOUZE, MICHEL DE   I-198
TOUR, CHARLOTTE MASSARD DE LA
    III-227
TOUR, GEORGES DE LA   I-530; II-
    296,316,346
TOUR, M. DE LA (musicologist)
    III-268
TOUR, MAURICE QUENTIN DE LA   III-
    195
TOURNEMINE, PÈRE   III-331
TOURNON, COUNT   I-312
TOYOHARA, SUMIAKI   I-163,275
TOZZI, PIETRO PAOLO   I-531
TRABACI, GIOVANNI MARIA   I-516;
    II-73,83,156,161,166,197,320
TRAETTA, TOMMASO   III-64,368,388,
    392,409,422
TRAINI, FRANCESCO   I-119
TRAJAN   I-22,23
TRAJANO   I-244
TŘANOVSKÝ, JIŘÍ   II-136,149,163,
    249,277,279
TRANSCHEL, CHRISTOPH   III-337
TRANSILLO, LUIGI   I-251
TRAPP III-194
TRASUNTINO, VITO   I-366,378; II-
    38,100
TRAVERS, JOHN   III-188,381
TRAXDORFF   I-179
TREBOR   I-142
TREGIAN, family   I-223,447,448
TREGIAN, CHARLES   I-536
TREGIAN, FRANCIS (I)   I-223,448,
    II-112
TREGIAN, FRANCIS (II)   I-391,485,
    487,516,523,534; II-112,187
TREGIAN, KATHERINE   I-223
TREIBER, J.P.   III-178,194

TRENCHMORE   I-398

TRESTI, FLAMINIO   II-38,149

TREU, ABDIAS   II-14,422

TREU, DANIEL GOTTLIEB   III-92,
    297,397

TREVISA, JOHN   I-126

TREVISO, GIOVANNI ZAPPOSORGO DA
    I-427

TRIAL, JEAN CLAUDE   III-452

TRIEMER, JOHANN   III-418

TRILLER   I-377

TRISSINO, GIAN GIORGIO   I-187,
    341

TRISTAN L'HERMITE   (see Hermite,
    L')

TRITHEMIUS   I-206

TRITONIUS, PETRUS   I-246,247,288

TRITTO, GIACOMO   III-462

TROIANO, MASSIMO   I-382,408,412,
    414,418,420

TROILO, ANTONIO   II-38,102,109,
    116

TROMBONCINO, BARTHOLOMAEUS   I-
    185,197,207,212,236,237,241,
    244,245,249,261,263,264,268,
    298,300

TROMLITZ, JOHANN GEORG   III-436

TROTTER, MRS.   III-156

TROY, FRANÇOIS DE   II-312; III-
    434

TROY, J.F. DE   II-484

TROYES, CRÉTIEN   I-71

TRUCHSESS VON WALDBURG, OTTO VON
    (see Waldburg, Otto Truchess
    Von)

TRYDELL, JOHN   III-138

TRYGGVASON, OLAF   I-58

TRZYCIELSKI, ANDREAS   I-402

TS'AI, LIU   I-108

TSAÏ -YÏ   I-2

TSAI-YII, CHU   (see Chu, Tsai-
    yii)

TSAI-YU, PRINCE (Chou Dynasty)
    I-301; II-9,134

427

TSAN, NI   I-109,121,124

TSCHUDI, BARON DE   (see Theodore, Jean Baptiste)

TSCHUDI, BURKHARD   (see Shudi, Burkat)

TSO, HUANG   I-199,406

TSUNG, HUI   I-68,75

TSWUIGA, SHINNAI   III-277

TUAN, CHU   I-229

TUBERVILLE   II-139

TUCK, JOHN   I-243

TUCKER, EDMUND   II-38

TUCKER, EDWARD   II-236

TUCKER, WILLIAM   II-478

TUCKEY, WILLIAM   III-225

TUDWAY, THOMAS   II-290,336,380, 428,450,482,490,497,513; III-138,197,205,212,218,282,384

TUFTS, JOHN   III-38

TUFTS, (Rev.) JOHN   III-262,283, 330,334,341,389,445

TUKE   II-434

TULLIO   III-312

TULP, DR.   II-262

TUMA, FRANZ   III-190

TUNDER, FRANZ   II-155,280,296,298, 412

TUNSTED, SIMON   I-120,123

TUOTILO   I-52,54

TURA, COSIMO   I-153,179,183,206, 208

TURCO, ANNIBALE   I-473

TURENNE   III-114

TURINI, FRANCESCO   I-510; II-6, 205,220,249,282,294,308,360; III-132

TURINI, GREGORIO   II-129

TURK   II-54; III-134,149

TURNER, (Sir) JAMES   II-515

TURNER, WILLIAM   II-340,400,423, 458,464; III-8,32,103,112,119, 130,157,256,299,300,367

TURNOWSKI, JAN   II-245,247

TUSCANY, GRAND DUKE OF (see Me-
    dici, Ferdinando II)
TUTANKHAMEN I-5
TYE, AGNES I-438
TYE, CHRISTOPHER I-213,269,301,
    316,317,319,331,336,356,379,
    388,398,409,420,429,431,438;
    II-96
TYLER, WAT I-126
TYLKOWSKI, WOJCIECH II-247,424,
    491; III-58,88
TYNDALE, WILLIAM I-299,310
TYRTAEUS I-7
TYTLER III-140
TZARTH, GEORGE III-225
TZU, WO LIANG I-25

U

UBERTI, ANTONIO III-110
UCCELLINI, (Don) MARCO II-85,
    131,303,314,328,329,336,352,
    353,378,415,420,424,429,447,
    458,471
UCCELLO, PAOLO (Doni) I-129,149,
    156,159,165,172,177,184
UDALL I-358
UGERI, STEFANO I-484,490
UGERI, STEFANO I-484,490
UGOLINI, BACCIO I-181
UGOLINO, COUNT I-457,467
UGOLINI, VINCENZO II-81,87,120,
    156,166,173,196,211,237,245,
    247,252,284
UHLARD I-330
UJEZD, NICHOLAS CHUZY VON I-145
ULBRECHT, JOHANN II-480
ULENBERG, CASPAR I-468,497
ULIEGER, SIMON II-73

UTRECHT, HENRIC VAN   II-125
UTTINI, FRANCESCO ANTONIO BALD-
    ASSARE   III-354
UZ, JOHANN PETER   III-332
UZZANO, NICCOLO DA   I-154

VACCHELLI, GIOVANNI BATTISTA
    (see Naufragante, Il)
VACHON, PIERRE   III-441
VAELET, NICOLAS   II-172
VAËT, JACQUES (Jacob)   I-216,268,
    361,369,375,396,398,399,408,
    412,415
VAILLANT, JEAN   I-123,131
VAIRASSE, DENIS   III-301
VAL BREMBANA, ZAMBO DEL   (see
    Brembana)
VALBEKE, LOUIS VAN   I-113
VALCARENGO, (Pater) Caninio   I-
    469
VALDERRABANO, ENRIQUEZ DE   I-216,
    335
VALDRIGHI   II-179
VALENTE, ANTONIO   I-443,446
VALENTI, GIUSEPPE   III-170
VALENTIN DE BAULLONGE   (see Baul-
    longe)
VALENTINE, POPE   I-49
VALENTINE, ROBERT   III-130,172,
    279,334,442
"VALENTINI"   (see Urbani, Valen-
    tino)
VALENTINI, GIOVANNI   II-156,327,
    328
VALENTINI, GIUSEPPE   II-497; III-
    187,280,291

432

PALME LE VIEUX.

VAN DEN GHEYN, family (see
   Gheyn)
VAN DYCK, ANTHONY (see Dyck,
   Anthony Van)
VAN GOYEN, JAN (see Goyen, Jan
   Van)
VAN HEEMSKERCK, MARTIN (see
   Heemskerck, Martin Van)
VAN NOORDT (see Noordt)
VAN OSTADE, ADRIAEN (see Ostade,
   Adriaen Van)
VAN RUISDAEL (see Ruisdael)
VANAVASI I-87
VANBURGH (architect) II-410;
   III-192,203,219,390
VANBRUGHE, GEORGE III-130,155,
   156,273,334,408
VANDENEDEN, HENRI (see Eeden,
   Heinrich)
VANDERBERG, CATHERINE III-297
VANDINI, ANTONIO III-356
VANINI, FRANCESCA (Boschi) III-
   243,252
VANNEUS, STEPHANUS I-295
VANNINI, ELIA III-59,65,78,126
VANNUCCI, PIETRO (see Perugino)
VANSTRYP, F. III-433
VANUCCI, DOMENICO FRANCESCO III-
   316
VAQUERAS I-193
VAQUIERAS, REIMBAUTZ DE I-80,89
VARGAS, LUIS DE I-236,387,413,
   416
VAROCAI, GIOVANNI III-397,442,
   485
VAROTTO, MICHELE I-326,394,458,
   512
VARRO, MARCUS TERENTIUS I-19
VÁSÁRHELI, ANDREAS I-193
VASARI, GIORGIO I-253,343,437
VASCON-CELLOS III-263
VASII, IACOBI I-451
VASQUEZ, JUAN I-351,352,360,
   368,379,381,386

436

VELDE, WILLEM VAN DE (the elder)
II-140, III-77
VELDE, WILLEM VAN DE (the younger)
II-266; III-220
VELEZ, JUAN II-389
VENDRAMIN, PAOLO II-288
VENEROLO I-244
VENETIA, SIGNURIA DI (see also
Bassano, Giovanni) I-480
VENETICUS, GEORGIUS I-49
VENEZIANO, DOMENICO I-130,156,
165,170,175
VENEZIANO, GAETANO III-190,214,
295
VENN II-438,440
VENTADOUR, BERNARD DE I-72,75,
77,80,82
VENTO, IVO DE I-317,419,438
VENTO, MATTIA III-486
VENTURA, IN COMIN I-493
VENTURE, JOHANNES À LA (see
Longueval, Antoine de)
VENTURI, POMPILIO I-427
VENTURI DEL NIBBIO, STEFANO
II-12,20,25,38,56,60
VENTURINI, C. II-414
VENTURINI, FRANCESCO III-111,
118,205,270
VENTURY (see Venturi)
VENUS I-17,19,195,196,286,294,
306,385
VERAEINI, ANTONIO II-336,459;
III-62,68,105
VERACINI, FRANCESCO MARIA III-
5,43,274,279,280,287,298,299,
334,342,356,407,485,487,489,
491,493
VÉRARD, ANTOINE I-235
VERBONNET (see Ghiselin)
VERBRUGGEN III-106
VERDELET (Jehan Boissard) I-
146
VERDELOT, PHILIPPE I-212,235,
252,278,281,287,288,290,293,

396,400,537; II-5,9,12,13,15,
21,77,90,106,120,123,143,146,
163,237,313

VICENTE, GIL   I-177,237,303

VICENTINO, NICOLA   I-253,301,333,
338,346,364,366,387,388,429,
430

VICENZO, PALLADIO   I-478

VICH, PEDRO ALBERCH   (see Vila)

VICTOR I, POPE   I-24

VICTOR II, POPE   I-66

VICTOR III, POPE   I-68

VICTOR AMADEUS II   III-187

VICTORIA, TOMÁS LUIS DE (Vittoria)
I-218,296,312,393,398,402,418,
426,432,440,445,446,450,451,
464,472,476,479,483,489,500,
504,509,527,534; II-26,43,60,
79,83,96,97,134,136,243; III-
139,364

VICTORINUS, GEORGIUS   II-11,13,
172,219,221,286

VIDAL, ANTOINE   II-364

VIDAL, PEIRE   I-83,85,90

VIDE, JACQUES   I-148,151,154

VIENNA, PIETRO DA   (see Alamania)

VIERDANCK, JOHANN   II-44,243,283,
300,301,303,308

VIÉVILLES, LE CERF DE LA   (see
Cerf, Le)

VIGARANI, CARLO   II-367

VIGILIUS   I-36

VIGNATI, GIUSEPPE   III-130,323

VIGNOLA (architect)I-246,416,433

VIGNOLA, GIUSEPPE   III-258

VILA, PEDRO ALBERCH (Vich)   I-
262,305,386,466

VILLALAR, ANDRÉS DE   I-393,529

VILLANI, FRANCESCO   III-418

VILLANI, GASPARO   II-39,127,129,
130,140,146

VILLARS   III-288

VILLESAVOYE, PAUL DE   II-581; III-
188

VILLIERS, (Sir) GEORGE II-103
VINACESI, BENEDETTO II-431; III-
    87,105,126,186,190,208,279,
    280
VINCENT, ISABELLA III-486
VINCENT, RICHARD (I) III-172
VINCENT, THOMAS, JR. III-333,
    489
VINCENTI, ALESSANDRO II-180,197,
    200,209,229,233,239,253,269,
    281,327,341
VINCENTI, GIACOMO I-471,477,488,
    493,500,507,521,522,526,529,
    531; II-4,11,18,32,39,76,94,
    122,164,165,176,180,183,184
VINCENTIUS, CASPAR II-136
VINCENZO I, DUKE (see Gonzaga,
    Vincenzo)
VINCENZO, ANTONIO (see Aldrovan-
    dini, G.A.)
VINCHANT I-401
VINCI, LEONARDO III-46,52,147,
    322,331,347,348,349,359,372,
    373,374,376,378,395,399,405,
    407,422,425,428,432,433,434,
    441,445,454,474
VINCI, LEONARDO DA (painter) I-
    139,170,179,184,186,188,191,
    193,195,199,206,210,213,244,
    245,251,256,266
VINCI, PIETRO I-290,416,458,465,
    474,477
VINER, WILLIAM III-188,247,295,
    402,432
VINTA, BELISARIO I-478
VIOLA, ALESSANDRO DELLA I-290
VIOLA, ALFONSO DELLA I-310,318,
    360,361,386,390,394,411,430,
    454
VIOLA, FRANCESCO I-377,390
VIOLA, GIAMPIETRO DELLA I-195
VIOLINO, CARLO DEL (see Caproli)
VIOLINO, MICHELANGELO DE (see
    Verovio)

444

299,300,301,308,314,315,316,
323,331,336,341,342,353,355,
356,358,359,364,368,376,378,
379,380,382,384,386,387,388,
390,391,392,394,397,399,400,
402,404,407,410,412,414,418,
420,421,423,447,450,453,464,
471,482,489,491,492

VIVALDI, FRANCESCO III-339

VIVALDI, GIOVANNI BATTISTA II-
356,466; III-6,270,414,418

VIVALDI, ISEPPO III-404

VIVIANI, GIOVANNI BONAVENTURA
II-475,493; III-34,50

VIVIEN, JOSEPH II-365; III-482

VLADIMIR I-78

VLADIMIR, PRINCE I-58

VLIEGER, SIMON II-350

VOELDERS, MARIE-FRANÇOISE III-
323

VOES, H. I-273

VOGEL I-365

VOGELWEIDE, WALTER VON DER I-
79,85,92,93

VOGLER, JOHANN CASPAR III-342

VOIGTLÄNDER, GABRIEL II-13,229,
266,304,305,399

VOLTAIRE III-87,429,482

VOLUMIER, JEAN BAPTISTE II-431;
III-62,207,227,232,235,403,
429

VON BRUCK (see Bruck, Arnold)

VOPELIUS, GOTTFRIED II-271,314,
456,505,506; III-283

VOS, CORNELIS DE I-490; II-206,
342

VOS, JEAN DE II-127

VOSS, GERHARD J. II-185,265,322,
327,333,447(?)

VOSS, ISAAC II-184,248,330,428,
442,447(?); III-35

VOSSIUS, G.J. (see Voss, G.J.)

VOUET, SIMON II-240

VREDMAN, JACOB II-184,201

VREDMAN, MICHAEL II-146,246
VUILLAUME, family II-44
VULPIUS, MELCHOIR I-384; II-75,
    77,84,90,96,116,123,124,130,
    146,152,160,162
VULTEJUS, HERMAN I-366

W

WACE I-74,89
WÄCHTER, CASPAR II-395,400,404
WACLAW, of Szamotuly II-227
WAELRANT, HUBERTO I-263,326,333,
    335,346,351,357,360,365,369,
    375,392,404,410,414,483,484,
    536; II-1,223
WAGAN, JAMES III-286
WAGENSEIL, GEORG CHRISTOPH III-
    283,422,459
WAGENSEIL, JOHANN CHRISTOPH II-
    263; III-113,223
WAGNER, GEORG GOTTFRIED III-115,
    263,387
WAGNER, GOTTHARD II-481; III-
    155,244,307,330,432
WAGNER, PAUL III-113,405
WAGNER, RICHARD I-226,412
WAISSEL, MATTHÄUS I-433,522,527
WAISSELIUS (see Waissel)
WAKE, WILLIAM II-296,391
WAKELEY, ANTHONY II-437
WALDBURG, (Cardinal) OTTO VON
    TRUCHSESS VON I-389,390,393,
    399,430
WALDECK, PRINCE VON III-441
WALDEN, LORD II-142
WALDIS, BURCHARD I-357
WALDKIRCH, HEINRICH II-94,196

WALICH, EISIK II-5
WALKELEY, A. III-118,310
WALKER, JOHN I-409
WALKER, (Dr.) JOHN III-278
WALKER, THOMAS III-409
WALLENSTEIN I-473; II-222,270
WALLER, (Sir) EDMUND II-102,
    379; III-18,23,25
WALLIS, (Dr.) JOHN II-168,261,
    328,470; III-120,127,132,186
WALLISER, CHRISTOPH THOMAS I-
    416; II-30,77,130,140,152,160,
    228,322
WALLNER, B.A. I-478
WALLOT, JAN I-300
WALMSLEY, PETER III-328,397,420
WALOND, WILLIAM (I) III-373
WALPERGEN, PETER II-415,513
WALPOLE, (Sir) EDWARD III-430
WALPOLE, HENRY I-463
WALPOLE, HORACE III-308
WALPURGIS, MARIA ANTONIA III-
    362
WALSH AND HARE III-94,100,104,
    198,199,290,330,358,437
WALSH, JOHN (I) III-65,94,99,
    126,128,152,179,193,206,208,
    218,224,228,232,243,247,250,
    254,309,321,350,365,448,472,
    491
WALSH, WILLIAM III-72
WALSINGHAM, THOMAS DE I-158
WALTER, ELIZABETH II-105
WALTER, JOHANN I-263
WALTER, (Rev.) THOMAS III-101,
    330,341,379
WALTERS, LUCY II-486
WALTERS, WILLIAM II-268
WALTHAM, (Bishop) JOHN I-312
WALTHER, JOHANN I-207,277,278,
    279,280,281,285,304,306,321,
    327,337,346,352,360,372,387,
    407,408,421; II-39,506; III-
    338

WEBER, CARL MARIA VON I-220;
    III-478
WEBER, FRANZ ANTON VON III-478
WEBER, FRIDOLIN III-56,465
WEBER, GEORG I-360,417,501; II-
    15,294,315,325,329,345,350
WEBER, JOHANN BAPTIST VON I-
    348; II-209
WEBSTER, DANIEL II-217
WEBSTER, JOHN I-460; II-9,160,
    228
WEBSTER, MAURICE II-276
WECKER, GEORG KASPAR II-260;
    III-15,89
WECKER, HANS JACOB I-354
WECKINGER, REGINA I-374
WECKMANN, MATTHIAS II-281,293,
    356,398,414,448
WEDDERBURN, JOHN I-316,452
WEDDERBURN, ROBERT I-316,452
WEDEMANN, CATHARINA (wife of
    Johann michael Bach, 4th gen-
    eration) II-331,455; III-190
WEDEMANN, MARIA ELISABETH (wife
    of Johann Christoph Bach, 4th
    generation) II-317,413; III-
    183
WEDEMANN, SUSANNA BARBARA (aunt
    of Maria Barbara Bach) II-
    490
WEDIGH, HERMANN I-294
WEELKES, THOMAS I-383,443; II-
    20,25,28,58,61,63,72,74,78,
    114,116,160,174,213,300
WEERBECKE, GASPAR VAN I-157,160,
    181,191,196,198,199,210,238,
    246,248,249,257
WEICHMANN, JOHANN II-307,321,
    330,343
WEIDMAN, KARL III-387
WEIDEMANN, MARGARET I-439
WEIGEL, CHRISTOPHER, JR. III-
    489
WEIGEL, J.C. III-120

452

IOH. WINKELMAN̄

WEILAND, JOHANN JULIUS   II-354, 356,391

WEIMANN, JOHANN   I-319

WEIMAR, GEORG PETER   III-476

WEINBRENNER, JOSEPH PAUL III-411

WEISHMANN, JOHANN   II-192

WEISS, CHRISTIAN   III-282,356, 366,382,398,443,456

WEISS, SYLVIUS LEOPOLD   III-12, 208,227,279,288,306,312,320, 356,407

WEISSE, CHRISTIAN FELIX   III-390

WEISSE, MICHAEL   I-292

WEISSEL, GEORG   II-272

WEISSENBURG, OTTFRIED VON   I-49

WEISSERSEE, FRIEDRICH   II-10,73, 208

WELCH, JOHN   (see Walsh, John)

WELCKER   I-267

WELDON, JOHN   II-461; III-74,79, 84,120,154,155,165,169,170, 176,178,185,192,194,228,284, 387,398

WELLESLEY, GARRETT C.   III-484

WELTMAN   III-302

WENCESLAUS, of Prachatitz   I-144

WENCESLAUS II, KING   I-102

WEND   III-460

WENDLING, JOHANN BAPTIST   III-333

WENDT, CRISTIAN GOTTLIEB   III-415

WENSSLER   I-197

WENTWORTH, PAWLE   I-469

WENZEL, FRANZ   (see Habermann, F.V.)

WERCKMEISTER, ANDREAS   II-313, 368,374,388,396,411,428,451, 456,499,500; III-16,103,113, 120,127,157,178,202,206,219

WERLIN   I-169

WERNER(?)   II-330

WERNER, GREGORIUS JOSEPH   III-92,407,409

WERRECORE, MATHIAS I-268,270,
    274,297,315,366,376
WERT, GIACHES DE I-279,298,345,
    348,374,375,382,384,386,388,
    394,405,406,411,417,449,459,
    464,465,467,470,473,474,478,
    483,487,489,492,501,508,516,
    522; II-8,10,15
WESLEY, CHARLES III-489
WESLEY, JOHN III-489
WESSTRÖM, ANDERS III-326
WEST, WILLIAM II-306,379
WESTCOTE, SEBASTIAN I-389
WESTHOFF, JOHANN II-360,434,
    451,482,490,506,522; III-57,
    86,192
WESTON I-485
WESTRUP, J.A. II-165
WEWEN, FRANZ HILVERDING VON III-
    241
WEYDEN, ROGIER VAN DER I-129,
    142,154,155,157,162,163,170,
    172,176,185
WEYSENBERGH, HEINRICH III-11
WEYWANOWSKY (see Vejvanovský)
WHARTON, LORD III-234
WHARTON, PHILIP II-262
WHARTON, THOMAS III-31
WHEELER, PAUL II-360
WHETHAMSTEDE, ABBOT I-164
WHICHELLO,ABIELL III-244,423,432
WHIGG, (Sir) BARNEBY II-499
WHITCHURCHE, EDWARD I-338,340
WHITE, JAMES II-445
WHITE, MAGISTER I-292,307
WHITE, MATTHEW II-81,134,149,
    156,186,246
WHITE, ROBERT I-216,228,290,
    379,381,388,414,415,423,424,
    434,435
WHITEFIELD, GEORGE III-435
WHYTBROKE, WILLIAM I-279,285
WHYTHORNE, THOMAS I-284,289,
    419,427,513,514

456

IACOBVS ZABARELLA.

WRIGHT, DANIEL III-437
WRIGHT, EDWARD III-347,434
WRIGHT, PETER II-174
WRIGHT, THOMAS I-356
WRIGHT, THOMAS (playwright) III-71,75
WRITTLE, PETRE LORD OF (see Petre)
WRONOWICZ, MACIEJ II-492
WU-LIANG-TSE I-23
WÜLKEN, ANNA MAGDALENA (see Bach Anna Magdalena)
WÜLKEN, JOHANN CASPAR III-153
WULSTAN I-56
WÜRTTEMBURG, DUKE OF (1575) I-439
WÜRTTEMBERG, DUKE OF (1657) II-364
WÜRTTEMBERG, DUKE OF (1719-1721) III-323
WUST, B.C. II-428
WYATT, (Sir) THOMAS I-239,321,373
WYCH, (Sir) CYRILL III-208
WYCHERLY, WILLIAM II-295,434,439,447,453; III-301
WYCLIFFE, JOHN I-116,126
WYDOW (Wydewe), ROBERT I-191,198,204,208,210,211,236,238,241
WYKEHAM, WILLIAM OF I-140
WYLDEBORE (Wylbore), JOHN I-291,317,320,356
WYNFRITH I-41,45
WYNGATES, COMPTON I-270
WYRSUNG I-267
WYSSENBACH, RUDOLF I-343

X

XERXES I-12
XIMENEZ DE CISNEROS (see Cisneros)

Y

YALDEN   III-76

YCAERT   (see Yeart, Bernardo)

YEART, BERNARDO   I-189,244

YOLANDA, of Aragon, QUEEN of
    Sicily   I-145

YONGE, JANE   I-478

YONGE, NICHOLAS-   I-478,496,497,
    501; II-20,61,186

YORK, DUKE OF (1679)   II-479

YOULL, HENRY   II-61,116

YOUNG, ANTHONY   III-216,330

YOUNG, CECILIA   III-251,424,440,
    489

YOUNG, EDWARD   II-516

YOUNG, JOHN   III-124,157,210,253,
    272,280,365

YOUNG, TALBOT   III-170,365

YOUNG, WILLIAM   II-228,347,348,
    350,384,432,442

YÜAN LO   I-340,363

YÜAN, MA   I-87

YÜAN, TUNG   I-53

YÜAN-TING, TS'AI   I-76,82

YUNG, TSAI   I-23

Z

ZABARELLA   II-399   *See illustration on p. 463*

ZACCONI, LUDOVICO   I-227,230,363,
    442,525,527,529; II-3,12,188,
    191,211,236

ZACH, JAN   III-123

ZACHARIA, NICOLA   I-146

ZACHARY, POPE   I-44   *See illustration on p. 467*

ZACHAU, FRIEDRICH WILHELM   II-
    391,520; III-66,74,102,258,
    267

ZACHERIE(O)   I-143,147

ZACHOW (see Zachau, Friedrich
   Wilhelm)
ZAGABRIA, NICOLAUS DE I-143
ZAHN II-45,325
ZALZAL, of Bagdad I-46
ZAMBELLI, ANTONIO III-123
ZAMBELLI, ANTONIA MARIA III-
   123
ZAMORA, ANTONIO DE III-383
ZAMPONI II-334
ZANETTA (see Casanova, Gianetta)
ZANETTI II-100
ZANETTO, GIOVITA RODIANI I-461
ZANETTO, MAGGINI I-461
ZANETTO, PEREGRINO I-457
ZANGIUS, N. II-78,124,143,185
ZANI, MATTEO II-365; III-3
ZAPPOSORGO DA TREVISO, GIOVANNI
   (see Treviso, Giovanni)
ZARABANDA (dancer) I-346
ZARANI, D. GIOVANNI BATTISTA
   III-424
ZARLINO, GIOSEFFO I-217,229,234,
   262,289,308,317,336,366,375,
   388,389,390,401,402,405,407,
   425,427,433,434,437,448,449,
   463,467,471,501,508,509,510,
   511,513,533; III-491
ZAROTUS, MICHAEL I-186
ZARTH, GEORGE (see Tzarth,
   George)
ZASINGER, MARTIN I-215
ZASZEWSKI, JOZEF III-78
ZAVAGLIOLI, SIMONE II-314
ZÁVIŠ, MAGISTER I-125,126,129,
   143; II-7
ZEDLER, J.H. III-460
ZEELANDIA, H. DE I-132
ZELENKA, JAN (Johann Dismas)
   II-479; III-235,243,298,301,
   358,418,468
ZELLBELL, F. III-38,288,306(?)
ZELLBELL, F. (II) III-241,306(?)
ZELLE, GEORG VAN I-266